# GOOD DAY, BAD DAY

## TEACHING AS A HIGH-WIRE ACT

*Ken Winograd*

**ScarecrowEducation**
Lanham, Maryland • Toronto • Oxford
2005

Published in the United States of America
by ScarecrowEducation
An imprint of The Rowman & Littlefield Publishing Group, Inc.
4501 Forbes Boulevard, Suite 200, Lanham, Maryland 20706
www.scarecroweducation.com

PO Box 317
Oxford
OX2 9RU, UK

British Library Cataloguing in Publication Information Available

**Library of Congress Cataloging-in-Publication Data**
Winograd, Ken, 1951–
    Good day, bad day : teaching as a high-wire act / Ken Winograd.
    p. cm.
    Includes bibliographical references and index.
    ISBN 1-57886-244-2 (pbk. : alk. paper)
    1. First year teachers. 2. Teacher effectiveness. I. Title.

    LB2844.1.N4W58 2005
    371.1—dc22
                                                        2004027368

∞™ The paper used in this publication meets the minimum requirements of
American National Standard for Information Sciences—Permanence of Paper
for Printed Library Materials, ANSI/NISO Z39.48-1992.
Manufactured in the United States of America.

To Ernest Lax,
who took a chance on a beginning teacher,
the first time around

# CONTENTS

# ACKNOWLEDGMENTS

Identity is socially constructed and historic, and this book is no different. My words here flow from the circuitous path of my experiences, parents and grandparents, brothers and cousins, wife and children, friends, coworkers, teachers, students, strangers, texts, and dreams imagined and real over the course of a lifetime. I've used the words of others to make the words in this book my own, reflecting *my* intentions in a collaboration in which I am first coauthor.

I want to first thank Elise Bradley for sharing her classroom with me. In her inimitable constructivist manner, she taught me much about teaching and children. Her daily reminder to me to "love those kids" was a powerful message of acceptance of children as children. Sharon Blackwell and Lori Paul helped me gain the confidence to take risks and fail in the very public space of classroom teaching. Karen Smith also provided me with unconditional support that enabled me to accept the inevitable miscues of beginning teaching. Elise, Sharon, Karen, and Lori read an early draft of the journal and provided me with feedback. It was perhaps the students who are most responsible for this book. They challenged, criticized, ignored, tuned in to, accepted, and sometimes reveled in my efforts to teach them. Without the disequilibrium that reflected my relations with the students, there would be no book. Without disequilibrium, there is no learning.

Friends and colleagues read sections of the book and gave me their feedback: Nora Cohen, George Copa, Tom Birdseye, Dominic Cusimano, Tom Birdseye, Karen Higgins, David Ferreiro, Nell O'Malley, Susan Klinkhammer, Donna Phillips, Blake Rodman, Kay Stephens, and Eileen Waldschmidt. My students at Oregon State read the chapters on emotions and negotiations, and they let me know when the writing was unreadable, interesting, or irrelevant. From day one, the teachers and staff at Woodbridge accepted me as a teacher, even before I believed I was one myself, and for this affirmation I am grateful. I also want to thank Hilda Weinberg, Dorothy and Arthur Traiger, Bud Roberts, Byron Pulliam, Rick Silverman, Tom Adams, Tom Evans, Pearl Winograd, and Vinnie for their support during the more formative stages of this project.

Finally, Melinda, Claire, and Sam were present for me every evening as I sought to understand myself as a teacher. Melinda encouraged me to take risks, and she was usually successful in keeping me from falling into the trap of self-flagellation. Claire and Sam listened to my teaching stories and, for the most part, found them interesting. I kept them in mind often as I imagined the experience of my students sitting in their chairs day after day, subjected to someone else's agenda and words, coping and hopefully learning.

# INTRODUCTION

I am a professor in the School of Education at Oregon State University. I teach in a program that prepares students to become elementary and middle school teachers. During the 1998–1999 school year, I went back to the classroom, on sabbatical, as a teacher of a nongraded primary class, of first, second, and third graders. Here is an excerpt from my journal describing my third day on the job.

**September 3:**

I have led several activities and lessons. Easy stuff. Some read-alouds. Some challenging lessons, like in math problem solving. When I try stand-up teaching, students don't listen past my first twenty-second introduction. Side conversations and papers fly across the room. Students intentionally fall out of their seats. As the students get more antsy, I speak faster and sometimes become incoherent. I'm not sure what to say to them when they misbehave. I try different verbal signals . . . "I'm looking for active listeners . . . please be quiet . . . I'll continue when you are quiet . . . please be quiet . . . I see Stevie is ready to move on . . . I see this table is ready to listen . . . please be quiet. . . ."

I don't know the kids, they don't know me, and I don't know yet what kind of curriculum is appropriate for them. In my stomach, I sense that this is going to be a difficult year. A feeling that I've had under my skin is now surfacing: I am almost like a beginning teacher . . . and I think the kids have already picked up on this fact. Uh, oh! The jig is up.

Although I was a veteran teacher educator with eight years as an elementary classroom teacher, it had been fourteen years since I had done full-time classroom teaching—alone, unassisted, in charge of everything. I had considerable theoretical knowledge of teaching and learning, given all the reading, teaching, and research I had done during eleven years as a doctoral student and professor. However, in terms of my practical knowledge, I was almost like a beginning teacher again. By September 1998, at the start of the sabbatical, I was out of practice and had lost the fluency of everyday teaching. The reader will notice early on in the reading of this book just how difficult the year was for me, especially the beginning of the year. I did develop teaching routines and an automaticity in the first few months. Still, the emotional gestalt of my days even in the second half of the year was still somewhat unpredictable and unstable. I was not much different from a novice teacher.

Most of my colleagues take sabbaticals that involve writing, research, or study, in the true spirit of the sabbatical, a year of leaving the proverbial field fallow, to give one's intellectual earth a year to rejuvenate. Instead, I aimed my sights on what I now refer to as the antisabbatical: a return to the trenches of everyday teaching. While local public school teachers lauded my proposed sabbatical, most of my university colleagues thought I was a glutton for punishment. Regarding my motivation for initiating this project, I did not return to the classroom because I was looking for glory, from any sense of idealism, or because I was "brave." I really did not know how difficult this work was going to be. I believed simply that my effectiveness as a teacher educator would be enhanced if I spent a year in the classroom.

I had taught methods classes to preservice elementary teachers for eleven years before the sabbatical. I was well versed in the theory of teaching. During the sabbatical year, I also read a good deal of educational sociology, especially the literatures that examine teacher–student interactions, emotions, and identity development (e.g., Goffman, 1959; A. Hargreaves, 1994a; D. Hargreaves, 1972; Nias, 1989; Pollard, 1985; Woods, 1990a, 1990b). Because of this reading, I believe that I developed a greater "theoretical sensitivity" to my experience, and I was more able to use a variety of theoretical perspectives to inform my teaching practice and felt experience. I believe the integration of theory makes the book more relevant to teachers and researchers who are looking for ideas about teaching that can be adapted to other settings and teaching situations.

## WHY AND FOR WHOM I WROTE THIS BOOK

The book represents my experience of beginning teaching as very difficult, often excruciatingly difficult, as it is for many beginning teachers. The book is a personal representation of the teaching experience, focused on the construction of teacher identity and how I managed to survive with an ego still intact. Now, I sometimes read my journal and feel embarrassed to have others glimpse the sensitive underside of my insecure self. Then I realize, after many conversations with my preservice teachers, that the experience of grappling with one's insecure self *is* one of the realities of beginning teaching. Instead of burying the more embarrassing events so my year does not look so grim or my ego so fragile, I believe that to have any value for beginning teachers this book must represent the experience honestly and fearlessly (without falling off the edge into excessive self-indulgence). Still, I realize that the experience of some beginning teachers is less problematic than mine was here. There are classes that are more conformist than mine; other beginning teachers will have different personalities than mine; or their skills might be more developed than mine were. Still, most beginning teachers do struggle, and the struggle is ultimately played out in their minds and with their bodies, as they work vigorously and anxiously to defend their selves from embarrassment and failure.

I wrote this book because I felt that there is a side of beginning teaching that is largely unaddressed in the teacher education canon. There *are* fine scholarly and popular books that chronicle the struggles of beginning teaching (e.g., Bullough, 1989; Codell, 1999; Danielewicz, 2001; Herndon, 1968; Huberman, 1993; Ryan, 1970; Ryan et al., 1980; Schoonmaker, 2002) as well as books that describe the struggles of experienced teachers (e.g., Dudley-Marling, 1997), including works of fiction (Blanchard & Ursula, 1996; Kidder, 1989).[1] Most studies of beginning teaching have been done by researchers on others who are the beginning teachers. I believe this book is unique since the scholarly studies here have been conducted by the researcher *on himself*. Furthermore, I was a beginning teacher in terms of my practical knowledge and *mature* in terms of my theoretical knowledge. I believe that the tensions and contradictions in my positions as both novice and expert gave me fresh perspectives with which to examine teaching. Given my theoretical sensitivity, I hope the reader finds the rendering of my experience to be interesting, useful, and trustworthy.

I wrote this book for preservice teachers and beginning teachers to provide them with some reference points and perspectives on the problems and struggles they may face in their first years in the classroom. Sections of this book, in which I share more intimate moments of anxiety, fear, and despair, are very personal. For preservice and beginning teachers, part of the value of this book may be in the catharsis involved in reading a personal account of teaching and gaining a deeper, though partial, understanding of the teaching experience. Certainly, I hope that young teachers also construct insights and wisdom as they connect my texts with their own experience and theories about teaching. I also wrote the book for teacher educators to use with preservice and graduate students. The recommendations in part II center on the work of teacher educators and how they can help young teachers learn to negotiate and manage the challenges of teaching. For a small audience of teacher educators who are considering a similar sabbatical experience, this book can provide some perspectives, caveats, and even motivation regarding the prospect of "going back." Finally, I expect that the book will be useful to individuals who are not involved in teaching and schools, so they can come to know (my sense of) the complexities of teaching.

## THE BOOK'S THESIS

Teaching is imperfect and frustrating work, perhaps inherently so. The teacher's task is to reconceptualize or reframe this imperfection in two ways that, on surface, appear to be contradictory. First, the task is to understand the imperfection that is *inherent* in teaching: there will always be a gap between the teacher's intentions and the outcome of her work. Our goal as teachers is to effect some intellectual, social, or emotional growth or change in the students. However, the inherent frustration comes from our inability to control students, especially large numbers of students simultaneously, and get them to do exactly or nearly what we intend. One, some, or most students will, at times, not do what we teachers want them to do. The task for the teacher here is, first, to understand the complexities of teaching and then to accept and even celebrate these realities. However, accepting imperfection does not mean that the teacher gives up and acquiesces, for example, to partial learning outcomes for students or to disorder. It is the gap between intention and outcome that motivates and incites the teacher to improve her practice, serve students more effectively and compassionately, and close that persistent but inevitable gap.

Teaching is partial and frustrating also because of working conditions, and this type of frustration is *not* inherent in the work. Instead, this frustration stems from political processes that, historically, have left teachers and schools marginalized in terms of power, resources, and control. Teachers' working conditions are both their own doing and the doing of others. In the book, I argue that teachers ought to resist, organize, and become politicized in response to frustrations that stem from inadequate funding, hierarchical power relations, and loss of curricular control. While frustration stemming from working conditions may appear to be taken for granted and not subject to critique and change, these conditions are historical and reflect certain economic, political, or cultural interests. Working conditions and school cultures can change, and teachers can be participants in the political process.

## CONCEPTUAL FRAMEWORK

The chapters in the second half of the book are all self-contained studies, and each examines research questions and data from clearly articulated theoretical frameworks. The reader can read the studies as well as the journal reflections to learn the specific theories I used to guide these studies. I used a theory called symbolic interactionism, as well as critical theories such as feminism and poststructural feminism, to place my thinking in a larger social and political context. From these perspectives, identity (including our behavior and emotions) is seen as a social construction, reflecting a mosaic of factors such as the individual's personality, biography, immediate situation and partners, the immediate and larger cultural and historical context, and material resources. We are shaped by our external circumstances, but we have agency in shaping our own destinies as well. Our identities are shaped by power relations at the local level of our personal interactions and at the larger societal level. Identity also is reflected by the individual's expression of personality and desires to negotiate the demands of particular situations. While we may have one somewhat stable core identity, across time and situations, we also have many identities that are constructed as our situations vary. Teacher identities, then, get constructed in the interaction between a complex set of microstructural dimensions (personality, personal history, school culture, colleagues, students, etc.) and macrostructural dimensions (history and culture of schooling, market economy, state laws and regulations, testing, gender, age, race, class, etc.) surrounding classrooms and schooling.

## A BRIEF WORD ABOUT RESEARCH METHOD

Every night, I wrote impressionistically in a journal about my day in the classroom. In the journal, I generated a description of my experience, developed personal theories, did much planning, and vented emotions. I kept the journal with the idea of eventually using it as a source for professional publication. The journal is the single source of data for this study. My role in the field was what Adler and Adler (1994) would call a "complete membership role," one in which researchers are "already members or those who become converted to genuine membership during the course of their research" (380). I was the teacher of the class, fully certified by the state, in charge of the curriculum and teaching for the afternoon.

In this self-study, I modified Clandinin and Connelly's model for narrative inquiry (2000), which "begins with the researcher's autobiographically-oriented narrative associated with the research puzzle" (41). As such, the purpose of this inquiry is not the creation of any new claims to knowledge but rather a representation of my experience so others may "imagine their own uses and applications" (Clandinin and Connelly, 2000, 42). Using some elements of autoethnography, my goal was

> to encourage compassion and promote dialogue. . . . The stories we write put us into conversations with ourselves as well as with our readers. In conversation with ourselves, we expose our vulnerabilities, conflicts, choices, and values. We take measure of our uncertainties, our mixed emotions, and the multiple layers of our experience. . . . Often our accounts are unflattering and imperfect, but human and believable. . . . In conversation with our readers, we use storytelling as a method for inviting them to put themselves in our place (Ellis and Bochner, 2000, 748).

I realize this is a self-study, autobiographical, and therefore loaded with the perils of subjectivity, self-indulgent polemics, and narrow-mindedness. Because self-studies present special validity problems (Feldman, 2003), I used some traditional strategies in qualitative research to enhance the trustworthiness of my observations and assertions: clear description of data collection and analysis; sharing my writing with other teachers for their feedback; prolonged engagement in the field; and informing the work with other research and theory. I have grounded my "thick descriptions" and personal theories with the research and theory of others, and it is this conversation between myself and others that may further enhance the book's credibility. Besides, I hope that my story alone resonates with the experiences of the readers. Still, following Clandinin, Connelly, Ellis, and Bochner, the believability of this study, in the end, will depend on the readers' ability to imagine themselves in my shoes.

## WOODBRIDGE ELEMENTARY SCHOOL

Woodbridge Elementary School (a pseudonym), situated in the U.S. Pacific Northwest, is a public school located in a low-income section of town; 90 percent of the school's students were on free or reduced lunches. About 85 percent of the students at the time of this study were Euro-American, and most of the others were Latino or Asian American.

In my state, like most other U.S. states, the legislature has mandated a huge set of standards and benchmarks, for all the subject areas, that students are required to meet at certain junctures of their school career. Students are formally tested at third, fifth, eighth, and tenth grades on these standards, and it is expected that teachers teach and assess their students on these benchmarks at all grade levels. The standards-based approach to schools puts pressure on teachers and students in several ways (e.g., see Ohanian, 1999). The first pressure represents a concern that challenges the logic of the standards. The next three do not critique the logic of the standards and, instead, reflect a functionalist concern for efficiency.

First, there is an impression among many teachers that the standards are too rigorous, and that large numbers of students (especially poor students, students of color, and the students whose native language is not English) will not meet the standards. Importantly, the standards and their tests do not represent the interests and perspectives of the poor, students of color, or second-language learners. Many teachers, myself included, have a sense that this framework poses extraordinary problems for poor students, given the resources currently available to schools and poor families. Second, there is a pressure on teachers by the public nature of accountability. Many states, including my own, publish ratings of schools based on how well their students do on the tests. Third, the management of this system for teachers is unwieldy and burdensome. Huge numbers of forms and assessments have to be generated on individual students for each set of standards that is mandated by the state. In my state, elementary teachers have to assess students based on a large set of benchmarks in mathematics, reading, writing, and speaking. And fourth, many teachers are frustrated that the state's mandate for "reform" is essentially unfunded, so the obvious resources needed to make the standards system work as intended are unavailable (Conley and Goldman, 1995). All of these pressures are particularly difficult for teachers and students in low-income school communities.

The school's curriculum reflected a child-centered approach typical of the English infant schools of the 1960s. Behind the leadership of the principal and a group of activist teachers, Woodbridge began to take a constructivist, child-centered approach in the early 1990s.[2] Textbooks were abandoned, and teachers developed curricula using collections of constructivist teaching materials (e.g., Burns, 1992). Classes were combined with mixed age groups of children in what is called "nongraded primary." At Woodbridge, classroom management practices tended to avoid extrinsic reward systems and, instead, relied on the notion of building community, appeals to group pressure, and "making good choices." (For example, when a student misbehaved, a typical adult response was, "What should you be doing now?" Or when one student hurt another, the victim was directed to tell the perpetrator, "Tell Joseph how that made you feel. What can you do to solve this problem?")

The school was (and still is) located in the low-income section of the town. In the early 1990s, the poverty rate of the school population was about 60 percent. It was about this time that the school district implemented school choice, so parents could send their children to any school in the district as long as there was room at the receiving school. Some middle-class parents were unhappy with Woodbridge's child-centered approaches, and they began to move their children to neighboring schools. As the school lost middle-class families, the increasing percentage of high-poverty families (along with the associated behavior problems) drove away even more middle-class families. By 1998, the year of my sabbatical, approximately 90 percent of the school's students were on free or reduced lunch.

I job shared with Dorothy, a veteran of about twenty years as a classroom teacher. Dorothy, who I knew from her work with our student teachers from the university, had just given birth to her second child, and she wanted to teach half-time for the first year of her daughter's life. I thought that a half-time position would give me time to read, reflect, and write about my return to the classroom. Dorothy taught the morning (reading and writing); I arrived at the school at 11:15 a.m., I debriefed with her for about ten minutes about the morning, and then the students entered the room after lunch recess, at 12:15 p.m. Between then and 2:35 p.m., I taught mathematics, social studies, science, and some language arts. I had a full-time instructional assistant, Barbara, who taught small groups and managed paperwork and materials for me. I had the support of a student teacher, Fran, who worked in the room on and off during the year.

I taught twenty-five students in a classroom typical in size and shape: a rectangular room that was twenty-five feet by thirty feet. Of my twenty-five students, about half showed signs of exceptionalities. These exceptionalities included attention deficit disorder, reactive attachment disorder, chronic depression, and conduct disorder. Two of my students were fetal alcohol babies whose behavior was volatile and frequently immature or irrational.

About twelve of the students were first graders, seven were second graders, and six were third graders. Of the third graders, only two were useful as role models as problem solvers and self-managers for the younger students.

## A SHORT BIOGRAPHICAL SKETCH

This book is a study of my identities as a teacher. One of the points I make in the book, especially in the chapter on teacher identity, is that one's biography is paradigmatically implicated in one's identities. Therefore, it is important for me to sketch a brief autobiography here. The purpose of this self-disclosure is to make visible to the reader some of my beliefs and values, grounded in my experience, that might be relevant to the teacher identities represented in the book.

I am a Euro-American Jewish male. I never experienced poverty or abuse. My family life was stable and nurturing. My parents stayed married until my father's death in 1982. I also benefited from the support of an extended family, since my father's brother and his family lived next door. My father always worried about money, and my mother chose to work as a secretary in the middle years. Still, we had enough food on the table, trips to Yankee Stadium, and the occasional summer vacations in the Catskills. I have lived most of my life in the second half of the twentieth century, so I was spared the explicit anti-Semitism that my grandparents and parents experienced in the first half of the century. Given the color of my skin, my maleness, my epoch, and an emotionally and economically stable family, I have had a privileged economic and cultural position. I recognize that my position is not my doing, but a matter of chance.

I was born in New Jersey in 1951, the youngest of three boys. My mother stayed home during the first twelve years of my life, and my father ran the family-owned mom and pop toy store. I was, at best, an average academic achiever. I grew up and went to public school in the same town. After high school, I went to Rider College in New Jersey, where I majored in political science. My plan had been to become a lawyer ever since I had read *Anatomy of a Murder* when I was in junior high school. However, after graduation I decided that, instead, I needed to travel and work odd jobs for a few years, which is what I did.

I was working the assembly line in a Revlon perfume factory near my home town when I saw *Conrack*, a movie about a young male elementary school teacher whose conception of his teaching self was that of change agent.[3] The image of *Conrack* as a change agent appealed to my desire to make a difference in the world. I figured, What better way to change the world than as an elementary school teacher? After the movie and a bit of nudging from Hilda, an old family friend and also a teacher, I began exploring teaching as a profession. I enrolled in a one-year master's program at Rutgers University. By the summer of 1976, I had my master's degree and teaching license. My approach to teaching included practices such as discovery learning, writing to learn, and the project approach.

I could not find a teaching job in New Jersey, and the school year had just started in September. I saw a help wanted ad in the *New York Times*: there were several teacher openings at the Stavanger American School in Norway. There had been a sudden rise in enrollment, and the school needed more teachers. Since I had a passport, was single, and could move to Stavanger on short notice, I found myself teaching a class of third graders a week later. In Stavanger, Norway! The school was funded by oil companies based in and around the North Sea. Unfortunately, the school provided me with little support as a beginning teacher, and I acknowledge that my performance as a first-year teacher was weak. I was not renewed after the one year.

I returned to the States a year later, ended up in Boulder, Colorado, and eventually found a job teaching fifth grade in Grand Junction. I had a successful teaching experience in Grand Junction; I taught fourth, fifth, and sixth grades during a six-year period. Looking back, I remember relying on the textbook exclusively to structure my teaching of mathematics. In reading, I used novels and other primary sources along with the basal series. In language arts, I did not use the textbook and had enough intuitive sense to have the students write every day about their experiences and from their imagination. In the early 1980s, my district designated me the "language arts person," and I received training in the writing process, which I then used to lead several workshops for my colleagues.

In my last year in Grand Junction, I was made an assistant principal in one of the larger elementary schools in the district. After a year of not quite knowing what to do with myself in this role, I married Melinda Michaels, and we both resigned our positions with the district. We spent two years traveling around the world. We worked for one year in Japan teaching con-versational English. In my spare time, I remember writing a handbook for teachers containing canned writing lessons, including one story prompt for each week of the school year. I also remember tossing the manuscript in the garbage when I realized that the whole premise of the book was to keep con-trol in the hands of the teacher. This was before I read the work of Donald Graves, who argued the importance of student control over the topic and content of writing.

My uncle, a retired New York City high school English teacher and prin-cipal, was also living in Japan. Driving around the countryside one day, he asked me about my plans after leaving Japan. I described my plan to return to Colorado and become a principal. He suggested that I first earn a doctor-ate in education, which would give me more options in the job market. I liked the idea of studying curriculum and teaching, and then as a principal I would have more credibility as the "instructional leader."

I enrolled at the University of Northern Colorado in Greeley. I loved the reading and writing one does in graduate school, and I immersed myself in literacy research and teaching, including whole language, writers work-shop, and holistic approaches to the teaching of mathematics. As a gradu-ate teaching assistant, I taught language arts, spelling, and even handwrit-ing methods classes. (I may have taught the last handwriting methods class in the history of the United States. I'm not sure.) Consistent with my student-centered philosophy, I developed a dissertation topic that exam-ined students' cognitive behavior when they wrote, solved, and shared orig-inal mathematics story problems. I was excited by this approach, since it neatly applied Donald Graves's ideas about student control in writing to the teaching of mathematics. Graves argued that it was possible to teach those skills and strategies required of good writing *in the context of stu-dents' self-generated writing*. Similarly, I speculated that it would be possi-ble to teach mathematics concepts in the context of students' self-generated mathematics stories and story problems.

As I read, wrote, and taught, I found myself more interested in a career in higher education than in school administration. I decided to become a teacher educator, and I came to Oregon State University in 1990. I have taught classes in action research, reading methods, and language arts meth-ods. I rarely teach the same course twice in quite the same way.

While my knowledge base and language ability has developed, my basic orientation to education has not changed much since I began this work in 1976. I still believe in the multicultural democratic ideal, and my teaching and writing reflect a social justice perspective. My approach to teaching and learning as a teacher educator has consistently reflected social constructivism, the idea that people learn by actively constructing their own knowledge in collaboration with more knowledgeable others around activity that is meaningful and relevant. I still want to change the world. Early in my career, I believed that education could be the great equalizer, that schools could be a catalyst for a more equitable and just society. I was enamored with the social reconstructionists of the 1930s, who aimed to democratize society by democratizing schools. I am more tentative now in my belief that schools and teachers alone can change the world and even change the destinies of most of our students. I realize now that there are influences on student performance and behavior that are beyond my control as a classroom teacher. I think the answer is alliances between teachers and their communities and between teacher unions and unions of other working people. I suppose this is why I believe that teachers can most effectively "make a difference" only when they more fully develop their understanding of the political dimensions of teaching. For the moment, I believe that we can make a difference in our students' lives, but the difference is small, incremental, and often not apparent. Still, the task for the teacher is to continue striving and working to achieve his ideals, perhaps with that familiar heuristic in mind: think globally—act locally.

## OVERVIEW OF THE BOOK

### Part I: The Journal and Reflections

Every night before going to bed, I trekked to my basement and wrote retrospectively about the day. On some nights, I wrote just a line or two, and at other times I wrote several pages. I wrote much description, I wrote interpretations, and I wrote plans for the next day. The journal in the next section is an abridged version. I have excised journal entries that were redundant, rambling, overly theoretical, or in my judgment, uninteresting. I also edited out extraneous entries that may have been embarrassing to my students, their families, colleagues, or others.

One year after the sabbatical, I returned to the journal, read each excerpt, and did some initial theorizing by basically asking myself, "What does this mean? Does my reading of this excerpt remind me of any other research or theory?" The theoretical reflections are italicized.

The reader will notice that I begin many of the entries with the phrase, "good day" or "bad day." This phrase provides a reasonable sense now of my emotional gestalt after each day. Fortunately, the proportion of good days to bad days increased as the year transpired, beginning in late January. The reader will also notice the absence of a strong narrative in the journal. Instead, it seems at times that each excerpt is topically unconnected from what came before it and what follows. Certainly, my struggle to achieve order is an ongoing topic, and there are some curricular initiatives that follow a narrative flow, such as my concern about student-led conferences in the spring. I wonder if the lack of narrative (topically) simply reflects the reality of beginning teaching as a matter of survival, living day to day, just focused on having a day devoid of power struggles, chaos, and anger. In retrospect, I imagine that my goals, especially in the first months, *were* short term: for example, to get through the day with my ego intact.

## Part II: Dimensions of Teaching—Three Studies

The second part of the book contains three separate studies on three aspects of teaching of great concern to me: teacher–student power relations, teacher emotions, and teacher identity. The first study—"The Negotiative Dimension of Teaching: Teachers Sharing Power with the Less Powerful"—examines teacher–student negotiations. This chapter and the next one, on teacher emotions, have been published elsewhere and are reprinted here.[4] I have revised the articles for this book, so the texts in this volume are different versions than those published in *Teachers College Record* and *Teaching and Teacher Education*.[5]

In the first chapter in this section, my thesis follows an idea from Foucault that power is not certain, stable, or simply a requisite of position. Instead, it circulates among different people and groups as situations change. I suggest that, while teachers have some power advantages because of their physical size, skill, and role, students have much power as well, and power in teacher-student relations circulates between them as situations change. I argue that teachers and students have fundamentally different goals for school, so teachers and students need to engage in an ongoing process of negotiation, leading most of the time to a working consensus. In this working consensus, teachers and students modify their goals somewhat by each giving up a little, so some work can get done. In the end, the negotiative demand on teachers depends on their skills, the kinds of students they have, and the size of their classes.

In the chapter on emotions, I examine the "feeling rules" that guided my display of emotions as a teacher and how my emotions can lead to functional and dysfunctional outcomes. The challenge for me, as it is for all teachers, was to manage the tension between my felt emotions (how I was really feeling) and the "rules" that suggested how I was supposed to feel in certain situations. In response to this tension, I engaged in emotional labor, or face work, to change my internal emotional state or to simply change the look on my face in order to follow a particular feeling rule. Finally, I explore anger and how teachers might use this emotion as a catalyst for taking action for change and social justice.

"Theorizing Flexibility: Teacher as High-Wire Dancer" studies teacher identity and how (I think) I came to know as a teacher. I began the sabbatical with a fairly stable sense of my teaching self. In the first weeks and months, my beliefs were challenged continuously by situations that were unfamiliar to me. I constructed my identity(ies) in the small spaces between my ideals for what it meant to be a teacher and the actual reality of my working conditions. I found my self-concept shaped by my students most profoundly, but also by my colleagues, the school ethos, and the resources available to me. At a larger structural level, I also was shaped by forces outside the school walls that imposed expectations and material constraints on me, such as shrinking school budgets and the imposition of standards and tests. I argue that the task for teacher education is to help preservice teachers develop a wide set of beliefs and perspectives (i.e., identities) with which to make sense of the many discourses and pressures that await them as first-year practitioners.

In the concluding chapter, I examine hope as a motivation that is central to teachers' beliefs about their work. I argue that teacher education works best when it leads young teachers to understand and critique many perspectives on teaching and schools, and the work of university teacher education is important and ought not be marginalized in the current climate of deregulation. Finally, I recognize the importance of the school as a learning organization, as a social-collaborative culture for its adults, especially for beginning teachers, who need more support to weather the Sturm und Drang of early teaching and to grow from this experience.

## ETHICS

In writing about my students, their families, my colleagues, and the school, I am concerned that I will inadvertently cause them some harm or embarrassment. I realize that I can never completely protect their anonymity. People in the town where the school is located will know which school I am referring to. My former colleagues at the school will know I am referring to their school as the high-poverty school with large numbers of "high-profile students." In the event parents read this book, I am concerned that they will infer that I am referring to their child when I talk about my special needs students who are out of control. In order to reduce harm or embarrassment to others, I have employed the following strategies:

1. This book will be published almost seven years after the end of the sabbatical. The stories I tell in the book have become vague memories to most of the participants. By the time the book is published, my first graders will be eighth graders, and the third graders will be in tenth grade. When Barbara, my instructional assistant, read the journal just before publication of this book, she could barely remember the stories or even the students to whom I refer.
2. I have given everyone involved pseudonyms. I have also fictionalized some of the students in the journal, so the descriptions of these students do not accurately represent the more "high-profile" students. I have also split some of the key students into two students; for example, one of my most memorable students has been morphed into two students: a boy and a girl. All of the events contained in the book happened, but the characters have changed in order to protect the privacy of the students.

I believe the fictionalization of some of the students does not reduce the veracity of this research. The focus of the book is me and my struggle to construct a teaching identity. Changing the identities and characteristics of the student characters does not change or compromise my questions and the goals of the research. Still, I realize that one trade-off in truncating some of the players in the story is that it reduces the narrative's potential as a compelling and interesting read.

3. I gave the journal to Dorothy (my job-share partner), Fran (the student teacher), Barbara (the instructional aide), Judy (the principal), Arthur (the counselor), and a parent of one of the children in the class. I asked them to read the document to determine instances in which information might appear embarrassing or hurtful to the participants. I excised more excerpts based on their feedback.

4. Fundamentally, the studies contained in the book are about me and my thinking and development as a teacher. The book is not about my students, my colleagues, or the school. This was my heuristic as I made decisions about excerpts from the journal to include here and the fictionalization of some of the characters.

## NOTES

1. Dudley-Marling's (1997) book is most similar to mine. Dudley-Marling is also a teacher educator who took a leave from his university position and returned to the classroom as a full-time third-grade teacher. Dudley-Marling's book is a self-study of his work as a literacy teacher, while my book focuses more generally on issues of identity, emotions, and power.

2. Constructivist teaching (i.e., child- or student-centered teaching) reflects the Piagetian idea that children construct their own knowledge through their interaction with materials and objects in the everyday environment. Teachers who share this perspective tend to engage their students in much hands-on activity leading to inductive, or discovery, learning experience; the teacher is viewed as a facilitator of student learning; students are invited to raise their own questions and curiosities, which then guide teachers' instructional planning; there is more emphasis on cognitive process than on content; there is relatively little didactic teaching, and instead, the teacher *guides* students' performance as they are engaged in self-managed work in small groups or alone; and the curriculum is more contextualized in everyday experience.

In teacher- or text-centered teaching, the teacher or textual materials control the content of the curriculum; there is more emphasis on content than on cognitive process; there is more direct instruction or didactic teaching; teaching reflects deductive approaches to learning; and the curriculum is more decontextualized, or disconnected, from everyday experience. See Katz and Chard (2000) for more description of constructivist teaching.

3. The movie *Conrack* is based on the book *The Water Is Wide*, by Pat Conroy. The book describes Conroy's first year as an elementary teacher.

4. Chapter 2, "The Negotiative Dimension of Teaching: Teachers Sharing Power with the Less Powerful" is reprinted from *Teaching and Teacher Education*, volume 18, "The Negotiative Dimension of Teaching: Teachers Sharing Power with the Less Powerful," pp. 343–362, with permission from Elsevier. Chapter 3, "The Functions of Teacher Emotions: The Good, the Bad, and the Ugly" is reprinted from *Teachers College Record*, volume 105, "The Functions of Teacher Emotions: The Good, the Bad, and the Ugly," pp. 1641–1673, with permission from Blackwell Publishing.

5. The reader may notice some minor discrepancies between the journal excerpts displayed in the three studies in the second half of the book and the journal presented in the first half of this book. The three chapters use journal entries that are contained in the original, unabridged journal. The journal that is displayed in this book is edited and abridged.

**I**

# THE JOURNAL
# AND REFLECTIONS

# 1

# THE JOURNAL:
# FROM FIRST DAY
# TO LAST

**September 1, 1998**

First day with kids. Exhausting. We had kids sitting too much, listening to directions: how to use the playground equipment, the bathroom, entering the room, exiting the room, on and on. I am sitting at the computer now, in the evening. I'm emotionally spent. Can't remember much. It was all a blur.

**September 2, 1998**

Two days back and I'm now feeling, in my gut, the immensity of the task ahead of me.

This morning, I woke up at 4:30 and wasn't able to go back to sleep. I don't know my students yet, and my first two math lessons missed the mark badly. I posed problems that were too difficult for most students. Today, I had an unnerving experience. I lost control of the students for about an hour. I was embarrassed. Luckily, I was able to bring it together for the last half hour of the day.

The day has shaken my confidence about the next 178 days. I got home and was impatient with my own children. I anxiously put my two-year-old to bed. I was scared because tonight I didn't have any psychic energy for my own children. Teaching. It's hard work.

The last time I was an everyday teacher was 1985. Since then, I have worked with elementary teachers, as doctoral student and then as a professor in a teacher education department at Oregon State. But I was never in charge.

*Reflection: The preservation of self is a central concern in teachers' lives (Nias, 1989). My core teaching self reflects an experienced, somewhat expert teacher who knows what he is doing! After two days in the field, it is apparent that my teacher educator self (who is confident and knowledgeable) is threatened by the difficulty of this teaching assignment. My confusion is leading to a host of dark emotions: guilt, embarrassment, sadness. Already, I sense that teaching is going to encroach on my family time, especially in terms of how much quality time I'll be able to spend with my own kids.*

## September 3, 1998

I have led several activities and lessons. Easy stuff. Some read-alouds. Some challenging lessons, like in math problem solving. When I try stand-up teaching, students don't listen past my first twenty-second introduction. Side conversations and papers fly across the room. Students intentionally fall out of their seats. As the students get more antsy, I speak faster and sometimes become incoherent. I'm not sure what to say to them when they misbehave. I try different verbal signals: "I'm looking for active listeners . . . please be quiet . . . I'll continue when you are quiet . . . please be quiet . . . I see Stevie is ready to move on . . . I see this table is ready to listen . . . please be quiet. . . ."

I don't know the kids, they don't know me, and I don't know yet what kind of curriculum is appropriate for them. In my stomach, I sense that this is going to be a difficult year. A feeling that I've had under my skin is now surfacing: I am almost like a beginning teacher, and I think the kids have already picked up on this fact. Uh, oh! The jig is up.

*Reflection: I entered today's lesson without any sense of my own definition of the situation: How did I want the students to raise hands, sit, share information, be active listeners? My indirect management strategies were ineffective, and I sense that I needed to have begun the year with a more forceful articulation of classroom rules and expectations.*

Teachers in the building pass me in the hallway and ask, "Isn't it fun?!" To be honest, I am not having fun at all. The class is out of control, and I am confused. I am scared as I envision, now, 177 more days of school. My student teacher has a way out: she can change her placement if she gets too stressed out, or she can make a case that she needs a different venue at midyear.

Me? I have no way out. No exit. If I bail out, I would bring shame to my department, colleagues, the university, and my good professional name. After school today, I did imagine two ways out of this teaching assignment. The first is to just disappear. Leave town, alone, in the middle of the night, move to another state, change my name, and start a whole new life. Maybe work with the FBI in helping me relocate with an entire new personality. People might think that I was kidnapped and then incinerated, ashes blown in the wind never to be seen again, by a gang of free-market extremists who want to privatize all of public education. The second is to become very sick, maybe even have a heart attack.

*Reflection: Part of the corporate identity of teaching is the notion that "teaching is fun." I think this idea derives from the original motivation of many teachers to go into teaching because they "love working with kids." Implicit in loving what one does is the notion that "fun" will follow. I wonder if a broader, more complex description of teaching is in order, reflecting beliefs such as teaching is fun and enjoyable at times, onerous and excruciating at other times, and just tolerable at other times. It's like any other profession that has a certain complexity and unpredictability.*

I had my first successful teaching episode with students. I put a piece of writing done by my daughter on the overhead. It was a good example of prephonetic writing, in which the writer represents one or two sounds in each word. I wanted to show my students that they can begin taking risks and not worry about standard spelling. I led the students through the piece, and I demonstrated how an emerging writer vocalizes the target word and then segments each phoneme so these sounds are more obvious. I invited the students to interact with me during this demonstration, and they were very interested.

### September 4, 1998

I'm tired. I woke up this morning at about 4:30. I've done this the past three mornings. I have a mantra that I usually use to fall back to sleep, but it's not working. I keep rehashing the day in my mind. I begin feeling a knot in my stomach. The kids are out of control, and I haven't yet instituted any rules or consequences.

Dorothy's style is remarkable and consistent and effective. She continually redirects the students whenever they stray off task. The students respond to her. Why? I am not sure, but here are some ideas.

Since this is a blended primary and the students stay with the same teacher for three years, Dorothy has had fourteen of the students for one or two years. They trust her and her routines. She knows the families and the families know her. And since she has been teaching for the past twenty years, she has an automaticity about her language and the directions to students. There is nothing tentative about what she says.

I don't know the students. In their eyes, I am still a *stiff off the street* whose role is ambiguous and more akin to that of a student teacher. Dorothy has had student teachers in the past, and we have one now. I don't think the students truly understand that I officially have the same status as Dorothy!

A second reason that students respond to Dorothy and not me is that I am still tentative about redirecting students when they need redirection. For example, when two students are fighting over a jump rope, I know that I want them to problem solve, but I am still unsure how to direct the students to solve their own problems. So I vacantly look at the kids fighting and tell them, "Stop and go back to your seats!" I don't sound like I know teachers sound.

The third reason has to do with the absence of clear consequences for student misbehavior. Gradually, we are instituting procedures, such as how to share information in whole group, sharpening pencils, etc. But so far we haven't instituted any clear system of consequences. I sense that Dorothy does not need these in order for the kids to stay orderly. She has her own system, but it's invisible and I don't recognize it. I look in the mirror, and of course, I'm *not* Dorothy! I will need my own system for the afternoon.

*Reflection: Coming into the situation totally "cold," I was entering what Ball (1984) calls "problematic definitional situations par excellence" (113). According to Woods (1990a), there are two essential tasks for the teacher in the first few weeks of school. First, he needs to establish the fact that he is, indeed, in charge and in control. During the establishment phase, the students need a clear articulation and demonstration by the teacher of his boundaries, expectations, and parameters for behavior in the room. Second, within the teacher's general structuring of behavioral expectations, there needs to be room for student negotiation and input into these rules and how they are enforced by the teacher.*

> *Pupils (began) to probe for "living space" for themselves, testing around the edges of the sharply drawn rules, to negotiate the ground rules that actually operated. . . . Pupils soon began to discover priorities—important and comparatively unimportant parts of the school day, what they (are) actually allowed and not allowed to do in lessons, high and low status subject areas of the curriculum, important and less important teachers. (Measor and Woods, 1984, 52)*

*In the first few days of school, the quintessential task of teachers is to forge a common "definition of the situation" with students (Hargreaves, 1972). Students do come to school each year with some common understandings about how school works, including how to relate to teachers. For example, students generally know to show certain manners with teachers, or they know they are supposed to ask permission for certain behaviors, or they know that they are required to comply overtly with teacher directions. But each teacher and classroom situation is different, so the question of asking permission is ambiguous and needs to be negotiated with students over time. Do students need to receive permission to get water at the fountain? Do students have to defer a trip to the water fountain when the teacher is doing a read-aloud to the whole class? Can they just go without permission during independent work time?*

*When the students are just entering the room after recess, what are the drinking rules? Does everyone go at once, individually, in table groups, with or without teacher direction? How many trips to the fountain are allowable each hour, each day? How long can someone stand and drink water when others are waiting on line and you have to begin the lesson? And many of these rules for the water fountain cannot be simply stated, a priori, explicitly and unequivocally by the teacher, because students inevitably challenge the rules, deviate from them, and politic for their modification, and actual situations require the rules to change over time. The rules for multitudinous behavioral and academic situations gradually take shape and become the basis of a working consensus between teachers and students. Inevitably, the beginning of the year is stressful for teachers because they have to engage in the relentless give and take with students, and often they have to impose their will on basically reluctant youngsters. Ball (1984) wasn't kidding when he said, "Initial encounters . . . constitute pessimistic social environments that necessitate, or are conducive to, the continual reflexive calibration of the congruence between the self and others" (118).*

I ran into Robert, the school's recently retired principal. He asked me, "So have you become a teacher, yet?" His tone was humorous but his question was sage. His question got under my skin.

Implicit in my role as a teacher educator is the assumption that I would *know* what to do if I was thrust into an elementary teaching situation. Of course. I am the "expert." The education professor!

I am not a teacher, yet. In a sense, I am more like Fran, our intern, than Dorothy, my wonderfully skilled partner. Certainly, when the class goes haywire and the kids are out of control or a lesson bombs, I have more theoretical knowledge than Fran with which to make sense of the experience. And given my theoretical background and background in schools working with students (I did teach elementary school for seven years), my ability to make adjustments and refinements in my teaching is more developed than Fran's.

Perhaps what is more difficult for me than for Fran is the fact that I am not *supposed* to be having problems. I mean, big problems, like not having a handle at all on classroom management or how to develop curriculum in math for a 1–3 blend. Fran is just starting out, so her problems are "developmentally appropriate." My biggest struggle is the mismatch between my professional self-concept and my abilities to teach at this point in time. Exacerbating this mismatch is the fact that my teaching performance is quite public, for my colleagues at Woodbridge and the university to see. I am struggling, and it is embarrassing. Instead of developing sophisticated strategies to implement literature circles and writing to learn mathematics, I am trying to figure out how to have the kids line up outside the door after recess and then enter the room quietly.

Robert is right. I am learning to be a teacher. Again. It's an exciting professional opportunity. But, most of all, I want to stop waking up at 4:30 every morning. With a knot in my stomach. I keep reminding myself that it's just the first week of school.

## September 6, 1998
Just got back from a weekend in the mountains. Spent too much time thinking about school. In fact, it was on my mind virtually the entire weekend. Melinda and I talked about ways to reduce the stress of teaching: be extremely planned; exercise every day; have twenty minutes of quiet time after coming home from work; monthly visit to the masseuse; get a sitter and go on a date one night each week; plan weekend retreats hiking, skiing, etc.

One of my former student teachers is now teaching next door to me. I go to her almost everyday for suggestions, materials, and feedback.

A big problem I have is in helping kids solve social problems. I tend to be inundated with complaints from kids that other kids have hurt their feelings or have done them wrong in some way. The orientation of Dorothy and the other teachers is to teach the kids to solve their own problems. There is a problem-solving structure that, on paper, makes sense and one that kids can often manage successfully.

## September 8, 1998
Math was hectic. I divided students into three groups, and the three available adults in the room each took a group. I worked with the

middle-range group. I directed students to go pick up their math journals, but I wasn't organized. We lost about ten minutes as the kids fought with each other to pass out the journals. On the rug, I posed open-ended math problems. Of the twelve kids in my group, about four kids did not participate. I am not sure if this was because they were bored or confused. I will do more assessment tomorrow. Here is a list of what went well and what did not go well:

- I directed students to get their math journals at outset of period. Some journals were missing, and some kids did not have journals, since they missed the day we had passed them out. This led to a chaotic opening.
- For about the first ten minutes, most of the students in my group were engaged in solving the problems I posed on the board.
- After ten minutes, most kids seemed to get tired. They stopped working. Instead, they did some major fidgeting.

I am beginning to get to know my students. I am concerned about the number of high-needs kids. It's a little overwhelming. Nothing that I taught preservice teachers would prepare me for this teaching assignment. In fact, very little that I know about teaching and curriculum prepares me for this.

I am slowly bonding with students. During circle time, I gave one boy sitting next to me a gentle touch on the top of his back. He proceeded to gently tap my back for about thirty seconds. This student does no work and does not initiate much conversation with me. Lately, however, he and I are trading banter.

*Reflection: In order to teach someone, I need to know how they think and feel. When schoolwork isn't intrinsically interesting, which it often isn't, a key factor in students doing the work is their relationship with the teacher. Woods (1990b) holds that students don't do work for the sake of the work; they do it as a result of a relationship with the teacher (or peers or parents). Particularly when the schoolwork is not interesting to kids, "Work in itself does not seem a natural activity to . . . pupils, but it might be a natural adjunct of sociation. . . . The activity of work is a joint, shared enterprise, subsumable under the general relation-ships—that is what makes it enjoyable" (167).*

## September 11, 1998

It's Friday. Walking around the building, teachers and aides greet each other with, "Hey, it's Friday!!!" When I was at the university, the weekend did not have the same meaning as it does now. My schedule was so flexible. But now, given the locked-in nature of a teachers' work schedule, the idea of "weekend" has far more significance for me than it has since 1985, my last year of classroom teaching.

Before the students entered room after lunch recess, I had an anx-iety attack. I broke out in a sweat, heart racing wildly. I panicked. Once they entered, I was lulled out of my angst quickly by the demands of managing the class. Anxiety was replaced by . . . high anxiety.

The afternoon was pretty much a disaster. I had a really hard time with transitions. The kids tend to lose focus, and I have diffi-culty getting their attention. I would try all sorts of attention-getting language that I've heard Dorothy use successfully.

"I need your eyes . . . I am looking for active listeners . . . we'll get started with the next activity when everyone is sitting down and looking at me . . . table four is ready, table three is ready . . . I'm wait-ing . . . one, two, three, eyes on me!" (to this the kids respond, almost in military cadence: "one two, eyes on you!").

Even when I use attention-getting strategies that get the stu-dents to quiet down for a few seconds, I lose them quickly again when I start giving some other directions and they sense tenta-tiveness in my voice. I wanted each table group to come up with team names and then devise a team sign that would be hung above the table group. Four of the six groups got bogged down. Through-out the room, students were arguing and shouting, and some kids were crying.

In one group, two first-grade girls wanted the name the Pink Ponies. The one boy, a second grader, wanted the name Warrior Dragons. The girls agreed to vote on a name, theirs, and the boy started screaming since this was the second year that his suggestion for a group name was voted down. He sat in his chair, hands over head, sobbing. In another group, a boy stormed away from his group when his proposed name, Titanics, lost. In another group, all four kids had their own proposed names. Among the groups that had decided on a group name, only a handful of kids were completing the assignment, composing a picture sign that would hang above the groups. I was too busy trying to mediate the major conflagrations, and I did not have the time to monitor what the other kids were doing. By the end of the period, not one group had posted a sign above their group.

*Reflection: The lesson was unexpectedly difficult. I think the big issue is that I didn't anticipate the importance of "name" to students, as they worked to name their table groups. Of course, I didn't consider the students' existing cooperative group skills or the need for me to provide more structure, a tighter "rule frame" (Pollard, 1985), so the students would have fewer tangents to take and the solution path to a negotiated name would have been more clear-cut.*

Around 2:00 p.m., I introduced the idea of pantomiming. I pantomimed eating a banana. I had the kids guess my food. Then I gave each table group a different food to act out. Students got very involved.

## September 13, 1998

It's Sunday night, and I am grieving. The weekend is coming to a close. Tomorrow, I enter the culture of at-risk children. I recall several times in the past few weeks when teachers at the school asked me if I am having fun, yet. I'm not having fun at all. (I wonder if they are having fun, but I don't have the nerve to ask them. I would be crushed if they said, "Yes.") I respond, with a smile on my face, "Teaching's hard work." It's one of an emerging set of mantras I use to cope with or frame this experience. Other mantras:

- I can do it. I can do it.
- It's just for one year.
- I am brave.
- This is going to make me a better teacher educator.
- The afternoons are just two hours and twenty minutes.

I started jogging today. Bought some fancy jogging shoes. First time in years. I hope I get a good night's sleep.

**September 14, 1998**

I changed a piece of the rule system. Previously, when students were disruptive, I asked them to go to "time out" and then return to the group when they were "ready to be cooperative." (The time-out spot was a desk in the back of the room.) Students did not like being separated from the group. However, I found that time out was not an effective consequence for disruptions. It worked for Dorothy, but not for me.

Today, I upped the ante on time out. Now, students had to copy a laborious form, which read something like, "I will work harder at not disrupting the learning of my friend's or Ken's teaching. I will work harder to stay in control of my behavior." Then the student has to explain how they are going to change their specific behavior. Today, it tended to work. When students were antsy, I held the form in front of them, and they calmed down. For the moment, this measure is helping me get a grip on student behavior.

*Reflection: Teaching folklore says that the teacher must start the year being tough on the students, to let them know "who is boss." Gradually, once the rules are in place and the teacher is confident that students are going to acquiesce to the teacher's definition of the situation, then the teacher can relax and be more personal with the student. Hargreaves (1972) argues the same idea. Essentially, the early stance of the teacher has to approximate the relationship that the kids have had with previous teachers or with other adults in their lives. Most classrooms and parent–child relationships are autocratic, with the adult dominating the child. Children are used to being told what to do and when to do it. After the teacher has established her dominance, the teacher can begin leaving more space for children to give voice and participate in classroom governance and the everyday negotiation typical of all relationships.*

*I really didn't know what kind of culture that I wanted in the room. For example, procedures are an essential way that kids learn the culture of a classroom. Questions of entering the room, sharing information, when to talk, when to be quiet, how to talk to me, how they should solve problems, and so forth. These are all questions of procedure, and I had only a fuzzy idea of what I wanted.*

**September 15, 1998** (evening)

I got home from an ice cream social at the school. It's 8:15 p.m. I thought about tomorrow afternoon. There was so much to do and think about. I put a poem about clouds on butcher paper for a whole-group choral reading. I also made a cloud painting, a model for the kids today when I want them to do the same. I couldn't find white paint in my school, so I drove to a store, only to find that they sold white paint in very small quantities at a high cost. I asked Melinda, my wife, if she had any in her classroom. She said yes, so tomorrow morning I will stop by her school to pick up some paint.

I practiced doing a math center as I prepared to introduce it to the students.

I perused several books on creative drama. I planned pantomiming activities for tomorrow.

I called Mary, one of the students who has been sick and is coming back to school tomorrow.

I watched a thirty-minute videotape on classroom management. I took notes. Before the tape ended, I got tired, turned off the TV, and went upstairs. All the lights were out. Melinda went to bed. I climbed into bed around 11:15 and was unable to fall asleep. I thought about the next day for about an hour. I woke up at 5:30 a.m. thinking about what I need to do.

*Reflection: A perennial problem for teachers is the lack of time for all the planning and preparation that they need to do (Coates & Thoresen, 1976; Dollase, 1992). Dollase (1992) found that beginning teachers worked an average of fifty-seven hours a week, and veterans worked just slightly less. I was teaching a constructivist math curriculum for the first time. I knew that I wanted to engage the kids in creative drama, but I hadn't taught this subject before. And, assuming that classroom management represents a curriculum, I certainly was in the embryonic stage of learning about this domain.*

*In the absence of textbooks, I was encumbered with inventing a curriculum each day and each week. On the one hand, this freedom was exhilarating, since I had some control over what and how I taught the kids. On the other hand, this freedom made for a workload that was exhausting, and it reduced my interest in professional issues outside the classroom.*

## September 16, 1998

Every day, or almost every day, when I say goodbye to Dorothy as she leaves the class at noon and I take over, her parting words to me are, "Love those kids!"

There are so many kids who need my individual time. So many of the kids have issues. Judy, a bright third grader, has been refusing to follow Fran's directions.

I talked to Nathan's dad last night, and we agreed to set up a highly structured behavior plan, one that Dorothy used with him last year. I need to get together with Dorothy and the counselor and discuss this.

Stevie appears to be encapsulated in his own little world. I need more time with him.

There are at least two students who were fetal alcohol babies, so their attention span and ability to grasp concepts and directions lags behind most of the others.

I have three kids who are chronic avoiders of assignments and, instead, tend to wander around the room.

There is another student who has bladder-control problems, so she might emit a small amount of smelly fecal matter.

Another boy, Joey, often cries when he is faced with a task that is either confusing or uninteresting. There are four or five very young first graders who need brief directions and well-defined tasks.

Bonnie is bright and interesting, but sometimes her idiosyncrasies take over: the other day, her two feet began a conversation with each other, and she could not (or would not) control the feet for about forty-five minutes.

So many of the kids are loud, and they externalize their anxiety and anger. I am exhausted at the end of each afternoon from the task of trying to keep the group focused on a common agenda. At the end of each day, I try to have the group stand in a circle, holding hands, and I say a brief meditation, "May we learn to find calm and peace in our lives, at home and at school; may we have eyes that see, hearts that feel, and hands ready to help those who need us." My meditation is a prayer for the kids but, mostly, for me.

In math, I have collaborated with the other primary teachers to implement a center approach to the teaching of mathematics. We agreed on the math strands for the year (patterns, numeration, measurement, probability, statistics, etc.), and we agreed to teach these strands at the same time. We will meet every other week and decide the types of centers we want in our classrooms, for each strand.

When I am alone with friends from the university, I share my second thoughts about the decision to return to the classroom. They tell me that I had overromanticized teaching. As much as I hate to admit it, I wonder if they are right.

*Reflection: Many accounts I've read by returning education professors have chronicled the difficulty, and often the pain, of what is essentially a novice teaching experience (e.g., Dudley-Marling, 1997; Hudson-Ross & McWhorter, 1995). I think that the most confusing dimension for the returning education professor is the mismatch between his/her self-concept as a teacher educator (successful, confident, expert) and the realities of being a novice classroom teacher again. The teacher educator was probably viewed as a successful classroom teacher years ago, before he entered higher education, and now he probably has a reputation as a successful teacher educator. And the public dimension of teaching makes it embarrassing when the so-called expert proceeds to fail again and again.*

*It is, perhaps, crucial that the returning professor redefine his self early in the experience and realize that he is again a novice and quite dependent on the support of colleagues.*

I wonder if there is a dispositional dimension to being a teacher. Educational researchers and other educators have written much about the pedagogical and curricular dimensions of teaching, such as the various knowledge bases of teaching or the studies that have examined the behaviors and cognitions of "expert" and "novice" teachers. I wake up each morning and feel an emotional response to getting out of bed, and I feel the butterflies at 12:15 as the kids are about to rush in. I wonder about how I *should* feel. I suppose I know that I am supposed to be excited and happy to see the kids. I worry a bit now, since I don't have a whole lot of positive feelings at 12:15.

I think that a so-called good teacher has a particular disposition about the task of teaching and the work with youngsters. This dispositional component might have the following criteria:

- wholeheartedly enjoys working with young people,
- desires to effect the intellectual and social development of young people,
- and looks forward to most days in the classroom as an opportunity to help young people further their development and learning.

The experience of being with a group of twenty-five kids every day, in an enclosed space, can be stressful for any adult. Children think differently than adults, and there is a culture represented in how youngsters think and behave that is different than adult culture. And when one considers classrooms composed of several ethnic or racial cultures, then the cultural mix is even more complicated for the lone adult teacher. The challenge for teachers in forging a learning culture among a group of twenty-five students is immense, and the sheer psychic demands of being in what, for an adult, is a foreign culture can be very stressful. I'm not sure right now if I have the dispositional "knowledge" to be a teacher.

*Reflection: It seems inevitable that the teacher is going to give more (more time, more care, more kind thoughts, more ideas) than he is going to get back from the students.*

*Constant giving in the constant context of vigilance required by the presence of many children is a demanding, draining, taxing affair that cannot be easily sustained. . . . To sustain the giving at a high level requires that the teacher experience getting. The sources for getting are surprisingly infrequent and indirect. (Sarason, 1971, 167)*

I introduced a math center on tessellations. I gave a five-minute explanation and then invited students to work at this center. The six students who worked on tessellations didn't get it. One girl just wanted to fill in the tessellation worksheet with random colors. Other kids thought that I wanted them to make simple patterns on the worksheet. I realized that this topic is more complex than I'd originally thought. I need to teach tessellations again. Tomorrow.

*Reflection: The kids found the activity either too easy (and boring) or too difficult. In these cases, it is natural for students to enact their own definition of the situation. They redefined it in a way that made sense to them and would also keep me off their backs, since they were doing* something. *It is common for teachers to ignore minor deviant behavior if it is not disrupting the general order of the class.*

The end-of-day procedure was chaotic. With ten minutes left in the day, I blanked out on what else to do. I brought the students to the rug for some sharing. I forgot to review my expectations for circle behavior. I struggled with many students to stay quiet when someone (like me!) was talking. My language was ineffective: "I am looking for quiet listeners. I need your eyes. How are we supposed to behave when we are in a circle?" With a minute before the bell, I tried to give my farewell meditation, "May we learn to find calm and peace in our lives, at school, and at home, etc." No one heard me, since there were too many other voices. I tried to have everyone sing a song. A lot of the kids used silly voices. Finally, the bell rang and I persisted with the end of day cheer. This led to group screaming. I was embarrassed when a parent stuck his head in the door, and he gave me a sympathetic look.

Tomorrow, I need to establish expectations and enforce them. I read a great chapter on time out, one strategy for enforcing rules, in a humanistic approach to classroom management by Ruth Charney (1992). I will try it tomorrow.

It sometimes feels as though Nathan is taking over the class. He is only eight years old, but his volatile responses to my directions have me on the defensive. He gets emotional when he is asked to do something that he doesn't want to do. He'll storm around the room, raise his voice, pout, and sometimes cry. Today, when he started cry-

ing and running around the room, I followed him and sympathetically asked, "What are you feeling? What's the problem? What can
we do about it?" I am taking a therapeutic approach with the kid, but
this strategy just seems to give him license to simply continue his
theatrical-hysterical behavior. He is sapping my psychic energy and
time. I went home today, and I have no idea what kind of work was
generated by half the class.

I want to try something new, with the cooperation of his father.
The next time Nathan has a tantrum, I will give him two minutes to
get himself reorganized and back to work or, when the timer rings,
he will be sent home.

### September 18, 1998

One girl has many physical problems. Today, she complained of a
rash on her leg, and she asked to go home so her mom could ad-
minister some ointment. I said no, since there was just one hour left
until the end of the day. A few minutes later, she disappeared. She
was in the office asking to use the phone. I brought her back to classroom. Five minutes later, she urinated in her pants. She really
*wanted* to be sent home! We found a new pair of pants for her. I am
perplexed by the kid's problems, which are considerable.

Deacon, a first-grade boy, does not listen to directions at all. I'll be
standing next to him, and I might ask him to sit down. It's like talking to a statue. I sent him to time out today. After school, he asked
me if the time-out slips are put in students' permanent records. I
said, no. Relieved, he indicated that his parents are stricter than I am.
When he misbehaves at home, he gets spanked with a wooden spoon.

*Reflection: It is now a given in education that students from differ-
ent cultural groups may need different participation and curricular
structures (e.g., Phillips, 1972), and perhaps gender ought to be considered in how teachers represent knowledge and activities. I am fast coming to the conclusion that the way our students have been parented
ought to be a factor in how we think about teacher–student negotiations.
A kid such as Deacon might require a more closed negotiating style.*

We did pantomiming at the end of the day. The students were focused. It's part of what I hope will be a year-long study of drama. I

am also finishing a read-aloud of the book *Shoeshine Girl*, by Robert Bullah. It's a compelling story of a girl who has emotional and social problems. She takes a job working as an assistant in a shoe-shine stand, and through her relationship with the shoe-shine man she begins to pull her life together. I want to read more good literature, reflecting the issues and problems of real kids, like the ones in this class!

I am still playing around with strategies to get students to "listen to directions." I have been employing a time-out sheet, which students fill out when they get sent to time out. However, students are being sent to time out two and three times in one day. Yesterday, another primary teacher described a second step that he uses. In the event of students' second time-out infraction, they have to take the time out form home and have their parent sign it. If they fail to do this, then they stay in for recesses until the form comes back. It's a real punitive approach, but I will try this today.

I found an idea in Charney for building classroom community and, specifically, to help kids be nicer to each other. We will sit in circle, and students share a kindness or good deed performed by a peer that they observed this week. The good citizen can then take a pretzel stick from a bowl in the middle of the circle. I'll try it next week.

## September 21, 1998

Yesterday was hellacious. Math went all right. I put up some models of math stories written by primary students with whom I've worked in the past. I asked students to generate a math story about their family, before they went off to centers. After math, things began to unravel. In science, I led a short discussion of the key ideas about weather. Then, I asked the students to think about wind, what they knew and what else they would like to learn. I had a short book on the topic of wind, which I tried to read.

Continuously, I had to ask the students to be active listeners and focus on the speaker (me!). I tried walking over to disruptive students (which sometimes calms them down), touching them lightly on the shoulder and asking them quietly to listen, and finally, I began administering time-out forms, sending kids to various parts of the room. Nathan argued with his being sent to time out, so I asked to him to leave the room and go to the alternative learning environment. In spite of Fran's directions, Crystal would not come out from under her desk. I indicated to Crystal that she could "choose" to go to the time-out room or come out from under the desk. She started to cry. I backed away from this threat and sent her back to her table. Meanwhile, I could not get the rest of the students to quiet down and focus enough for me to read the wind book. I finally gave up and directed the students to put their heads on the tables and relax for a few minutes before break.

After break, at 2:00 p.m., it was time for creative drama. We were beginning with pantomime. One of the student's parents, Jill, comes each Monday at this time to help out. She is interested in drama. Again, the kids were disruptive. They were loud, physically out of control, and often oblivious to adult instructions. I presented a scenario, such as eating an ice cream cone on a hot day, and then invited students in small groups to the front to act out. I invited anyone who wanted to come to the front to pretend to hold a bird with a broken wing. Twenty students came to the front. I should have had them come to the front in small groups. I am not sure how to structure drama differently. But I am sure that it needs to change. By 2:25, when I asked Fran to read a story, I was physically and emotionally exhausted. I felt like a policeman—one who did a very poor job.

I think these kids need different structures. Things to do:

1. Review behavioral expectations before each lesson. I did it before math but not before science and creative drama.
2. In the first part of the science lesson, get students more involved. Have groups brainstorm their knowledge of questions about wind. Assign one student in each group as recorder, who then reports back to whole group. Then, do a whole-class read-aloud. Find a book on wind that has larger pictures. Or use overheads of key illustrations.
3. Creative drama was too freewheeling. I am a bit perplexed how to organize this.

Jeff does no work, unless I sit with him and "force his hand." I called his mom last night and asked permission to keep him after school, when I would have the time to sit with him. She agreed.

I called Crystal's mom last night. We talked of Crystal's recalcitrance and, at times, complete insubordination. The mom agreed that her daughter needs to be held accountable for the choices she makes. I feel more comfortable in dealing with her after this phone conversation.

There are many other parents I want to call, to address issues. About seventeen of my twenty-five students have "issues," which is a euphemism for behavior or academic difficulties. I feel that before I can meaningfully and confidently address the issues in school, I need parents to be informed, and I need their support.

I am making my first visit to a psychotherapist tomorrow. I keep fantasizing how I can get out of this teaching assignment, and I realize that this isn't a useful coping strategy. Teaching is getting to me. I fixate on work, am a lot tenser with my own children when I come home, and am having trouble sleeping. Work is seeping into my consciousness almost twenty-four hours a day. Everyday conversations with friends and neighbors are impeded when my mind switches to work, as when I was having a conversation with neighbor Ian about the price of oranges.

A friend who is a therapist described me as suffering from anxious depression. I do feel anxious and depressed. I get anxious when I think about facing the students. And I get down in the dumps when I dwell on the difficulty of my situation. As lousy as I feel, it is crucial that I be "up" with the students. I need to laugh, smile, and stay grounded when teaching. The work to maintain a positive outward persona is, itself, stressful, since my authentic feelings are anxiety, depression, and sometimes anger.

Ironically, in spite of my dissatisfaction with my mental health, my teaching, and the progress of the students, the students all seem to be happy; they like me and their parents feel the same way. Go figure.

I need to be more systematic and explicit in defining the classroom culture. Today, I am going to be articulating an image of the "good math student," as someone who writes math problems or math stories, shows their problem-solving work, and completes their work. I will post these ideas on the wall, and I will show overheads of several exemplary student stories and story problems written yesterday.

*Reflection: Maslow (1973) argued that the "best helpers of other people are the most highly evolved, healthiest, strongest, . . . most fully developed people" (153). I think that I am a somewhat (psychologically) healthy person, but certainly I am not without hang-ups or ego problems. In most situations in life, my mental health is sound and stable. However, when I am put in a situation like this that is unfamiliar, my ego is at risk of attack and I have inadequate resources to reduce the risks. I now realize mental illness is a sensible outcome for many people.*

## September 22, 1998

Today went well. I was very organized. I reviewed some new management expectations. The math assignment was clear. The science activity was hands-on. While the kids were on task, I was concerned about the superficiality of the activity in terms of science content. The manipulation of materials dominated students' attention, and they were attentive. However, when we debriefed at the end of the period, very few kids were willing or ready to make observations about the experience. I'll return to this activity tomorrow.

At the end of the day, the circle activity was calm and effective. I placed a bowl of pretzels in the middle of the floor and invited students to point out peers whom they observed to have done some kindness or good deed. The doer of the good deed then got one pretzel stick. Nathan was not mentioned once. At the end, he complained that it wasn't fair, since he didn't get any pretzels. I asked him to speculate why he didn't get pretzels. He ignored me. Over the long term, I am interested to see if this circle activity has an effect on his peer relations.

I posted "consequences for disruptive behavior." Fran indicated to me that she read about this practice in Harry Wong's book for beginning teachers. She asked me if I was going to post "consequences for positive behavior." I overlooked this.

I watched Jeff in math. Again, he sat and did nothing. I reminded him of my conversation with his mom and her agreement that he could stay after school and do math. I asked him, "You can do the math now or after school. It's your choice."

He said, "I'll do it after school."

Fifteen minutes later, he turned in his math assignment.

I am reading Charney's book with great enthusiasm. It's a very practical book on classroom management from a humanistic perspective. I read portions of it last summer. I found it interesting, but it was hard to read cover to cover, and its suggestions and ideas did not stick. Now, as I struggle with transitions, I write crib sheets of transition language that Charney suggests, keep the "cheat sheets" in my shirt pocket, and take them out as reminders when the class is in transition. The section on sending students to time out is helping me to revise how I approach this strategy. I have been having power struggles with several students with whom time out does not work, and Charney's suggestions for power struggles seem sensible.

*Reflection: I began using Harry and Rosemary Wong's (1998) handbook for beginning teachers. It is a traditional approach to classroom management in which the teacher imposes the structure on the students and, in effect, takes strong direct leadership in establishing the classroom culture. In this book, there is little room for a negotiated culture, at least in the first few months of school. At first glance, the book offended my student-centered sensibilities. My belief has been that classroom culture, although ultimately controlled by the teacher, should provide more space for student input and initiatives. However, my teaching self in this situation demanded a more structured, teacher-centered approach. Why? Two reasons:*

1. *I didn't yet have the skills to facilitate a more democratic classroom.*
2. *Many of my students were so behaviorally challenging that, even if I had had more skills at implementing a democratic classroom, these kids would still have needed more top-down structure.*

## September 24, 1998

Yesterday, I had students do a story problem in which they had to fill in the blanks for the numerical information.

I have _____ friends. Their names are _____.
Each friend ate _____ cookies. How many cookies did they eat altogether?

Wanda could not complete the blanks. She called out plaintively, "I don't have any friends." I did not have the heart to tell her to simply make up some names and make this an imaginative story problem. She *doesn't* have any friends, and I cannot imagine the pain of not having any friends. I need to spend more time with her, talking about this issue, and I need to do more work with the class on having them develop class-based friendships.

As difficult a time as I am having, it is crucial that I'm upbeat and happy with the students, at least on the surface. When I let them in the room after lunch break, and I feel a knot in my stomach, I greet each individual student with a handshake or hug. When things go awry, I almost force myself to laugh. When students really bug me, I will occasionally hug them. When I make a major miscalculation, I've begun to ask myself, "What can I learn from this." When things go totally awry, I might look at Barbara, laugh, and say, "I love this class!" We smile at each other and I am able to let the tension fall away.

A basic condition for my succeeding with these kids is that I genuinely enjoy them, and I am able to share this pleasure with them. If I don't like them, it is silly and hopeless to think that I can fake it.

## September 26, 1998

I got to school yesterday and saw one of my students, sitting in the office. He explained, "I have lice." His parents were unavailable, so he had to sit in the office all day. In the rush of the afternoon, I forgot about him. I didn't go back once to visit him and see how he was doing. I realized this oversight after I had gotten home. I tried to call the student at home, but all I got was his father's voice mail. I felt guilty that I'd forgotten him.

I sure would want my daughter's teacher to treat her more compassionately if she had to sit in the office all day, with head lice. As a criterion for how I ought to interact with my students, I think about how I want my daughter's teachers to interact with her. The Golden Rule. . . .

We are four weeks into the school year, and I am not sure what my students have learned. I am having some anxiety that they haven't learned much. Thank God for Dorothy and her morning program.

I am focusing on three curricular areas: science, math, and creative drama. In science, I am using a structured science program provided by the school district. I am comfortable with this system. It's hands-on, well organized, and developmentally appropriate for a multiage classroom. Meanwhile, I have not figured out how I want to organize the math program. I feel as though much of what I do represents a "holding" strategy, until I figure out what will work for me and with these students.

The biggest problem for me in this (grades 1–3) nongraded primary school is the range of needs and backgrounds represented by these students. I have some students who are operating at a prekindergarten level, and then I have some third graders who have some rather mature mathematical understandings. Besides the range of math background, the students represent a wide range of dispositional and emotional stances toward school, sitting in a chair, engaging in academic tasks, and so forth. The students sit in table groups of about four to a table. Unless Barbara or I am sitting alongside certain students, five or six of them usually do not do any work. About six other students dawdle in getting the assignment done, and the period often ends before they are done. Some of the students tend to engage in disruptive behavior (loudness, argument, roaming around the room, falling out of chairs) that requires our attention.

*Reflection: I am troubled by the mismatch between my belief that the teacher takes care of the needs of all his children and the reality of teaching. At this time, I cannot possibly meet all my kids' needs, academic and social/emotional. I am responding with the emotion guilt. Hargreaves (1994a) defined my feeling as "depressive guilt," when we "realize that we may be harming or neglecting those for whom we care, by not meeting their needs or by not giving them enough attention" (144). Guilt is not an uncommon emotion for teachers.*

## September 28, 1998

Good day.

We did creative drama today. The kids broke up into groups of four and acted out "Three Billy Goats Gruff." I had Barbara and Jill, a parent volunteer, help out. We each took two groups and worked with them in different parts of the building.

Sarah is very quiet, almost painfully shy. During Sarah's performance as the troll, I was impressed with her willingness to play the part and even verbalize the minimum language required to play it. She seemed a bit pained when doing the lines, but I saw a smile crease her face when she was done.

Math went well. I am still mismatching students and academic tasks. Still, the tasks I assign, for some students, often are either too difficult or too easy.

Emma has missed the past six days of school. I don't know why. Is she sick, or has the family moved? The family has no phone. I will check with Dorothy tomorrow to see what she knows.

I still have trouble with transitions. If I am not particularly entertaining or interesting, I tend to lose many of the students. As I look around, I watch students' heads move closer to each other, and a low indecipherable mumble of conversation can be heard. Off to my right, Stevie and Sally might be wrestling over a marker. Nathan and Billy might be blowing crayons to each other, across their table. Several students might still be playing with manipulatives from the math period.

I go through my litany of verbal attention-getting signals, and these have a moderate effect on most students. Recently, I might assume an exasperated look on my face, fold my arms, and give an I-message: e.g., "I feel frustrated when people are talking when I want to give directions." Again, this would have a slight moderating effect on perhaps one or two students. Meanwhile, I am spending five minutes trying to get near silence, so I can begin the next lesson, but the sheer length of time spent in getting the students' attention is having a negative effect on my desired outcome. Students who earlier had been ready to move on are now losing it.

**September 29, 1998** (evening)
Melinda and I both feel itching on our heads, itching that won't go away. Within the past few days, we both had students who had to be sent home because of head lice. I have a sinking feeling in my stomach that we're infected. We are about to check each other's hair. Another occupational hazard.

**October 1, 1998**
I've noticed some changes in my relationship with the students. I've been with them for twenty-two days. I sense that the students look forward to seeing me, and I am beginning to look forward to seeing them. It's still really hard, matching them up with curricular experience that is developmentally appropriate, interesting, and significant. When I make mistakes, the group can still go haywire. But now, the pandemonium is only for a few seconds until I make an adjustment. Earlier in the month, when I gave a verbal direction, it was often as if I was whistling in the wind. No one heard me.

I remember the first few days of school I wore funny ties, like with Mickey Mouse or Cat-in-the-Hat themes. None of the students made any comments about these ties. Yesterday, I wore one of these ties and some of the students made a fuss. When the students see me, at 12:15, I am beginning to feel some genuine affection. Most of them will either call out my name or give me a hug. In the morning, when I am not working, they will sometimes forget the schedule and ask Dorothy, "Where's Ken?"

At 12:15, when they walk in from lunch recess, I greet them at the door, touch their hands, smile, say their names, and give them a full-voiced, "Hey, Cesar, how ya doin'?" They enter the room, sit down, and I then do a status check. They give me two thumbs up if they are having a great day, two thumbs sideways if they are having an average day, and two thumbs down if they are having a bad day.

"Hey, it's great that your day is going so well."

"Ooh, a so-so day so far. Let's see what we can do to make it better this afternoon."

"Oh, I'm sorry your day isn't going well so far. Let's turn it around this afternoon, so you can go home feeling great."

Yesterday, we had a fire drill. I spoke to the students beforehand about behavioral expectations. When they went out, their line was perfectly straight, and they were quiet. I wasn't aware of the significance of this event until several adults in the building commented, "This is the first time I've ever seen this class line up so quietly." Ordinarily, I would be disdainful of a compliment on my students' lining up skills. For now, I do not care about the curriculum, the state tests next spring, math problem writing, and the other heady features of the explicit curriculum. My head swelled with pride. My kids know how to line up for fire drills!

When the kids go crazy, I work hard to never lose my cool. On surface, I stay calm and work to redirect, either my own teaching moves or the students. When I send a student to time out, I try to do it with an empathetic face. I sometimes work to laugh at their jokes. When I commit a teaching faux pas, I might let my hair down with them. For example, I was drinking iced coke in an unmarked cup. It was sitting on the overhead projector, and in my excitement I knocked it over. The students were horrified that I put ice in my "coffee." Concerned that they would find out that I drink Coke when teaching, I lied and said that I drink iced coffee. I then volunteered to go to time out, where I filled out a time-out form. The students had a good time with this.

## October 2, 1998

Yesterday, we had a special education staffing for one of our second-grade girls. Her life is totally discombobulated, with physical handicaps, emotional traumas, social problems, and academic problems. It came out in the meeting that she is skillful at storytelling. Tomorrow, I have made time at the end of the day so she can present a story to the class. She is excited.

I am planning to have the students act out the story, *Caps for Sale*. I will read it aloud to them twice today and then, during a second reading, have the entire group, in chorus, join me for the key dialogue sections. On Monday, I will have students act out the story in pairs. Barbara and I will model for them first.

I am still perplexed with the planning for math. I know what I have to do, but now it is a matter of accessing resources that fit my objectives. The focus for the next four or five weeks is numeracy. I am using materials from many sources (Quest 2000, Math in Stride, Mathland, etc.). I have a wide range of students who need some differentiated instruction and math tasks, beginning with a group of six first graders who are operating on a pre-K level. But then, given the fact that this is a nongraded primary, I want to exploit this organizational feature by having the students work on common tasks. I want to pose tasks to the whole group, which the olders are more ready to handle, so the youngers can watch the olders model more mature problem-solving behavior. I realize that the youngers will not grasp the actual meaning of some of these more complex problems. However, I want them to watch the olders demonstrate the macrofeatures of problem solving such as volunteering to come to the board to share a solution, drawing solutions, and giving verbal explanations.

I want everyone to work problems that are *low entry, high ceiling*, the ones that everyone can make sense of *at their own particular developmental level*: For example, there are four people in the room. They all shook each other's hands once. How many handshakes were there?

Most first graders can understand the meaning of this problem and begin working on the solution.

Other dilemmas I face in math have to do with some of the following:

- balancing problem-solving tasks with drill and practice.
- teaching for meaning versus drill and practice
- balancing all the math strands (such as geometry, measurement, statistics/probability, calculations, patterns and functions, and problem solving)

Mathematics curriculum has become a black hole, especially since the publication of the National Council of Teachers of Mathematics (NCTM) in 1989. In this report, NCTM advocated for a broader conception of math knowledge. I agree with this new image of mathematics curriculum. The quintessential question has to do with time:

how do we fit all this curriculum into the school day so each strand is addressed in a deliberative and thoughtful manner?

I wonder how many teachers in my building love coming to work most days.

I had a lot of trouble maintaining the focus of the students. I wrote an open-ended problem on the blackboard, passed out one poster paper to each table group, and then directed the groups to work the problem together. I asked that the oldest person in each group be the scribe.

The problem: There were four raccoons that went for a picnic near the lake. Two raccoons got their front feet wet. One raccoon got its back feet wet. How many dry feet were there?

I suggested that the groups draw raccoons and use the pictures to eliminate the wet feet. Many of the students redefined the task to be artistic. In some groups, the kids pulled out the crayons and focused their attention on the visual dimensions of the task. Two groups fought over which member was the oldest. There were youngers in many of the groups who did not attend at all to the task, so these students played at off-task activities. One group spent ten minutes writing down the problem and group member names on its paper.

Once most groups had completed even partial representations of the solution, I asked groups to come to the front to explain their ideas. It was extremely difficult for students, sitting at their desks, to focus on the sharing groups who stood in front of the room with their poster paper. Some of the illustrated solutions were visually indecipherable from more than three feet away, and almost all the speakers did not express themselves clearly so anyone could hear them. I tried to repeat their explanations, but most of the audience was tuned out and, in many cases, engaged in off-task conversations. I tried my litany of attention-getting techniques. Given the unfamiliarity of the task and the fact that it was Friday afternoon and many of the students were tired and ready to go home, the students did not ever truly sit still and listen to the presenting groups.

It was a good problem, and I think that many of the students did engage meaningfully in its solution. The social dimension of the task (sharing ideas in small group and in whole group) may be essentially a new routine for them, especially the thirteen first graders. Of course, the first attempts at this structure are going to be just an approximation of what it can be if I continue this structure for the next few months. I could take an expedient course of action and avoid these kinds of activities by rationalizing that these students *need* more structured tasks and that this task fell apart because it was mismatched with these particular students. Or I can resolve to pursue this type of activity, since I believe it is important for their math learning and for their learning in general.

Later in the day, a half hour before the students went home, I had them sit in a circle on the floor. I posed the question, inspired by Vivian Gussin Paley (1992), "Can you say you can't play?" Lately, there had been incidents in which some kids had excluded others from outside games during recess. I was holding the talking stick, so that anyone else who talked was breaking a circle rule and had to leave the circle and go to time out. In the two minutes I needed to explain the question to the students, I sent eight kids out to time out. So, there was a circle of fifteen kids.

Half of the remaining students "passed" when the talking stick came to them. The other half was divided on the question. Some kids agreed with Paley's idea. The other half disagreed. The oppositionists generally agreed with Paley, but they didn't think it would work when the kid asking to play was someone they despised or disliked. They also indicated that, sometimes, it is dangerous to allow too many kids to play a game, especially when the game is a physical one.

I spent too much time managing the kids who were in time out, while I simultaneously tried to listen and manage the circle. Besides, the remaining circle participants did not seem to be particularly interested in the topic. I guess the bottom line on my afternoon is the role of structure, especially the role of familiar structures on the students and the classroom climate. The activity in math was unfamiliar to the kids. Compounding the students' confusion was my own unfamiliarity with leading these activities: hence, an afternoon that was marked by antsy kids and an uptight teacher.

*Reflection: What I don't have now is what Grimmett and MacKinnon (1992) refer to as general pedagogic knowledge and knowledge of learners, or "procedural ways in which teachers deal rigorously and supportively with learners" (387). They refer to this as craft knowledge, a deeply contextualized knowledge of the kinds of practices that will be effective with particular learners. My theoretical knowledge was worthless in the world of action in which I was most abruptly thrown. Perhaps I had anticipated that my theoretical background and knowledge would be an adequate basis for my beginning efforts to teach. Instead, Ryle maintained that "efficient practice precedes the theory of it" (in Grimmett & MacKinnon, 1992). Similarly, Grimmett and MacKinnon (1992) argue that "intelligent performance does not follow automatically from knowing a set of procedures and maxims" (395).*

*So, the repeated miscues of today make sense. The only recourse I have is to come back tomorrow, continue making miscues, learn from them, adjust, refine, make more miscues, learn from them, and so on.*

## October 5, 1998

Last Thursday, I invited Wanda to stand up in front of class and do some improvisational storytelling. She spun a yarn about a magic rock. The students were entranced, and Wanda was amazed by the positive response and all the attention. When she finished, the students raised their hands to share what they liked about her performance. Susie came back and told me that she had a story she wanted to tell.

I realize that all these kids have stories to tell. So many of them have damaged self-concepts, and I wonder about the effect that a storytelling curriculum could have on them. What could be more affirming than to stand up and perform storytelling before an interested audience of peers, younger and older children as well as adults?

One place to start might be with family stories. Today, I will invite Wanda and Susie to tell more stories. I will tell some of my own family stories and then will invite the rest of the students to do the same.

About once a week, during lunch, a group of primary teachers meet in order to share ideas for the teaching of math. Usually, the attendees are Saul, Colleen, Eileen and me. Saul is the most experienced in teaching math in a nongraded primary, Colleen is slightly less experienced, and Eileen has been teaching at this level for just one year. I have the least practical experience.

*Reflection: I worried early on about my inexperience and inadequacy at "carrying my weight" with my colleagues. The group is a great idea. Concern about my ego inhibited my participation in the group. Besides, the group never could agree on a common focus. Shortly after the year began, we all tended to veer off and address different math strands. Without this common focus, the sharing of ideas became more unrealistic.*

*Second, the group never had a common planning time, except for a twenty-minute period during lunch. However, I was never relaxed during this time, as my concern was to get ready for the afternoon. After school, everyone almost always had other meetings with parents or teachers. The lunchtime meeting time didn't work. We rarely got full attendance.*

## October 6, 1998

I introduced family stories today. It went well. I told my own story, about how I learned to ride a bike without training wheels when I was six years old. Susie got up and told a story about a giant wave at the beach and her fear of getting swept away. I invited Wanda to do more improvisational storytelling. Today, she got morbid. She talked about an abusive parent who threatens to kill the boy's puppy; the puppy then gets sick and is taken to the hospital, where everyone is overcome by the stench of death. I watched Wanda as she generated this gruesome tale. Her eyes lit up like I hadn't observed before. She had the stage, and her peers were rapt in attention. When she was done, students shared what they liked about her story. I wonder about the value, for Wanda, of her dredging up these dark images of her life. I don't think it would be a good model for the rest of the class. I realize that many of the family stories that these kids tell will reflect the darker side of life, and I don't want to restrict stories to the bright and sunny side. Obviously, if the students feel safe with the group, the honesty of their stories will only be enhanced. I am not sure where this is headed, but I want to move ahead with story-telling.

Tomorrow, the students are going to the kindergarten class. Each student will have practiced the story, *How the Rabbit Lost Its Tail*, and they will meet, one-on-one, with kinders to tell the story. It should take no more than one minute to tell this story. I'm excited. Some of my students have indicated fear of this activity, and they want to drop out. I realize that stand-in-front-of-a-group storytelling is not for everyone, so I'm not going to force my students to do this. However, it is important that everyone have experience standing before a group and speaking in some fashion: to tell a brief family story, to tell a joke, etc.

Nathan received an in-school suspension today. He threatened another child before school. This is part of the school district's new zero-tolerance policy on violence or the threat of violence. I visited him to leave some math work. He didn't express sadness at being left out of the class for the day. When I told him that I'd missed him, he said, "Well, I didn't miss you." He may have sensed that I was lying.

## October 7, 1998

A problem was presented by Judy at the staff meeting today. The "alternative learning environment," a room staffed by the two counselors and two aides, is getting overrun with students. The room was intended as a place to work with students who had learning and behavioral needs. Students can be sent there for a range of behavioral problems, on a continuum from . . . they need some quiet time to . . . they need to do some extra work to . . . they are out of control. Yesterday was a wild day for this staff: twenty-five kids spent time in the ALE! The counselors are frustrated because this load prevents them from doing any counseling with individuals and groups. The principal is frustrated because she spends much of her time in the ALE to support its staff. The ALE has become a kind of stockade for troubled youth.

Mark, a first-grade teacher, noted that the problem was essentially a political one, since it derived from foot-dragging or insensitive central administrators who just "don't get it" or don't care about this situation. We simply have too many students with behavioral problems who cannot effectively cope with or adjust to a regular classroom scene. Mark's solution was to go public with the problem, thereby embarrassing the administration to take action. However, other teachers worried that the strategy of confrontation would scare some of the remaining middle-class families away from Woodbridge.

*Reflection: I think teachers are apt to avoid political action for two reasons. First, as Lortie (1975) suggests, the motives teachers have for going into the profession tend to influence a more conservative worldview. Many teachers enter teaching because of an affinity for children, a favorite teacher who inspired him or her, or a parent or relative who is a teacher. Rarely do people go into teaching for political reasons, such as to make society more equitable or democratic.*

*Second, everyday teaching is so intense that, by the end of the day at a staff meeting, teachers are exhausted. At staff meetings, when social or political issues come up, teachers may be thinking instead about work that needs to be taken home, or they may be thinking about some struggle they had with kids or parents that day, or they may be simply thinking that their own kids need to be picked up at the day-care provider and that dinner has to be made.*

*Exacerbating a naturally difficult job is the increasing encroachment on education by the standards movement. This movement requires a top-heavy system of testing, accountability, record keeping, teaching to the tests and assessments, and the stress of assessing difficult learning outcomes that are unrealistic for, perhaps, 40–60 percent of our students. Apple (1989) describes the increasing "intensification" of teachers' work a result of "curriculum reforms":*

> [C]urricular practice required that teachers spend a large portion of their time evaluating student "mastery" of each of the various objectives and recording the results of these multiple evaluations for later discussion with parents or decisions on whether or not the student could "go on." . . . The recording and evaluation made it imperative that a significant amount of time be spent on administrative arrangements for giving tests, then grading them, organizing lessons, . . . and so on. One also found

*teachers busy with these tasks before and after school and, very often, during their lunch hour. Teachers began to come in at 7:15 in the morning and leave at 4:30 in the afternoon. Two hours more work at home each night was not unusual, as well. (Apple, 1989, 44)*

*Perhaps I should not rush to judgment by attributing teachers' political inaction simply to some basic core conservatism. The material and institutional context of teaching has much to do with how they make sense of political action.*

I am beginning to look forward to school. At least I'm not dreading it as I did a few weeks ago. I open the door at 12:15 and walk outside to greet the students as they line up. I am relaxed. Most of the first kids to line up greet me. Some shout their hellos or some information about their day or moment. Especially Cesar and Joey. They don't talk; they shout. It's a pattern that I may be able to moderate but one that I may have to live with. Some of the kids come up to me for a hug. I hug them (but I can't get the idea of head lice out of my head). I walk down the line and try to high five as many as I can. I lead the way into the room with my arms raised high and hands cupped down, as if to indicate "let's be calm." They're becoming calmer. I don't allow trips to the fountain until after I've begun math and have completed my whole-group minilesson, otherwise it'd take fifteen minutes for everyone to get water.

The students are moving to their seats and tending to get ready for math more easily than they did a few weeks ago. Reflecting the revelations of other beginning teachers (Bullough, 1989), my sense of satisfaction with work stems from three clear changes I have made in my teaching performance. First, I have developed a grasp of the routines that I want to implement, and I have been more consistent about implementing these routines (such as moving right to their seats after they enter the room, how to ask me for help, how to ask a peer for help, the end of day procedure, etc.). Second, I think that I know the students better and they know me better. I sense that they trust me and like me. Third, I know the students' background knowledge a bit more, so I am better able to match students with curricula. The work that I give students is *closer to the mark* of what they can do and what they are interested in.

*Reflection: My increasing comfort has much to do with the implementation of some basic routines, like how students are to enter the room, go to the bathroom, sharpen their pencils, etc. The establishment of routines is, perhaps, the essential task facing teachers in the first days and weeks of school.*

*Another reason that I am beginning to look forward to school is the warm response of the children. Our students are important "reference groups" for teachers (Nias, 1989). By far, we see them more than our colleagues or principal; they do indeed create our reality as much as we create their reality (Riseborough, 1985).*

I am concerned with getting colds and head lice. Some of these kids have no sense of personal hygiene, so unless the teachers direct them otherwise, they will just let snot run down their faces, soak into their shirts, and then eventually spill onto the floor in a puddle of disgusting body fluid. I am working with them to cover their mouths before they sneeze and cough into my face. I need to work with them on washing their hands after they sneeze. I haven't gotten sick yet, and I take a daily overdose of vitamins, minerals, echinacea tea, and tablets. Knock on wood.

*Reflection: I am often concerned about my physical health. Teachers are particularly vulnerable to illnesses transmitted by students. Especially colds. And it is a common practice for teachers to come to work when sick. ("It's just more trouble to get ready for a sub" is a typical teacher rationale.)*

### October 9, 1998

Yesterday, the students were very talky. It was a continuous struggle to get them to attend to my directions. The weather yesterday was cold and wet. I wonder if a change in weather can affect students' behavior. I know that this idea is part of teacher folklore, but I am curious about its scientific basis. I've heard that animals become more agitated or animated just before inclement weather. After school, I talked with other teachers. They said their kids were wild. I feel a bit relieved when I find out it's just not me.

It was Pak's last day. He is moving back to Tibet. His mother brought in some treats at 2:05. She called to say that she was bringing in some juice and a cookie for each child. No problem. At 2:10, she arrived with five bags of goodies: chips, cookies, Hershey bars, candy, more candy, juice, etc. It is also Pak's birthday on Sunday, the travel day back to Tibet. We had a nice time saying adieu to him. We presented him with a shirt signed by everyone, a big card, and some songs. At the end, we stood in a circle and cheered, "Hip hip, Pak!" three times. I am sorry to see him go. He has been a model of the hard-working, calm, and friendly student. Always a smile on his face.

*Reflection: I wonder how teacher behavior is a factor in how kids do or do not get ansty before holidays or days off. I wonder if teachers consciously and unconsciously give kids signals that a vacation is looming, so rules and expectations will be more loosely enforced. There seems to be what Pollard (1985) calls temporal rule framing: time is a factor in how rules are framed, with either sharp boundaries (strictly enforced) or weak boundaries (loosely enforced).*

*It seems that teachers do frame expectations differently before vacations. Friday afternoons are often occasions for art activities or movies; the days and weeks before Christmas break are dominated by the weak curricular boundary represented by craft activities. (A sharply curricularly bounded activity would be to have students do some pages in the math textbook that are routinely evaluated by the teacher.) In many schools, it is a common practice for teachers to dress less formally on Fridays. This change in attire might cue students that rule frames are going to be looser. And teachers' moods tend to be more easy and tolerant of student antsiness just before holidays.*

*A holiday is imminent, teachers and students are both anxious for a break of the routine, and already the anticipation of the break influences both parties to let their guard down a bit (by weakening the rule frames). Teachers and students' past experiences with preholiday school days come into play, and teachers and students then cue each other to define the situation so the Friday afternoon of "talky kids" makes sense. Kids sense the acquiescence of teachers, so this gives them license to "be excited about the weekend." The important idea here is that this redefinition is a mutual and dialectic process between teachers and students, informed by their past experiences, in which teachers and students "take each other into account when they act and are thus at least partially affected by each other" (Charon, 1979, 133).*

> *Human beings in interacting with one another have to take account of what each . . . is doing or is about to do; they are forced to direct their own conduct or handle their situations in terms of what they take into account. Thus, the activities of others enter as positive factors in the formation of their own conduct; in the face of the actions of others one may abandon an intention or purpose, revisit, check or suspend it, intensify it, or replace it. . . . One has to fit one's own line of activity in some manner to the actions of others. The actions of others have to be taken into account and cannot be regarded as merely an arena for the expression of what one is disposed to do or sets out to do. (Blumer, 1969, 8)*

*There are certainly particular expectations teachers use to inform their responses to antsy kids, such as the "fact" that some kids may feel anxious before a long weekend or the mysterious effect of weather on kids' behavior. Often, teachers just know to go with the flow when forces seem to be out of their control, like when the kids are really talkative. I suppose that "good" teachers are able to make adjustments in the curriculum and in their own mood, so they avoid unnecessary conflict and subsequent damage to their relationship with the students.*

## October 14, 1998

Yesterday, I had a good day. Today was the opposite. I am learning how unpredictable life is for me as a beginning teacher.

I seemed to be in a policeman mode the entire afternoon. In math, one of the assignments was to write (and solve) a math story problem. Three boys asked if they could sit and draw a picture of a toy tractor that one of the boys had brought in. They wanted to use the drawing as the basis of their math story problem. I agreed. This was a mistake. The boys spent about 75 percent of their time socializing, examining the tractor, and only marginally focused on math story problems. Once I agreed to let them go to the back table for the tractor gazing, I became inundated with a plethora of other behavioral and academic questions from students who were either off task or on task. Kathleen pulled out manipulatives to help her solve some math problems, but she merely played with them. After I told her that she'd need to get some work done before recess, I noticed that she was copying answers from Deacon. Donna generated sloppy work, and I asked her to redo it. Again, she did it sloppily. She wanted to *sit* and help Kathleen, which is code for *socialize with Kathleen*. I looked in the back of the room, and Bonnie was lying on the floor relaxing—apparently done with math. For the entire period, my focus was on getting the students to focus. Exhausting!

*Reflection: The assigned tasks were not intrinsically interesting to the students, and I hadn't adequately "sold" them on the idea, or manipulated them into thinking, that the tasks were, indeed, worth their time. My strategy here is what Pollard (1985) calls "manipulation to evasion." Using this strategy, the teacher resorts to "motivation" strategies to get kids to do things that they naturally would be disinclined to do. The teacher here conveys previous good work and the potential enjoyment and value of the task. The strategy is enhanced if the teacher has good acting ability and is facile at using praise, flattery, and appeals to personal relationship (e.g., "Do it for me, kids, and I will be pleased").*

*However, according to Pollard (1985), if manipulation is to work, the teacher must not use his power if things don't go well and the kids don't follow directions. And manipulation doesn't work when the teacher is poorly skilled, as I was at the moment, and the kids were able to see through my "excitement" mask about the tasks. In addition, I hadn't adequately negotiated with the students a working consensus, so the consequences (positive and negative) for the students' completing or not completing the task were ambiguous. The students interpreted the assignments as not meeting their interests (related to enjoyment or learning), so a majority of the students basically withdrew from the activity. I persisted in cajoling here as a response to student withdrawal, but given my lack of relationship with the students, the absence of a working consensus, the aridity of the tasks (from the students' perspective), and my unwillingness to resort to power to change their behavior, this math period was doomed.*

Lately, I've become confused with how to manage student–student conflict, especially when the two antagonists have two versions of the conflict and there are no corroborating witnesses. For example, I found Timmy crying on the ground outside. He had crashed into Nathan, who claims it was an accident. A witness claimed that Nathan purposely tripped the boy. Timmy had no idea whether or not it was an accident.

Later in the day, Nathan and Crystal had a problem. I observed Nathan screaming in her ear, apparently in response to one of her actions. Crystal came in the room in tears, with a splitting headache from his scream. I sense that Nathan is the responsible player in most of these disturbances, and I am acquiescing to him in order to keep him calm. Ironically, by placating Nathan, I am enabling him to become out of control. It seems that I sometimes ignore student conflict until it sorts itself out without my intervention. This is one way for me to reduce the complexity of everything I have to do. However, I am uncomfortable with this strategy of expedience. When students sense that I am going to ignore peer conflict, then it sends a message "anything goes."

*Reflection: It is not unusual for beginning teachers to sometimes ignore important classroom events when they are otherwise overwhelmed with the task of teaching (Bullough, 1989).*

*Martin (1976) found that teachers' assumptions about students guided their negotiation style with students. He identified three groups: the nonnegotiable students, the intermittently negotiable students, and the continuously negotiable students. Since the philosophy of most teachers values supporting the self-esteem of students, engaging in open negotiations with students is an especially satisfying part of teaching. However, for a kid such as Nathan, who is a nonnegotiable student, the appropriate strategy is the closed negotiation routine, which consists of "explicitly given directions and explicitly stated consequences" (Martin, 1976, 34). This may be more appropriate for students who show extreme deviant behavior as well as an unwillingness to recognize the perspectives of others. Early in the year, I mistook Nathan as someone with whom I could negotiate.*

I need to be more aware of high-risk periods, when disturbances are likely to occur, such as the five minutes during which students line up outside after the lunch-break bell rings. I think that I will discreetly go outside during this time and observe students as they line up.

I need to watch Timmy more, especially during recess. Recently, he has been a victim of a series of episodes with peers. Dorothy told me that his mother and he were "kicked out of their home" by the father, whatever this means. I need to check out what is going on in his life.

I called Joey's mom last night and asked her what is going on with her son. He is on extreme "edge" in school: he is recalcitrant, defensive, and loud. She indicated that there is a small gang of older boys in the neighborhood who have been harassing the younger boys. Joey has been a victim of these neighborhood kids. She encouraged me to be firm with him, not giving him an inch. I will. Lately, I have been giving him a lot of "inches," and he is running all over me.

I called Kathleen's dad last night. I told him that I was concerned that she was coming to school sleepy. He responded positively.

Wanda stunk from unwashed clothes, or perhaps she'd produced some feces during the day. After school, I spoke to her about it, which she admitted to me was an embarrassing subject. During a pregnant pause in the conversation, she blurted out, "Can I pass out my birthday invitations." Realizing my body odor talk was going nowhere, I said yes. She jumped for joy and proceeded to place an invitation in each child's mailbox. As she walked out the door with her mom, I called out, "See you later, *Birthday Girl*." I could hear her walking down the parking lot, happy as a lark, chanting, "Ken called me a birthday girl! Ken called me a birthday girl!" The counselor and mom are trying to get her hooked up with the Big Sister Program in town.

This morning, I drove Sam to the sitter and then Claire to school. On the way to the sitter, I kept *running the tape* of yesterday's debacle in my head, and I focused especially on one student who took up about 50 percent of my time during the afternoon. My two lovely children were in the back seat talking to each other and listening to the radio. I was quietly brooding, getting more and more tense as we approached the sitter's house. My kids had no idea what

I was thinking about. My stomach was in knots when we pulled up to the house, and Claire asked me to keep the car running when I took Sam in so she could listen to the radio. I forgot to press the clutch, so the car engine jerked and jumped to an abrupt stop. I snapped emotionally, and I hit the steering wheel a couple of times and screamed a profanity. I immediately became scared that I'd frightened my children. I turned around, told Claire that my outburst had nothing to do with her. Obviously uptight, she said, "I know. I know." Sam, at two years old, seemed to be oblivious to me and my outburst. I dropped Sam off and then took Claire to school. She was quiet most of the way to school.

I want my kids to experience a father who likes his work. I want them to experience me as a relaxed, confident, and happy person. I feel sad when I am not able to give them what I know they need from me. I feel sad when I don't have the psychic space that I need to care for Melinda like I want to. And then I have all these learning goals for my students and professional goals for me. Given my inexperience and the extraordinary needs of the students, I am frustrated that I have to (in some cases, radically) alter these goals. The daily struggle of maintaining balance at home and school is draining me emotionally. I read a poem written by the Buddha that is a nice reminder to me to keep things in perspective.

> How wonderful!
> How wonderful!
> All things are
> perfect
> exactly as they
> are!

Distance. Distance. I need to remember to distance myself emotionally from what happens at work. I need to do my best, read, reflect, and then engage in coherent and rational problem solving. All I can expect to do is work hard and be earnest about my work. Then things will be wonderful, wonderful, and perfect exactly as they are, as the Buddha suggests.

**October 15, 1998** (morning)
A parent called me just a few minutes ago. His son is not getting challenged in the classroom. The boy is the most mature thinker in the class and, along with several other students, an effective self-manager. The boy had been complaining to me that the work hasn't been challenging and that I don't give homework. I tend to agree with the father and son. I have let the norms of the group slow down or reduce the kind of curriculum that I could be setting up for the handful of more mature students. The father intimated that he would remove his son from the class in the afternoon if he continued to complain. I am comfortable with this problem. The boy is capable, and this is a good reminder to me that I have to take care of the more able in the class.

Donnie is lucky to have a parent who is aware of what's happening in his school life and has the ability and confidence to voice his concerns to the teacher. I find the father's concerns to be legitimate, and I will act on them. I worry about the rest of my students, whose parents don't have the wherewithal to advocate for their children. For these children, I need to be their advocate. I need to critique my curriculum and continually ask myself, "Am I challenging these kids? Am I meeting their needs? Would I be happy with their school experience if I were their parent?"

*Reflection: The parent's criticism of my teaching hurt more than the journal entry shows. I rationalized the criticism by trying to analyze the problem in a larger social context. First, I critiqued the problems of a nongraded primary in meeting the needs of all kids, especially the more able ones. And then I responded to the criticism by recognizing the legitimacy and dignity of the "involved" parent who advocates for the child. This is all well and good, but the criticism made me feel embarrassed. Kelchtermans (1996) believes that "being a good teacher" is essential to a teacher's professional self: "good teacher" implies a certain degree of technical skill and moral integrity. Teachers' values influence the kinds of pedagogical decisions made in particular situations, so choices we make are not simply technical matters. "Rather, they are moral in character, because they involve the need to do justice to children's educational needs" (318).*

*When a teacher is questioned or criticized, it is the teacher's moral position that is threatened.*

> *[B]ehind teachers' emotional relations to apparently trivial incidents lies a moral perception of their task and therefore of their "selves" that is particularly vulnerable to challenge because it is supported by neither shared knowledge nor agreed normative principles. Individuals have repeatedly to make decisions that are not just complex but are also set in a morally ambiguous context. Invariably, they fall back on their own beliefs about what it is to be a teacher and act in accordance with this perspective. The depth of teachers' feelings, especially when their practice is challenged, reflects not an immature emotionality but, on the one hand, their attachment to their own moral values and, on the other hand, the normative isolation in which they often work. (Nias, 1996, 299)*

## October 15, 1998

It's interesting how an event that, to me, is trivial, takes on greater significance to kids. And this kind of mismatch between the adult and students can cause a crack in the relationship. For example:

Each day, I send a student outside to measure the thermometer. It's a two-minute operation. The student, or meteorologist, holds a thermometer, steps outside, stands in the shade for a count of 100, reenters the room, walks to the front, and reads the temperature on the thermometer. I then record the temperature on the calendar. After several months of this, we will construct a line graph in order to examine trends in the weather.

I had assigned students to do the job of "meteorologist" by randomly writing one name for each day on the calendar for the two months. However, I often spaced this out, and there would be two or three days in a row that I forgot to have the meteorologist go outside for her/his job. I then decided to change the plan. I simply posted a list of students, in alphabetical order, to do the job. We would work our way down the list. We moved to this plan on October 13, after several weeks of not using the names posted on the class calendar. Kathleen, however, still was watching the calendar intently, since she was scheduled to be meteorologist on October 15.

I changed the schedule two days before Kathleen's turn (as indicated by the original plan). She suddenly was thrust to the bottom of the list, since her last name begins with "Z." She was upset by the change in plan, and her grandfather also indicated on the phone that he felt this was grossly unfair. In retrospect, I realize that the meteorologist job is a big deal to the students, and any sense they had that they were being cheated out of a turn or some kids were getting more turns than they deserved is a significant breach of ethics (to them).

The student is angry at me, for this and several other reasons. Yesterday, she sat and sulked for most of the afternoon.

I am still learning the culture of childhood: how children think and the issues that are important to them. Dealing with the emotional and social needs of twenty-five students, who are simultaneously reacting or playing off each other, presents more complex questions of children's thinking. I am sometimes inundated with students approaching me with conversation about important issues in their life, happening at *that moment*. Spontaneously, during independent work time in math, for example, I might encounter the following events within a several-minute period:

- one child asks me to look at a book he has brought from home
- five students need help on a math problem
- a student is upset she is being cheated out of a turn
- a student wants to sing a song to the class
- a student needs a hug and spontaneously hugs me
- a student walks up to me and starts telling me a family story
- three students are playing and are off task
- two students are fighting over "scarce" resources (e.g., a marker)
- a student tells me that she doesn't want to sit near another, because he picks his nose constantly and is, in general, disgusting (which he is)
- a student approaches me with a science book on air, and he argues for more hands-on experiments
- a student is angry at me and sits, sulking, doing nothing, wanting to get into a power struggle with me

- a student with a speech problem gives me a message, and I don't understand him

Each event represents a non sequitur, since it's math time. But each event also represents a potentially important issue in each student's life. I don't want to "blow off" students, but it *is* math. If I give time to every student-initiated conversation, the curriculum will be completely diverted. But in my rush to keep the program going, there are many student initiatives that I have to deflect. I wonder when I am inadvertently harming a student or causing a hurt feeling that is not readily apparent to me. I am concerned because I believe that my students, these students, need a caring adult who is going to listen to them. Really listen. Often, I have to say, "Oh, I'm sorry. We just don't have the time today," or "Can we talk about this after math?" or "Can I look at your work later?" Stevie brings a book that he wants me to read to the class. It is inappropriate for the class, and I have other read-alouds planned that would have more positive impact on the group. But if I read his book, his heart would swell and he would feel like a million dollars. I could deflect his request by reading his book privately and talking with him about the book. Still, he would feel a slight disappointment because he wanted me to read this favorite book to the whole class.

What taxes my mind is not the number of decisions that I have to make every day. Rather, it is the number of decisions that have no easy answer. Do I read Stevie's book? Do I let William stay in the room during recess and work on the computer (other kids would notice and want to stay in, too, at a time I need fifteen minutes of silence)? Do I have Joey stay in during recess to catch up on math work he avoided during the math period, or do I send it home with him for homework? Do I call Nathan's father for the umpteenth time this year about a concern, only to have nothing change as a result of the call? Justin asks if he could read to the class at the end of the day, to show his growth as a reader (there are ten other kids who would like to do the same). Wanda asks me if she can turn on the overhead projector when I need it, and so have half a dozen other kids. I probably say "no" thirty or forty times an afternoon. Much of my confusion certainly stems from my own inexperience. If our procedures were more routine for the students, I would be getting fewer questions and problems.

I don't know. I'm confused. I'm inexperienced. The kids are really needy. I don't have many self-managers in the group. And many of these issues are typical *and insoluble*, even for veteran teachers. The question is one of *trade-offs* and finding balance among the needs of individual students, the needs of the group, and of course, the needs of the curriculum. As in any class, there is incredible diversity in my class: diversity in their interests, academic needs, and psychological needs. In a three-graded class such as mine, the diversity is accentuated.

I have several doctoral students whom I am still advising. One of them, Erin, a veteran elementary teacher, assured me last night that "it'll come together in January." Never have I looked forward to a January as I do this one!

## October 16, 1998

Today went really well.

I have been anxious lately about the impact my teaching has had on the students. Given my concern for classroom control issues, perhaps I've overlooked much evidence of academic and social learning. Today, here are some observations that suggest my work is having a positive effect on the students' learning.

- Several boys have indicated that they want to be elementary teachers. These boys are two of the most challenging kids. In math, however, they are very task-focused. I realize their interests are unstable and, most likely, they will not become teachers, although I am thrilled to encourage them. However, their interest in teaching now suggests that they see me (and Dorothy) as interesting role models, people who enjoy their work and enjoy children. And that they see school as a good place to spend time.
- In the lunch line, Deacon gave me the weather forecast for the day, based on his reading of the newspaper weather page. He

was excited about sharing this information. I had been encouraging the students to do this.

- Math class was calm, and I was calm. Students worked hard to finish their work. Students who were done played math games. I observed several students who usually do not show great effort working hard without my continuous admonishment. About five students voluntarily brought their math work home on Thursday for homework.
- The storytelling unit is successful. Students are bringing the written copy of the story home, and their parents are helping them practice. Yesterday, we practiced the most recent story. I told it but left out important parts. The students, using choral response, helped fill in the blanks. On Tuesday, we go to Colleen's class, next door, also a 1–2–3 blend, and my students will tell the story to her students.
- The students love the activities in the science program. We are studying weather. I sense that some of the targeted concepts get "lost" in the midst of the frantic rush of the hands-on activities. Still, the students are getting exposure to some important ideas, and some students are actually developing some meaningful understandings about weather.

Jeff asked me if I would take him to a movie. I was taken aback by his request. He said that his mother asked if I would do this. It would be risky if I agreed. First, I don't have enough time for my own children. Second, if I take him to a movie, the other kids will eventually find out and be hurt that I didn't take them. At Jeff's special education staffing a few weeks ago, the counselor indicated that she was working on finding him a Big Brother, a college student who would engage the boy in social activities weekly. I need to speak to her on Monday.

*Reflection: Nias (1989) found the following sources of job satisfaction, listed in order of frequency mentioned by teachers: affective rewards of kids' company; sense of competence by effecting students' learning; extension of personal skills and qualities through teaching and through work with colleagues; and feeling autonomous. Clearly, in the above excerpt, I am feeling satisfaction from the first two factors: enjoying the kids' company and a sense that I am affecting their learning.*

### October 19, 1998

Another good day. I'm increasingly comfortable with the students. I like them more. I am beginning to *know* them. Now when they bug me, I am able to smile at them, or at least I'm able to step back and accept them as young kids who are prone to behavior that is naturally at variance with my adult, middle-class sensitivities. Increasingly, when student behavior goes awry, I am (in my head) asking myself, "Isn't this interesting?" while I simultaneously work to redirect the errant behavior. When I as teacher like my students, it's easier to accept their peccadilloes.

*Reflection: In at least two ways I am different from my students: age (all of them) and social class (most of them). There are Latino students in the class, and I have not really considered the language differences between them and me. I wonder how much my maleness also presents a cultural gap between the girls and me in our relations. I think this question warrants more study.*

*The age difference and social class difference between my students and me are considerable problems for a teacher. I am able to relate to my middle-class students and their parents with more ease than I am with working-class kids. The middle-class kids are more apt to acquiesce or conform to my agenda, while working-class kids are more apt to challenge the legitimacy of my authority. The parents who are like me know what I mean when I cajole them to read to their kids. I am more effectively able to understand the needs of my kids who are middle class like me. "The more remote the child is from the teacher's common sense, the less will intersubjectivity be a feature of their relationship and the less individuality a feature of the teacher's perception of the child" (Sharp & Green, 1975, 121).*

### October 21, 1998 (predawn insomnia)

I woke up at 4:30 this morning. Couldn't fall back to sleep. There are three things on my mind.

First, our first class trip is today. After lunch, we will take the city bus to the public library. The children's librarian will do a presentation, and then the students will borrow books. I have three parent volunteers/chaperones, in addition to Fran, Barbara, and me. We have enough adult support for this trip. Still, I am ruminating on every step of the trip: walking from the school, along busy 3rd Street, to the bus stop, getting the kids on the bus, etc.

Second, I have heard students putting down other students, often from a distance, but I haven't been responding to this problem. In the rush to manage math and the rush to just keep students working on tasks, I again realize that I am ignoring the plethora of "penny-ante" interpersonal problems that crop up in the course of the day. I think that the students may realize that I sometimes take a laissez-faire attitude toward this interpersonal dimension, and my stance may give some of them license to really act out. So I sit here now and plan how I can teach more proactively to reduce put-downs and then more actively respond when put-downs occur. If I let put-downs happen with impunity, the class is going to become unsafe very quickly for all students.

Third, Donnie has become difficult. He has complained, probably for the last month, that the math curriculum does not offer enough challenge. Both his parents seem to have a problem with my math program, and they have communicated this lack of confidence to their son. I have tried to increase the complexity of his work in math, but it has not been enough. With me, the child has become obnoxious and argumentative. I ask him to do something that he doesn't want to do, so he argues. I tend to back off and let him have his way. When I have used my authority to force him to work, twice he has cried and hidden under a table.

Generally, the boy has the power. I don't. I call on him more than I do other kids, to keep him from being unpleasant. I give him preferential treatment, like in answering the classroom phone. And I look the other way more when he engages in deviant behavior, mostly penny-ante violations, but the kinds of deviance that I would censure everyone else for. So he talked more when he wasn't supposed to, he walked around the room more than other kids, and he called out when other kids were not allowed. I know that other kids noticed the differential treatment.

## October 21, 1998

Today was the trip to the public library. Since we were in a public place, my awareness of the students' behavior was heightened. The entire time, I had to remove kids, give dirty looks, remind the class about active listening, etc. After the librarian's presentation, the kids had an opportunity to peruse the shelves and check out books. Four or five kids could not control themselves. They fought with each other at the water fountain. They ran through the aisles. They raised their voices. One parent volunteer had to physically remove a boy who was disruptive. I had to drag Nathan by the arm away from an altercation with a peer. While most of the students behaved appropriately, my focus was the errant children. According to my tunnel vision, the trip was a bomb, stressful, and not fun. When I surveyed the class later, all but one of the children asserted that they'd behaved appropriately, and that they had had a good time.

I think it's hard for some children, especially from homes that are not calm, to understand my middle-class (and middle-aged) notion of *calm*. Perhaps they *do* understand what it means to be calm. However, they are lacking in the metacognitive strategic knowledge to monitor and regulate their behavior. My common sense tells me that it is home environment. Homes that are calm and environments that support civil conversations . . . children who come from these homes will come to school able to be calm and engage in civil conversations.

*Reflection: I blamed kids' home environment for the debacle at the library. I know of many instances when "good" classes (and kids from "good" homes) went berserk for a substitute teacher. Home experiences certainly do influence kids to behave only in general ways much of the time. I sense now that it isn't the disorder of kids' home lives that makes for particularly stressful class trips (cf., Rosser & Harre, 1984). Rather, I think teachers have to examine the presence of a negotiated order that is situated in specific settings. My kids and I did not have a common definition of the situation, a shared understanding of how to behave in the library. During the trip, I maintained an open-negotiating style, by appealing to reason and common sense when I laid out my behavioral expectations. I could have been much more dominating in how I managed the trip. For example, I could have asked each of my eight adult volunteers to physically attach themselves to one of my eight most unpredictable students, and then I would have had the adult physically restrain or remove the student if he or she acted out. I didn't resort to this power strategy since (a) I didn't think it was necessary and (b) this strategy is in opposition to my substantial self.*

*In the absence of this "socially constructed order," some kids will act quite naturally: by running, talking, fighting, and shouting—mostly at inappropriate times. Not surprisingly, without a clear set of rules (implicit and explicit) for behavior, the students will have no way to evaluate their behavior in a way that makes sense to the teacher. It is no wonder that my students thought that they actually behaved well during the trip!*

## October 22, 1998

We went to Colleen's room next door so my students could tell this week's story ("How the Boy Turned into a Peanut") to her students. It went well. My students paired up with students in Colleen's class. So one student sat with another student and told a thirty- to sixty-second story. Most of my students accomplished the storytelling task quite well. Even students who struggle with the rest of the curriculum excelled. I allowed shy students to tell the story with a peer. One or two students still did not want to do the activity (too shy), so they were allowed to watch. Tomorrow, we do it again in the kindergarten.

I sat down with Judy, the principal, to do goal setting. I want to focus on classroom management, especially the question: How do I teach children to solve their own social problems? I am inundated with student–student conflict. I often fail to help children resolve these problems because of my own limited skills and lack of time. Judy is going to do an informal observation of me on Monday.

I am reading the book *Tuesdays with Maurie*. An easy read. It's about coming to terms with death and, in the process, life. Maurie suggests one practice he learned from Buddhism. Imagine a bird on your shoulder that continuously reminds you, "Today is the last day of your life." If this were the last day of my life, I know that I would ignore the small details and, instead, focus on the wondrous aspects of my existence. I started to talk to the imaginary bird on my shoulder yesterday in class. It worked.

## October 24, 1998

I have been having the kids write original math story problems. During math, I ask kids, "What's your problem?" when referring to their self-generated math problems.

Today, at recess, Nathan was fighting with another kid. I happened to be outside when the duty teacher called me over to mediate. I asked Nathan, "What's the problem?" referring of course to the playground altercation. He stopped and stared off into space. After a few seconds, he said, "I went to K-Mart with my dad. He had $20 and I had $5. We bought some things that cost $12. How much do we get back?" I was pleased with his response.

There continues to be an excessive amount of put-downs among the students, more than I have time to manage. When I "manage" these events, I mediate as the students confront each other. There also seems to be a continuous stream of conflicts when the students line up (e.g., cutting, fighting). I am noticing a pattern, that the same students get hurt all the time, victims of their peers who tend to be the same ones who are doing the hurting.

My daughter's aikido teacher told me his three principles that guide his teaching. First and most important, the kids need to be safe. Second, they should have fun. And third, they should learn. He suggested that these principles would make sense for public schools as well as aikido clubs! Safety, fun, and learning—in this order. It *can* work! Monday, I'll work on the first goal. It's only October. There's time. Still. I know the kids want to be safe. The kids need us adults to provide the kinds of structures that'll signal a safe environment.

## October 26, 1998

It's early morning. My son, Sam, woke up at 5:00 a.m. and wouldn't go back to sleep. I have a pit in the center of my stomach. The week looms ahead. I feel trapped, anxious, and depressed. I once read that Monday morning is the riskiest time of the week for working men, when they are most susceptible to heart attacks. After a weekend of peace and quiet, the immediate prospect of the week's beginning is psychologically daunting. In a few hours, I'll be facing twenty-three kids, many whose weekends were chaotic. The transition to school on Monday, for these kids, is usually difficult. They are louder than usual, less focused on academic tasks than usual, and more emotional than usual. I feel that I need to be more structured on Mondays than the other days.

I am beginning to sense the kinds of activities that work for my class. These activities fall into two types. The first type is the academic, highly structured, well-defined activity such as working alone on math worksheets; it could be drill and practice sheets or it could even be open-ended math problems. When the students work collaboratively on these tasks, they tend to veer off task quickly. The second type is hands-on construction activities, in which the students are designing and building some technology. In the weather unit, many of the lessons have had a "design technology" focus, so this unit has been successful. The students have built objects such as propellers, pinwheels, and anemometers. Open-ended activities with no concrete outcome, such as creative dramatics or discussions, tend to stimulate off-focus behavior. Part of the problem is the developmental range. We have first through third graders, and some of the first graders have the social or intellectual temperament of kindergartners. Having whole-class discussions has been difficult.

## October 27, 1998

Donnie has fallen off the edge, or at least my relationship with him has. If he doesn't want to do something, such as clean up his table area, he ignores me or argues with me. He is continuously out of his seat or engaged in inappropriate behavior.

Even as I struggled with curriculum and management, I have always had the sense that the students and I liked each other. Now I struggle with interpersonal conflict with a student and parents who are giving their children negative signals about me. My immediate response to this is anxiety. Yesterday, after school, I couldn't enjoy my own children, because my two-hour power struggle with Donnie had rattled my peace of mind. This kind of problem diminishes my motivation: to teach, to work hard. I counted the number of student contact days between now and winter break. There were thirty-two days. With the passing of each day, I put an "X" on that calendar date in my mind. I am counting days, already. This isn't a good sign.

*Reflection: In my relationship with Donnie, I haven't established myself as an adult with reasonable rules and expectations. First, I certainly have to act on my prerogatives as an adult in our culture: that, as an adult, I have more power than children do. Second, accompanying this power, I have to show that my regime can be fair, consistent, and sensitive to individual student differences. With Donnie, and I suspect most of the kids, I have not accomplished either task. I am too hesitant and insecure to establish my power as an adult. And I haven't yet established my own consistent understandings of what it means to be fair, consistent, and student-sensitive. I am inconsistent. I still don't know how to respond effectively to students in a way that will meet their individual needs as well as my need to maintain order.*

*Kelchtermans (1996), like Nias (1996), argues that teacher vulnerability and teacher emotions have their origins in "moral and political roots in the workplace conditions" (308). It is teacher's "experiential and value-laden knowledge . . . [that] constitutes a weak basis from which to defend practice, if this is attacked or questioned by others" (314). Donnie and his mother were basically rejecting my program as being irrelevant and even dysfunctional for him. I did acknowledge that the problem of Donnie and a nongraded primary was a difficult one for me, and I also felt that I was still trying to figure out how I might serve him in this situation. However, my indecision was interpreted as a show of weakness (inconsistent with Donnie's notion that adults are confident and assertive). My strategy with Donnie was to be patient with him, to listen to his concerns, and to be responsive to him when an activity was "too easy" for him.*

**November 4, 1998**

bushed tired with lingering cold.
no energy, head's floating
like water lily on a pond
of flagellated phlegm.
the kids are loving
to me and to school . . .
but so out of balance.
Jeff gives silent cry,
a victim of bullies.
Nathan yells at Barbara
and does a sentence
of time outs.
Bonnie throws up
and dances in her vomit.
Billy's head
full of sawdust
from a recess
of down pouring rain.
Deacon doesn't stop talking.
Sally's mind
stuck on painting her hands
with markers.
I'm tired and it's so real.
day in and day out.
the occasional day off
like veteran's day,
welcome respite from being awake.
keep drinking that
echinacea tea.

first legs of a marathon,
the wall is yet to come.

Today was a sluggish day. I'm fighting a cold, so I had little energy and less patience than I usually do. In math, I have the students working independently in math folders, collections of work that they need to complete by the end of the week. They need to do a minimum of two assignments, or jobs, in the folder each day. Then they can play math games, such as chess, checkers, or cards. Naturally, many of the kids rush through their work, often sloppily, so they can play games.

*Reflection: As much as I tried to jazz up the curriculum by having the students write their own problems in math, as much as I worked to embed academic work in small-group activity, I can't get away from the conclusion that the kids were working only because they were a subordinated group—they had no choice—and that they would bail out through the door and not come back if they had their druthers. Much of how I present curricular activity is emotionally flat and conventional. However, the "most meaningful activit[ies] to many of these pupils[were] those which made sense within their own culture, and which pertained to their private sphere" (Woods, 1984, 233), such as child care, social crafts, sports, or games. Woods goes on to suggest that teachers transform school "work" into a play or game context—"in keeping with the private sphere" (234).*

I want to revamp much of what I am doing in math. In order to bring some order to the class, I have the students do more drill and practice worksheets than I am comfortable with. I do have students individually working on story problems, even problems that they write themselves, which is a piece of my curriculum about which I feel good.

I also want to revise my storytelling curriculum. Interest in storytelling is waning. I need to give the students a bit of choice in the stories they practice and tell. Right now, everyone is doing the same story.

*Reflection: My overreliance on drill and practice of arithmetic doesn't reflect my ideal math program, and I would be embarrassed if the world saw what I was doing. Luckily, I am somewhat sequestered from my colleagues, so they can't see my teaching (nor can I watch them).*

Today, I asked the students at the end of the day to draw or write about how they were feeling. Wanda sat looking very forlorn. The kid's family is experiencing great economic stress. The mother is divorced with three kids, and she doesn't have much in the way of parenting skills. Wanda lives on junk food and television, and she is a victim at school. She has a really bad speech impediment. Her years of school speech therapy have done little good. Twenty percent of the time she doesn't come to school.

I asked her, "How are you feeling?"

She replied, "Pretty bad. Kids at lunch said I stink." I asked her for names, and she implicated students in three classrooms. I reckoned that my first strategy has to focus on Wanda and the fact that she, indeed, does have pungent body odor. I am going to drive over to her house after school tomorrow and chat with the mother (She doesn't have a phone). We've got to get her to shower every day and to wear clean clothes.

At the end of the day, I couldn't get all the kids to be quiet, as I stood in front of the class ready to give a direction. One section of the class would get quiet, and then a student in another corner of the room would start talking. Nothing loud. Just incessant, low-humming conversations. I was tired and wasn't responding decisively to the chatter, so Barbara called out in a no-nonsense manner, "All right, everybody. That's enough talking!" I then proceeded to threaten individual kids with a loss of recess if they talked when I was talking. I looked and talked as though I was really angry (I wasn't), and they really responded. It was so quiet you could hear a pin drop. Barbara said that's how many of the kids are treated at home, so this ad hoc tough-guy strategy is a management approach with which students are familiar and responsive.

Ugh! I don't want to play the tough guy every day. It'd be exhausting. I will follow through with the recess consequence. They care about their recesses, and I care about having a quiet classroom when people are talking, especially me!

*Reflection: Perhaps from these kids' perspectives, Barbara acted like an adult: in charge and volatile. Anger can be a hostile and violent emotion. In my relations with a subordinate group (the students), my use of anger and threat is a clear show of my power. This tact is obviously in contradiction with my teaching self. Our adult outburst resulted in a temporary retreat by the students. As a result of this experience, I felt the usual cacophony of dark emotions.*

## November 5, 1998

Saul, another primary teacher, stopped by before math and asked if he could observe me teaching. He was genuinely interested in what I was doing in this subject area. I have known Saul for eight years, and he is someone I hold in great esteem and trust. Actually, people who know both of us tell me that Saul views me as one of his "gurus."

However, when he asked if he could observe me, I felt my face flush, and I became embarrassed. My voice said, "Yeah, sure, any time." But I suppose my nonverbal signal was obvious to him, so he backed off, saying, "Great . . . uh . . . I can't observe today, but I'll come back soon." And he was out the door.

I was embarrassed to have him observe me, because I don't feel good about my math program. I have a fuzzy image of what it should look like, but I am light years away from this image. I was also embarrassed at being embarrassed. I will talk to him and explain why my response to him was so unenthusiastic.

*Reflection: I was mortified when Saul almost stayed in the room and observed me teach. If I was more adept at impression management in this situation, I would have shown a front that was more "excited" about his coming in: "But," I would say to Saul, "at the moment, this isn't a good day since we are doing bla bla bla . . ." or something like this. We use impression management to avoid embarrassment or shame when our "self" is threatened (Goffman, 1959). I failed to manage the impression today. It was obvious to Saul that I was embarrassed to have him stay in the room, and this obviousness worked to double my feeling of embarrassment.*

I spoke to a school counselor, now at Melinda's school, who spent a year at Woodbridge about four years ago. His first words to me were something like, "I heard from Melinda, and it sounds like you're really getting scarred." I hadn't viewed the experience as a scarring one. I realize that I am under stress every day, and that it takes enormous psychic energy to work with these students. I also sometimes feel a bit depressed before I go in to work. But I don't feel as if I am getting scarred by the experience. Maybe I am fooling myself.

*Reflection: I remember years ago, as a beginning teacher with no confidence, our principal would always open staff meetings with a declaration that "This staff has the finest, and I mean the finest, teachers in the entire district. That's why I picked you!" Of course, I got other messages that I was a good teacher, from my students, their parents, and even colleagues, and the accumulation of these messages powerfully defined how I viewed myself as a teacher. But the rhetoric of my principal really affected my self-concept. I believed that he was talking just about me! So my willingness to believe his message fit in well with a history of messages.*

*I had respect for the school counselor, and his diagnosis bothered me. His message didn't fit with my preexisting teaching self-concept. I don't want to be viewed as someone who is mentally unstable or suffering from psychological damage. Given his status, his assessment shook my sense that I was still, indeed, distanced, professional, and analytic about my teaching experience. Maybe I wasn't examining myself clearly, at an emotional level, about how the teaching experience was affecting my mental health. My work was so intense and frenzied, I didn't have the time or mental space to reflect on the emotional and psychic toll that teaching was having on me.*

## November 6, 1998

A difficult day. I got sucked into a power struggle with Donnie regarding his math assignments. The assignment was to write an original math problem, solve it, and then share it with a same-age peer. He said that he didn't want to do it since he had already done two math tasks. (In math, the rule is that once kids have done two tasks, they can play a math game.) I argued that one of the tasks he claimed to have done was completed yesterday. He argued that he had done most of it today.

When he and I reached an impasse in the power struggle, I wasn't able to distance myself from the situation, so my behavior toward him was angry and histrionic. I need to distance myself from these problems and, instead, respond dispassionately—and with a pleasant face.

*Reflection: Donnie and I did not share a definition of the situation. My negotiating strategy was an open one, in which I tried reasoning and logic. He also tried to use reasoning and logic with me, reflecting his nine-year-old framework for reason and logic. Neither of us was willing to compromise, so we were at an impasse. I was frustrated with my inability to resolve the problem using my preferred strategy (an open negotiating style). I used anger to intimidate the boy, but this didn't work. He simply refused to talk. His response to my emotional outburst was a sane one, and one that I use in my everyday life. (If someone won't talk to me calmly, I often refuse to engage him in further discussion.)*

*Donnie doesn't respect me as a teacher, so he doesn't care to do the negotiation necessary to forge a working consensus. Rosser and Harre (1984) identified the key ways that teachers can offend high school students. I was astounded by the similarity between their theory and my experience with Donnie.*

1. *Getting on nerves, being boring (Donnie was always claiming that I reminded him of a "wicked neighbor" and that my program was not motivating him.)*
2. *Students were "deeply contemptuous to be treated as anonymous" (205) by teachers (Donnie had a high need for preferential treatment, and he resented my attempts to give my attention to all students.)*
3. *Weakness (So far, I did not show the will to stand up to his resistance.)*
4. *Overt insult (As far as I knew, I hadn't insulted him but, who knows?)*

5. Unfairness ( Much. He views me as unpredictable and at times unfair.)

Rosser and Harre's students wanted structure and discipline at school (and home). At school, they wanted a teacher "who'll take a good joke but will make us work. . . . [E]verybody's happy and you don't realize you're getting your work done" (206). According to the criteria for offending students, I was not doing a good job, and this resulted in, at best, a fragile working consensus with the class in general. Other impeding factors were at play in my particular relationship with Donnie, so he was more prone to resist my power than were other kids.

During math, the power in the building went out, and so did the lights. The bathroom lights, especially, were intriguing to the kids since the bathroom has no windows. Suddenly, everyone had bathroom emergencies. Everyone wanted to run to the bathroom or the darkened hallway. I foolishly tried to maintain an orderly, on-task math period. It was a struggle, and my stomach turned to knots. This is when I started dispensing "loss of recess" consequences on students who did not comply with my directives. Then, at the end of math, I learned that my "ace in the hole" was lost. I was going to show a Bill Nye video on flight, but the teacher next door hadn't been able to finish her video because of the power outage. Her aide came in and said, "Do you really need the video?" I knew that Eileen needed it as much as I did, so how could I take it from her? I didn't have a contingency plan for science, so I ended up giving the students a free choice time during this period.

*Reflection: I had a definition of the situation that persisted in viewing this as a learning situation: kids will continue working on their math. However, when the lights went out, the kids' definition changed radically: the building is dark and the bathroom is black. "Yeah," chorused the kids in my imagination. "Let's party!!"*

*I tried reasoning and cajoling to get kids to stay in their seats and get back to work. It didn't work, so I reverted to domination and power, by taking away their recess. In retrospect, I should have respected the children's natural curiosity and loosened up with the work definition. By not modifying my definition of the situation, when the actual situation changed dramatically, I unnecessarily subjected myself to a cacophony of negative emotions, which worked effectively to ruin my day.*

## November 8, 1998

It's Sunday night.

I've got to distance myself emotionally when I am working with the kids. I can't respond to them when I have a knot in my stomach or tightness in the chest. It'd be terrible if I suddenly keeled over in class, victim of a heart attack, or if I incurred any kind of physical disability. Besides, when there is that tightness in my body, the students must certainly feel my tension, and this doesn't bode well for the class climate. I've got to relax, distance myself, reframe . . . all that jazz.

Here's a list of heuristics I've made up for getting perspective:

1. Remind myself of
that bird on the shoulder whispering
tomorrow you die.
2. Don't sweat the small stuff . . .
and its all small stuff.
3. Take deep breaths
and smile and
remind myself that the gig
is just for one year
and half time at that!
4. Don't worry, be happy.
5. Que sera, sera,
whatever will be will be.
6. Everything is perfect.
7. Remember my mother
who at eighty is due for bypass surgery
along with a nodule in her breast.
8. Nothing matters
say the existentialists.

9. I can only do my best
and that's all.
10. It's alright.
11. Let it be.
12. Let it go.

I feel good about the coming week. I have planned, and the plans appear on surface to be interesting and worthwhile. Some other heuristics I use for surviving this year include: keep my nose to the grindstone, focus on developing an interesting curriculum, care about my students, stay calm, keep on problem solving, stay calm, focus on an interesting curriculum, care about my students, yadda yadda.

*Reflection: I am taking an individualistic/psychological spin on my mental health. I don't consider the material/structural conditions of my teaching, such as the fact that I have twenty-five kids total in a 1–3 blend, eighteen high-needs students, and several high-resistance kids, that the curriculum is totally ill-defined and needs to be constructed by me each week, that there are no textbooks, and that the state is strangling the budget of local school districts and strangling our control over the curriculum.*

*Still . . . even while I shift my focus to the structural impediments of teaching, I wonder how much of it has to do with me. My personality. My skills. My disposition. I suspect that a different person, in my identical teaching situation, would be having a different emotional experience than the one I am having. I do notice wide variation among my colleagues in how they experience teaching.*

## November 12, 1998

Good day. No power struggles. I was much more sensitive to the issue of student safety, and I especially watched the behavior of Nathan. He intimidates physically and verbally. He is an effective deliverer of put-downs. At each of the afternoon breaks, I made sure that I was outside and able to observe him surreptitiously as he approached the building and entered the class.

Today, I had one student who suddenly transformed himself into a fish. He lay over his chair pretending to swim. He would only stop when I led him by the arm to the time-out table. Another boy, in the middle of class, started calling out, "We suck, we suck!" Another boy came to school with bad body odor, and he was taunted by the other kids.

The learning resource teacher in our school has been warned by the district special services director to *not* encourage our parents to advocate. If these parents don't know that they *can* advocate, or they don't have the common sense or confidence or skill or time to speak out on behalf of their children, their children are at a clear disadvantage, especially when compared to the children of their middle-class parent counterparts.

Recently, Wanda's speech has deteriorated so much that it is usually difficult to understand her. Her behavior also is so weird that the rest of the students avoid her. She picks her nose compulsively, and puts her face a few inches from other kids and utters incomprehensible messages. She often falls out of her chair, and she often shouts when she has conflict with peers. She is continuously poking, interfering with, or bothering people at her table group. She ignores adult redirection, and she has to be redirected physically by our taking her arm and leading her away.

Another student shows all the signs of depression. He has more physical and psychological problems than I could imagine in my worst nightmare. He does no work unless an adult is sitting with him, and he has performed like this since he was in kindergarten.

I believe that these two kids need individual, full-time, adult aides. Otherwise, the existing educational support system is not adequately meeting their needs. If these kids had parents who were articulate and assertive and could *get in the faces of the special services administrators*, I have confidence that we could get these kids a significant increase in support. But these kids don't have parents who can do this. What is my responsibility? Do *I* take a stronger advocacy role? Should I begin working directly with the parents to help them advocate, which may be in opposition to school district policy? Do I get in the faces of the administrators downtown? Do I go to the school board and speak of the inequities of the system? How do I work with the special services staff at Woodbridge to deal with these problems? Do we need to organize the Woodbridge community in response to these problems? Do I bring these problems to our site council?

I work with these kids every day, and I feel frustrated that I can't meet their needs. I am not comfortable in acknowledging this.

## November 16, 1998

A good day.

Today was the first day of independent research reports. Students can select any topic, and most have chosen an animal. I went to the university and public libraries and collected almost a hundred books on a variety of animals. I had the students simply peruse the books and begin identifying topics. Eight fifth graders came in and worked as "research assistants" for my nonreaders. They read text to students who were not able to read this material independently. Since I have about thirteen nonreaders, the collaboration with the fifth graders is essential.

The students were excited about looking at these books. Since they have choice over their topic of inquiry, I think that they are even more interested in this project. The outcome of the project is some kind of display, consisting of text and nontext information, in which the student shows what he or she has learned as a result of the independent inquiry. I want them to learn to find the answers to their own questions.

## November 17, 1998

Bad day. After the 1:45 break, I tried to have a discussion about a newspaper article about a new dinosaur discovered in Niger. I placed the article and picture on the overhead. I kept the discussion going too long, and some of the students either got tired or lost attention. I failed to monitor the failing energy of the group, and I continued with the discussion in spite of continuous flare-ups of misbehavior and student–student conflict around the room. I struggled, and it was my own fault. I realized my mistake afterward. I left school exhausted and frustrated. Ah, tomorrow is another day.

## November 18, 1998

The students worked on their independent projects again. Most have chosen animal topics, such as snakes, frogs, polar bears, or snails. I have about ten fourth- and fifth-grade students coming to the room during this time to help my nonreaders. I spent about a half hour last week showing the tutors how to read to and take notes for the youngers. Unfortunately, I overestimated the potential effectiveness of the fifth-grade readers. They weren't able to monitor and redirect the attention of my younger students, nor did they have a clear sense of what I wanted them to do.

We have six computers in the room, and half are hooked up to the Internet. The kids are trying to get on the Web to find information. It's a messy project. I find that most of my time is taken up with helping kids resolve computer/Internet glitches and with dealing with three or four kids who can't focus on the task at hand. Especially Billy. He can't sit still and, surrounded by large groups of loudly talking peers, it is virtually impossible for him to focus on the assignment. If he had a full-time aide who would force his hand (perhaps literally!), at least he'd get more work done. Wishful thinking. I spent 20 percent of my time keeping Billy in his seat.

The state tests in math and reading are given in the spring. This year, the state department is offering cash incentives to schools if they improve their tests scores in relation to last year's scores. So the top 20 percent of most-improved schools will receive approximately $2,000 per classroom teacher as a reward. Given that Woodbridge's scores were so low last year, it is clearly within our school's grasp to be in the top 20 percent of schools that experience the greatest gain over the prior year.

However, some teachers on the staff consider this to be "dirty money," given their rejection of the state tests as the ultimate measure of school effectiveness or student performance, as it has become in the state. Some of the teachers are insulted that they have to be bribed in order for them to work hard to help the students do well on the tests! One assumption of the money incentive is that teachers are driven by money. Most teachers I know are motivated by intellectual and moral goals: they teach because they aim for the intellectual and moral development of their students.

I am concerned that the state is manipulating teachers and schools to reorient their entire curriculum to the tests. I am embarrassed that the test is driving my teaching of math. The math test, for example, is a multiple choice/one right answer test in which the students fill in a computer-scored bubble sheet to indicate the answer. On the positive side, the math test reflects many strands of mathematics, as recommended by the National Council of Teachers of Mathematics. However, the test alone represents a narrow view of mathematics. There are a lot of items on the test that could be answered correctly *without* the students understanding the meaning of the math contained in the item!

Since school funding shifted away from local to state responsibility about ten years ago, the state has increasingly asserted its prerogative to control curriculum and assessment decisions and policy. Already, I am looking at the (April) test specifications and planning my year in mathematics according to the specifications. The test is influencing me to reduce the time I'd otherwise spend on problem writing and problem solving.

*Reflection: I have begun to feel some role strain, which Hargreaves (1972) describes as when an "actor has difficulty in conforming to the expectations that make up his role" (74). On the one hand, I agree with my colleagues in the need for a constructivist approach to the learning and teaching of math. However, I also believe that it is in my students' best interest to do well on the tests. Especially with my third graders, I do much less hands-on math, much more work focused on the test. I do more nonconstructivist teaching in math than I am comfortable with. In order to reduce role strain, I don't talk to my colleagues about this.*

Our intern, Fran, is stressed. She has difficulty getting the students to listen, be calm, and follow directions. Dorothy and I are worried that we are going to lose her, and that she will request a change in placement. We both agree that an intern in our room needs to have two qualities: first, a thick skin, and second, a strong desire to work with at-risk students. I have no doubt that Fran is *not* going to have an opportunity to do the kind of teaching here that she would do in a middle-class school. Undeniably, we need another adult in the room, to help us meet as many needs as possible. But we would understand if she left. Teaching *is* hard work.

In my head, I sometimes relate this teaching experience to the experience of the infantry in the boats as they were about to disembark on the beaches of Normandy in 1944. I just saw the movie *Saving Private Ryan*. The soldiers know that they are most likely going to die, so they sit in the boats smoking cigarettes, praying, vomiting, or crying. Early in the year, before I had a handle on management, I had the same feeling when I opened the door to let the kids in after lunch recess. It's scary when you are the teacher and you do not have control, especially control of a class of high-needs kids. Things have moderated, and I have established some routines for coming in and getting to work, but I still have a twang of tension in my stomach when the kids come in. I never know what energy and stresses they are going to bring into the classroom. I sense that Fran could develop the pedagogic wherewithal so the class climate would be conducive to learning. But she'll need to gut it out. It takes time to negotiate a working consensus.

## November 19, 1998

My birthday. Dorothy and Barbara organized the kids to do several lovely presentations. They made a book in which the kids drew pictures and wrote what they liked about me. Most of the kids wrote about the science activities. I got a lot of individual cards. They were sweet. There were many hugs.

One day a few weeks ago when the class was going awry, I smiled, looked at Barbara, and sarcastically said, "I love this class." Since then, we'd used this phrase to reframe our mood when things got out of control. The phrase, when used, became a way for us to blow off some tension and have a laugh. Barbara organized the construction of a life-size figure of me, on poster paper, with the words bubbling out of my mouth, "I love this class."

I love this class, especially today. The kids were so responsive to my directions and assignments. They even seemed to take a break from interpersonal conflict. Overall, I feel great affection from the kids. Only Donnie doesn't come over and spontaneously hug me, kid around, or do a high five when we see each other at the start of day.

*Reflection: The students emerged as a powerful reference group for me by affirming my personal competence, although not my professional competence (Nias, 1989). Student exhibitions of affection toward me were constant. Particularly in light of my difficulties in teaching and management, I found some solace in our emerging personal relationships. Parents reported how their children would talk about me endearingly at home. This affirmation of my personal self as warm, caring, and friendly provided a counterweight to the pounding that my teaching self was taking. However, the limited influence that my personal relationship had on students' definitions of the situation (i.e., to significantly effect students' willingness to conform to my teaching agenda) illustrates the complexity of factors that influence students' behavior and performance.*

## November 22, 1998

Just got back from an overnight trip to Elizabeth City with Melinda, Claire, and Sam. We took the kids to a science museum, to bookstores, downtown to see the holiday lights, and to several restaurants. We stayed in a nice hotel that served a continental breakfast. We walked to the roof and inspected the panorama of the city. We went to Sam Goody's and bought a CD of the *Wizard of Oz* soundtrack. At the museum, we saw an incredible movie about dinosaurs, filmed in Kenya. The museum and movie were expensive. It was all very stimulating for my kids.

The thought of bringing my class to the museum crossed my mind. It'd be a real pain, to raise money for the bus and then to transport these kids on a ninety-minute bus ride. But I know that most of my students' families do not have the money or wherewithal to bring their kids to this wonderfully stimulating world-class museum.

Many of my students are poor, through no fault of their own, and their poverty undeniably affects their parents' ability and time to provide the kinds of enriching experiences that, with a little more time and money, they *could* provide.

*Reflection: I am conflicted over my social class position in relation to my students' position. I see myself as a caring teacher who also looks ahead to my students' educational and economic prospects and doesn't see a huge transformation taking place for them. I do sometimes contrast my life and the life of my children with the lives of my students. I feel guilty because I do feel relief that I am where I am and not in their shoes.*

### November 23, 1998

Bad day. To kick off my unit on probability and statistics, Saul (another primary teacher) offered to do a lesson/story on the topic. He forgot to come. I went with plan B and got the math class started with another activity. The change in plans put me on edge, so during math I tended to overreact to students' off-taskness.

At 1:00, about seven students from Larry's 4–5 class came in to read to my students, who were working on independent research projects. About five of my students did not know what to do, or they knew what to do but were uninterested in doing it. I did a whole-class minilesson on how to transform notes to the final report. I forgot to remind students to do their final copy in pencil, so spelling miscues could be repaired. Donnie asked if he could go get poster paper so he could begin his display. I asked to see his notes, but he wasn't able to find his folder. He insisted that he be allowed to begin the poster display work. I said no, and he persisted in arguing that he was ready to do this task. When Donnie's plans were derailed by me, he roamed about the room, disrupting other students. I asked him to stop, and he snarled at me. Tomorrow, I'll talk to him about his obnoxious behavior.

At 2:00, after the break, the students returned. Jill, one of my parents who come every Monday at this time, was here. I wanted to show my students how they might rehearse their telling of the story "Abiyoyo." I placed on the overhead a skeleton of the plot structure and showed how this could be used as a prompt during storytelling. I placed one line from the story, and then attempted to have students generate the details following. As I worked my way through the story, fewer and fewer students attended to my lesson. As I looked around the room, pockets of students were engaged in small conversations, and some students simply were not looking up or participating. Billy, several times, fell out of his chair. The last time, I had to pick him up. Tomorrow, I will remove him from the room when this happens.

I asked Jill to read to the children at 2:20, and her reading of "Sideways Stories from Wayside School" closed out the day.

The entire afternoon was a struggle. I am having problems with the open-ended research projects. None of the students appear to have had much experience doing independent projects. The grade 4–5 students who worked the room as readers to my nonreaders need more training.

*Reflection: I mismanaged the research project. I inadequately laid out instructions and guidelines. Because of the absence of clear expectations, students naturally came up with their own expectations. I realize that once students fill the void by generating their own rules for behavior, and if their rules make sense to them, then it is very difficult to get them to change.*

### November 24, 1998

Another bad day.

I went through the motions in the afternoon, but I didn't want to be at school. I felt lethargic during math. I ended math a few minutes early so we could watch a *Reading Rainbow* video about Thanksgiving. I hadn't reviewed the film, but everyone on the staff was showing it, so I wasn't too worried. Still, I had no other intention for showing the film other than killing time. At the end of the day, we had "stone soup." The students had cut up vegetables when they arrived in the morning, and vegetable soup had been cooking all day in slow cookers. During our feast, the kids were normally antsy, given the upcoming five days off without school. This was the first afternoon since I began last August that I watched the clock. I couldn't wait for the day to end.

I realized today that I need to do three things. First, develop a curriculum that I am excited about. Second, make sure the curriculum is well structured and hands-on. Third, implement a system of outcomes (positive and negative) for student behavior.

*Reflection: More emotional laboring. The appropriate emotional stance of the teacher educator, related to the work of teaching, is excitement, interest, optimism, and joy. My emotions now are the antithesis of these; right now, I feel worn out, pessimistic, and depressed. My days are dominated by dark emotions. I am not having fun or finding much satisfaction in this work. In order to reduce the anxiety that I am having about my anxiety, there are a few things I should be thinking about: First, rethink my conception of the role of teacher educator to one that accepts the idea that teaching has a dark side, and this is acceptable and normal; it is alright to acknowledge that one occasionally has depression or dispair as a teacher. Second, I can work at being more analytical about my everyday experience instead of being self-accusatory and self-blaming (Lortie, 1975). Third, I can work to improve my teaching so I can have better days. Certainly, more "good days" will influence a more positive emotional state and self-efficacy as a teacher (and teacher educator).*

## November 25, 1998

Staff development day. No kids. The focus of the day is reading and the assessment of student reading performance.

## November 30, 1998

Good day.

The kids were very antsy, especially after the 1:45 break. After they came in from outside, it took about ten minutes to get them settled down. I was a little embarrassed, since one of the student's parents was in the room, her weekly Monday afternoon volunteer time. I talked to Barbara after school, and we decided that there needed to be clearer rewards and "punishments." I'd become slightly lax during the past several weeks in utilizing punitive consequences for disruptive behavior. Earlier in the year, my vigilant use of "time out" tended to be effective in moderating students' behavior. I stopped using the time-out strategy and, instead, have been managing the students by using indirect verbal techniques and positive reinforcement. (For example, I am looking for active listeners. I like the way that Nick's table is sitting and listening. I'll wait. I feel frustrated when I am trying to give directions and you are talking. Etc.)

Today, I announced a new lunch program called the Active Listener Lunch Bunch. Students who consistently exhibit positive behavior will be invited to eat lunch with me in the classroom. The students generally hate eating in the cafeteria, since it is loud and impersonal. During the afternoon, as I taught, I held a clipboard in my hand and wrote the names of students who did not follow directions. At the end of the day, I read the list of students whose names I had not written down. These nine students were invited to have lunch with me tomorrow. Most of the fourteen students who weren't invited to eat in the room tomorrow either disagreed with me or simply didn't understand why they were being excluded.

I don't think that many of the students understand or have the metacognitive wherewithal related to their behavior. I'll do some role-plays of appropriate and inappropriate behavior tomorrow so my expectations are clearer. It boggles my mind that it is December already and I am still teaching the students how to conduct themselves in the class. I should have focused on this more systematically in the first five weeks of school (thank you very much, Harry Wong). The problem was that, in the first five weeks of school, I didn't have a sense, myself, of how I wanted the students to be.

Still, all in all, I didn't have any power struggles with students, so I went home feeling pretty good.

Math is going well. I have an adequate organization for this subject area. I put together a packet of student work for the week. The packet consists of open-ended problem solving (e.g., story problems), drill and practice of arithmetic operations, and hands-on center work. This week, we are beginning the study of probability and statistics. I consulted some of the Marilyn Burns material, along with other curricula, and have come up with a set of hands-on experiences that support the learning of probability. While they are working in their packets of assignments, I call individuals or groups of students to the front of the room for instruction.

I require that they do at least two "jobs," or tasks, each day. Then, they can play math games. I am concerned that many students rush through their tasks so they can get to the math games.

I've resorted to sending Billy out of the room when he is unmanageable. Today, I think he got the sense that I will actually remove him if he doesn't listen. I made him sit by the office for about twenty minutes, near the end of the day. He came back much more subdued. He wants to be a part of the class. For this student, the *possibility* of removal from the group may be sufficient.

The last half hour of the day has become a problem for me. The kids are tired by this time. Usually, when I persist in trying to have them sit and listen to me, I can see their eyes move away from me and their hands get busy with table stuff, and my intentions are thwarted.

On Thanksgiving, we had dinner at a friend's house. Many school teachers were there. I made the mistake of speaking a bit too frankly about my teaching experience. Judy, my principal, shared a conversation she had with one of the people at the dinner. Judy was told by this person that I was "sinking" and having a "terrible year." Although I have been struggling, this characterization is a gross oversimplification of my experience. Besides, in a small town and as the resident teacher educator at the college, it probably isn't a good idea to bare my soul in the public arena. I need to be more careful with how I talk about my teaching and I how I talk about my students. I don't want to violate my privacy or the privacy of my students and colleagues.

*Reflection: I was embarrassed at the apparent rumor around town that I was failing as a teacher. I failed at "impression management" (Goffman, 1959) when I let my guard down and spoke honestly about the experience. I was still holding on to some vestiges of feelings that I was a "good teacher," and much of this self-image was connected to my standing in the community as the teacher educator, the accomplished and expert practitioner who supposedly knew what he was doing. Wide-spread knowledge of my struggle in the community would pose a real threat to my self-concept, and it is a threat that I want to minimize.*

## December 1, 1998

Bad day. I get angry when the students don't do what I want them to do. Lately, I've been showing my anger. My voice gets tight and I've started getting in kids' faces. I need to relax. I will ask Barbara to observe me and give me a signal when she hears tension in my voice.

I've had students working on independent research projects during the past week. It has been fun for most of the students and hellacious for me. There are almost fifteen nonreaders in the class. I overestimated the students' ability to glean information from nonfiction text, even with the assistance of fifth-grade readers. During the periods when kids are working on these projects, I am moving like a chicken with its head cut off. I have a continuous circle of students around me, all in need of help. I am spending maybe 80 percent of my time with five or six kids who either have no idea what to do or have no interest in my agenda.

*Reflection: The assignment as I have conceptualized it is totally inappropriate for these students and me at this time. Independent research projects presume students who can engage effectively in independent activity. Some of the students do not have the academic skills to do this project (for example, they can't read, and I don't have enough tutor readers), some students do not have the attentional/ motivational skills to stay focused on the task, and some students simply do not care.*

## December 2, 1998

Good day.

Mary and Dina are joys. They are consistently focused, task oriented, and positive. They are bosom buddies, and they usually ask to work together in math. When stuck on a math problem, they might spend twenty to thirty minutes struggling to make sense of it. There are about four other kids who show this type of task persistence.

*Reflection: Mary, Dina, and about four other kids are conformists. They do everything I ask them to without a whit of resistance. I suppose this is why they are "joys," although I can't say that I find them to be particularly memorable. My most memorable kids are the ones who listen to me for the most part but who engage in a bit of deviance. These kids joke around a bit more and challenge my authority more than the conformists, but I am still able to engage them in open negotiation with reason and discussion. I find the challenge of these kids to be the most satisfying part of the job (cf., Pollard, 1985).*

Billy has been extremely difficult, probably since the beginning of school. I asked for a care team meeting back in September, but it has taken a few months to organize a meeting of his parents, the speech therapist, counselor, resource teacher, Dorothy, and me. Just before the meeting, I spoke with the father on the phone. He was angry, since his son had reported that I had grabbed him by the arm on several occasions. The father was also incensed that Billy is being sent to a time-out space in the hallway, which is embarrassing him. The father acknowledged that his son is a "handful," but he wondered if I was considering Billy's perspective when he acts out.

I had grabbed Billy by the arm a few times, particularly as he acted out and then did not respond to redirection. "Billy, please sit down (no response). Billy, either sit down or go back to the time-out table (no response). Look at me Billy, you are interrupting the class. You need to go in the back of the room. Join us when you are ready to be an active listener (no response)."

At this point, I would become tense, since the kid was completely unresponsive. I would grab his arm with a slight squeeze, like I am holding a baseball bat, and lead him to the back of the room. On other occasions, when Billy would fall out of his seat and then refuse to get up, I would bend down, grab him under the armpits and pick him up, and place his body back in the chair.

At the care team meeting, both parents and I acknowledged that we could all improve our work with Billy. The father affirmed his need to be more patient with his son; I affirmed the same thing. Since the meeting, when Billy acts out, I give him an arm hug, whisper my redirection in his ear, and then give him a few seconds to respond. If he doesn't respond, I remind him that his father is home, only four blocks away, and will come in and sit with him if need be. I think, "No, I *know* that his father, when angry, scares him, and this may be my ace in the hole with this kid."

Another teacher visited me after school and admitted feeling guilty because of her recent more autocratic, martinet-type behavior with the students. This teacher was schooled in Glasser and Dreikers and had always worked at implementing humanistic forms of governance in her classroom. Recently, however, many of her kids had become completely unresponsive to her indirect signals and her appeals to kids' sense of what it means to be a "good citizen." I empathized with her and told her of my own sleepless nights as I worried about the same problem.

I think that one key way to managing this irreconcilable problem is to have other adults nearby who can listen to us and watch us as we teach and who can remind us when we are straying too far from our ideals. It's so difficult to reflect on experience alone, in isolation of other interested adults who share a common experience. I think that our ideals, philosophy, and ethics are a powerful vehicle to help us reflect on experience. For example, how do I want to treat people in my everyday life, and how do I want to treat kids in my everyday teaching, including the treatment of challenging kids such as Billy. By continuously comparing my ideals with my experience, I make more thoughtful assessments of my behavior and, in effect, become a better teacher and a better person for my students. But I needed the conversations with Billy's father and Judy to remind me to reflect, to remind me of the gap between my ideals and my reality.

*Reflection: Teachers are often reluctant to admit failure or self-doubt for fear of being thought incompetent by their colleagues. I was affirmed by my colleague's confessional. It acknowledged my own self-doubts.*

A recurring problem. Students sit at tables, but their actual seats are up for grabs. No assigned seats. Four or five times a day, there is a fight over a seat. One student will have left her/his seat temporarily and then s/he returns only to find another student sitting in the seat s/he had been using. I need to hold a classroom meeting and have the students' problem solve this situation. But certainly I'd need to do much peer mediation and additional discussion to help the kids learn to deal with this problem. The problem actually involves only about five or six students!

*Reflection: The time required to help kids more effectively manage peer conflict resolution around the issue of chair ownership is enormous. The question then becomes, "Do I want to spend the precious scarce time on this issue or do I want, instead, to solve the problem for the students so we can get on with academic learning?" By solving the problem for students, I can simply assign them their permanent seat. So, where's the emphasis: social skills or academic skills? I am inundated with peer conflict and I can easily devote much of the day to social skills and community building. But at what costs to the kids' learning of the academics?*

## December 6, 1998

State testing is coming. We'll collect assessment data on our third graders in math, reading, writing, and speaking. I am responsible for math. Dorothy and I haven't talked about how we will prepare our students for the speaking test. In January, I need to begin collecting work samples of the third graders on open-ended problem solving. I am anxious, since I don't know if I have done enough to prepare the kids for this.

A mammogram found a dark shadow in my mother's breast, so she went in for a biopsy last Thursday. Given her eighty years and the fact that she went under a general anesthetic, it was a serious procedure for her. She lives in Phoenix and we speak on the phone every week. I have a vague recollection that she told me about the surgery. I forgot about it. I spoke with my in-laws yesterday, and they reminded me of the biopsy. I was horrified to realize that I had forgotten the surgery. I spaced it out! Feeling guilty and sad, I called her. She had the sense to not lay on the guilt, since she knew that I have enough natural guilt for this filial faux pas.

I suppose that my forgetfulness is a manifestation of my busyness. I am on overload. Work, writing, planning, complaining, wife, children, the holidays, bills, the messy house.

Transitions have always been a problem for me. Recently, I have stumbled across a strategy that has improved my ability to manage transitions. I have established a consistent signal for "it's time to be quiet and listen to directions." I put my hand in the air and chant backwards from five. Between each number, I remind the kids that I expect "eyes on me and closed mouths." By the time I reach zero, most students are in their seats, watching me and ready for the next direction. I stand with a clipboard and note any students who have not responded to my direction. If students persist in noncompliance, I invite them to go to the time-out table in the room and then return to the group when they think that they can more effectively cooperate.

This system holds the students accountable for their behavior. I just have to be careful that I give feedback to the noncompliant students, so that on the day that I announce the students who are invited to eat in the room, they are not surprised and confused by their nonparticipation. This way, when I give them feedback that their behavior is jeopardizing their opportunity to eat in the room, they still have time to turn it around.

*Reflection: My strategies for control rely almost explicitly on my power as teacher (temporarily remove a student from the group or withhold an incentive that is appealing to most of them). The use of my power to regulate student behavior almost always contradicts my ideal of a more communitarian model of living, in which people tend to self-manage their behavior out of a sense of responsibility to the group and a commitment to the group's goals.*

The superintendent was scheduled to visit the staff at our regular meeting last week, but he couldn't come, due to a conflicting appointment. The staff was disappointed. We are the only school he has yet to visit. He has rescheduled to visit in January. I flew off the handle. I had been reading about the organizational and structural impediments to good teaching, such as large class sizes, large numbers of special needs students, planning time, and lack of resources. It has always perplexed me, since I came to Woodbridge, how uniform class size formulas are used when schools have different populations and vastly different needs.

We are about to end independent project work. The students have loved this activity. For me, it has been stressful. I was always over-loaded during these periods. There were always more students who could not work independently than I had extra support available. Usually, we had the eight fifth graders working with eight of my youngers, Barbara would be working with one of the youngers, and I would be putting out fires (such as students fooling around, students having computer problems, students who wanted help reading or taking notes).

Most students enjoyed the freedom to pursue their own topics, and particularly, they enjoyed the social dimension of the activity. During the work time, they would have great latitude to walk and talk about the room, looking for and sharing information. I decided that I would take a developmental perspective on their final written displays, almost like we accept young students' spelling miscues as a normal phase of their spelling development. Some of the reports were mature looking, with coherent categories (e.g., in a report on ants, one student framed coherent paragraphs on the enemies, breeding, food, habitat, and physical characteristics of ants). On the other end of the continuum, the adults had to do most of the writing for the students who were still writing at a precommunicative level. I realize that I could have more effectively prepared the students for this project, but I did my best, and all in all, their final products were both adequate (from my perspective) and superlative (from theirs).

### December 7, 1998
The afternoons this week will be shortened by holiday programs. Today was a dress rehearsal of the winter program. In the gym. The students had to sit for about forty-five minutes as they waited their turn to sing. My students were antsy. I felt like I was doing guard duty, as the rest of the teachers and I stood around the perimeter of the students, watching for the slightest student provocation, and then we'd swoop down on them with a finger in the face and a stern warning to "sit on your bottom." My kids were bored and restless. I noticed that the other classes were all more subdued than mine. I

wondered if it was my teaching or the students? I was embarrassed that I did not have complete control over my students.

*Reflection: I like kids, and I have a self-image as someone who is warm, friendly, and loving. However, the situation requires that I play the role of custodian, making sure that the kids sit quietly and comply with an uncomfortable hour of sitting on a hard floor doing nothing. Of course, it makes sense that the kids are going to get antsy. Who in their right mind would not get restless after sitting on the floor with nothing to do but look at some boring rehearsal? The anxiety here for me was the thought that I was being evaluated by my ability to control my kids, especially as I observed other classes to be more subdued than mine. It was an emotional strain being a hard-ass with my kids, and a double strain given the fact that I was doing a poor job of it.*

Alone, in the privacy of my basement in the evening, I reviewed the specifications for the state math test, administered in April. Any idea of "teaching to the test" among the teachers here is anathema. This year, the legislature is awarding sizable grants to schools that show the greatest increase in scores from the year before. While the items on the math test represent a set of bare-bones, "basic" knowledge about math, it certainly does represent mathematical knowledge that all elementary kids ought to know.

A new intern who will be working in our class for three weeks in January visited today. She immediately got into a power struggle with Nathan. She lost. Later, she asked me what I did when he refused compliance with a teacher directive.

I said, "Just give them a choice: to comply or leave the group. Be very matter of fact about it. Don't get explicitly emotional. Calmly give them the choice. Say 'thank you' and walk away. This strategy tends to work for me. It is simple and effective."

I realize that the student's motive has to be taken in consideration. Also, how important is your directive? Are you asking the student to do something that has no "valid educational purpose"? If you can't justify the directive in a way that'll make sense to most of the students, it is probably best to let sleeping dogs lie.

*Reflection: The pressures of maintaining order has had a powerful effect on my thinking about teacher–student relations. My first response to a serious act of student deviance is to resort to power: "Comply or leave the group!" I tend to use this close negotiation style with students who, for some reason, do not choose to engage me in the give and take of negotiations. Clearly, who I am becoming as a teacher reflects in large part my students—these particular students. Riseborough (1985) argues that the student is the "critical reality definer, as the teacher career gatekeeper, who constructs and sustains, through interaction, the identities and careers of teachers" (262).*

## December 9, 1998

Today, Justin went crazy. He threatened to body slam Bonnie when he suspected her of cheating in a game of dreidel. Barbara gave him the choice of quieting down or leaving the room. He refused to leave and went off on a wild tantrum, so Barbara had to *carry* him out of the room. Bonnie, herself, is inflexible when she has conflict with peers. Instead of engaging in negotiation or discussion, she usually won't talk and, instead, will run under a desk and refuse to come out.

In math, we explored vocabulary related to probability. I placed three words on the board: *certain, maybe,* and *impossible.* I posed several situations and asked students to name their probability, using one of the three vocabulary words. The first situation read, "The sun will rise tomorrow." About half the class said "Maybe" and several students said "Impossible." I don't think that these students had a schema for a "rising sun," so the question didn't make sense to them (or at least it made a different "sense" to them than it did to me). The next situation read, "It's going to snow tomorrow." Most students said "Certain." I looked around and it was the first graders and some second graders whose theories about these probability questions were most askew from the third graders' and mine. I wondered about the developmental readiness of this activity for most of the students. I also wondered about the difficulty of doing whole-class presentations of specific close-ended academic content, such as this, in the multiage classroom. I realize that there is much I don't know about developing multiage primary curricula. I'll try it again tomorrow.

*Reflection: Again, the quality of my relations with the students is having a profound effect on how I see myself as a teacher. Riseborough*

*(1985) is particularly interested in the effects students have on how teachers define themselves and how teachers' careers are framed. Teachers are sandwiched between their supervisors (or colleagues) and students, who each exert influence on how they conceptualize themselves as teacher.*

> *The social construction of "good" and "bad" teachers in schools and the social distribution of their competencies is related to the ideological and cultural hegemony exercised by their superiors and the counter-hegemony exercised by their inferiors [the students]. . . . It has been argued that a teacher's framework of imagery for judging him/herself and his/her pupils is to be understood partially in the activity of pupils. Equally, the pupil's framework of imagery for judging him/herself and his/her teachers is to be understood partially in terms of the activity of teachers. (Riseborough, 1985, 262)*

*My self-conception as a teacher reflects my experience in this particular situation, with these children and with my colleagues, the presence of the state tests, the existing curriculum, and so forth.*

## December 10, 1998

I can't believe how fast the year has gone so far. In a week and a half, we have two weeks off for the winter holidays, and then it's January! I am optimistic that I will begin consolidating my new-found pedagogic knowledge, and that my students will experience significant learning gains. In math, I will be doing a month-long unit on measurement. In science, I will begin a unit on food webs. I also want to explore the study of racism and sexism with the kids. I am excited about what lies ahead. I am excited about how far I've come as a teacher. I am excited that I have survived the first four months of school, with a portion of my professional ego still intact (I think).

## December 15, 1998

The kids walk in at 12:15, ready to begin the afternoon. Within a minute, often, I am swamped with kids who want to talk to me. Here is a not unusual scenario.

Timmy: Stevie pushed me outside.
Wilma: Ken, here is my math homework.
Donna: Ken, I have an idea for what we can do at the end of the day.
Jeff: Hey, you wanna hear a joke. Can I tell a story to the class?
Cesar and Nathan: Crystal ruined our game outside. She took our ball and called us assholes.
Goldie (whining): I don't feel well. I want to go home.
Stevie: Is it time to go home yet?
*The counselor walks in and takes two kids who were fighting outside.*
Crystal (screaming): Nathan called me stupid!!!

## December 15, 1998 (evening)

Three more days to go until winter break. Two weeks off. I am trying not to count the minutes. I am tired—mostly mental fatigue, although I have been fighting a cold for the past two weeks. I am having trouble sleeping again. I think that the biggest stressor on teachers is the mental fatigue that comes from everyday teaching, six hours a day, twenty days a month, month after month. If a teacher desires to teach something to someone, a truly collaborative learning situation would mean that the student agrees to be "taught." Achieving this agreement from twenty-five students, day after day, is a truly colossal task, and a task that, essentially, is rarely achievable with all or even most students at all times. Students' lethargy or passive refusal to listen to directions is stressful for teachers.

*Reflection: The assumptions of mass public schooling reflect a conflict model for adult–student relations. School attendance is compulsory, educational experience is done in large groups, and the learner has little control over curriculum. Teachers can control the overt behavior of students, but they can't control students' covert behavior. Given the macro- and micropolitical conditions of schooling, I think that student resistance to school, at least in part, is a sign of sanity.*

This week has been filled with holiday craft activities and readings of holiday children's literature. I've worked to maintain the integrity of the math period. But after 1:15, it's time for crafts. Yesterday, the kids made stockings. On Monday, they made menorahs. They also painted the outside windows with winter scenes. This was actually fun.

Goldie was a fetal alcohol baby. She is a third grader, but she is smaller than most of our first graders. She has a high-pitched voice, becomes excited at the slightest provocation, and is often sick. She is on medication for some "disorder." When she is upset over something, which is often, it is difficult to reason with her. Often, Goldie will storm away from the altercation, pushing chairs over and screaming, when it is apparent that she isn't getting her way. Sometimes she will threaten or even carry out physical assault of a peer who has "crossed her." Goldie is always begging me to be first in line or to be able to pull down the overhead, turn on the VCR, or plug in the television. Her psyche is turned taut like a cable on the Golden Gate Bridge. Nathan knows how to push Goldie's button. He consciously provokes her. Nathan will walk up to her and call her stupid. Or he will stick his tongue out at her. Most of Nathan's harassing behavior is done out of the sight of adults.

*Reflection: Nathan is a low-status student. On a sociogram, he turned out to be one of the least appealing kids in the class. My hunch is that his persecution of Goldie is a way of achieving some status. Goldie's outbursts may show the group that Goldie is even more bizarre than Nathan, and this may distract the group from making negative judgments of Nathan.*

## December 16, 1998

Good day. Math was conventional. The kids worked on a variety of tasks; I worked with individuals, reviewed their work, etc. Then, another craft activity. The kids made a gift for their parents—a minestrone soup mix—which they put together by moving around the room to different stations, collecting spices, beans, noodles etc. I spent an hour at the grocery store last night shopping for the ingredients. Tomorrow morning, I'll spend an hour cutting paper in preparation for a few craft activities tomorrow afternoon. Mark, another primary teacher, avoids crafts since he's chosen not to allocate his scarce time for this. I wonder what he is doing in the afternoons. The usual academic agenda? I'll ask him. I find that the crafts are a useful bargaining tool, to get kids to accomplish their math. Each day, I have been framing the math tasks with, "And *after* you finish your math work, we will begin on the next craft activity."

*Reflection: Open-ended, nonacademic activity is a common bargaining chip for teachers trying to get their kids to do academic work. The culture of schools tends to promote the practice of crafts and other loosely bounded activity (e.g., assemblies and programs) almost daily during the last two weeks before winter break. While some teachers complain about the reduction of academic work during this period, I find myself using the daily craft work as an incentive for kids to do academic work.*

This afternoon, after school, I joined the staff in wrapping Christmas presents. We wrapped about four hundred presents. An anonymous person donated $3,000 for Christmas gifts for the poorest kids in the school. Each teacher identified seven kids in their room who are most in need. Last week, a group of teachers went to Target and bought clothes and toys for these kids. On Saturday, teachers and aides are going to deliver the toys around the neighborhood. Merry Christmas, from the Woodbridge Elves!

Two more days to go. I have been fighting a cold for the past week or so.

I spoke with Debbie, a friend, who teaches in another high-poverty school in town. Last year, she had a class like mine. I asked her what she did to survive the year, because I knew that she had become depressed from her daily struggle with a difficult class. She said, "I began looking for the smallest progress or growth. For example, by the end of the year, my kids would be able to sit quietly as I read aloud from a picture book, and then a few kids would generate some coherent comments about the book, and most of the class would be paying attention for maybe thirty seconds. When I saw positive changes like this—I lived for this. This is what I looked for."

One dimension of my work that sustains me is my relationship with the students. We genuinely like each other. I enjoy talking to them and being with them. Some kids clap when I enter the room. I get many hugs. I just read a study that examined students' perceptions of the "good teacher." The data pointed to the interpersonal dimension of the teacher–student relationship. Students said that good teachers care for them, have a sense of humor, treat them fairly, don't lose their temper, etc. In spite of my struggle to implement an academic curriculum, and in spite of my struggle to help them control their social behavior, I recognize the imperative of a caring and easygoing persona for me as teacher. Of course, I still need to be clear and firm about discipline and academic expectations, but when my structures are ineffective (i.e., students are off task), it is important that I maintain a caring relationship with the students. Perhaps one essential benefit of my work with the students this year will be their association with an adult (me) who is caring, thoughtful, and easygoing. Perhaps the model of who I am as a person is the most significant lesson for my students.

There is a small group of students in the room who are consistently focused on academic tasks. Maybe seven kids. They are consistently focused as active listeners and cooperative workers. They never engage in deviant behavior. It seems that most of their school experience (at this school, at least) is one in which they sit and wait as teachers work to keep most of the other kids sitting still. I think the deep lesson for the "good" kids is on how to defer gratification (Jackson, 1968). How to wait. I suppose this is an important life skill.

Students are still fighting over chairs. They sit at tables, in groups of four to five. Specific chair assignments are fluid. So a student sitting in a chair at her table in the morning may find that someone else is sitting in her chair after she comes back from a five-minute visit to the bathroom. A fight ensues. Usually, it is the older child who wins the fight. I will call a class meeting on January 4 so the students can deliberate on this problem and generate some solutions.

**December 18, 1998**
Whew! No school for two weeks.

**January 4, 1999**
First day back after two weeks off. Picking up Sam (my son) at a weird angle, I strained my back. I called in sick. My back hurt, but I must admit that I was not saddened about missing the first day back.

Melinda, walking out the door on her way to her kindergarten job, looked back and asked, "Are you kinda glad to be staying home?" I turned away from her and smiled.

*Reflection: The prevailing discourse that teachers just love their work is, perhaps, the system's way of countering the utterly challenging and exhausting reality of teachers' work. It also reflects a maternal conception of teaching, in which love is the mediating emotion between teacher and students. However, when I am sick and I can't go in to work, I do feel a bit of relief. Who wouldn't feel relief at the prospect of a day off? Sometimes, I wonder if there is something wrong with me, since I don't feel guilt when I am not able to work.*

## January 6–7, 1999

These two days have been hellacious. It's almost like the first days of school last September, when I was usually an "invisible" presence, haplessly trying to manage a class that was oblivious to my directions. It is a maxim among teachers that a two-week vacation does havoc to kids' memory of "good behavior." In a school with a lot of special needs kids, this is especially the case.

A typical scene: I would ask for their "eyes," but only three or four kids would look up. Or I would ask someone to sit down, and she would ignore me. There was both passive-aggressive behavior and aggressive behavior toward me by students. A lot of kids would simply ignore me, and some kids were openly defiant. The defiant kids were the usual suspects, such as Donnie and Nathan. For example, Nathan would be sitting in Rob's seat. Rob protests. I say, "Nathan, you need to sit in your seat." Nathan replies, "Why?" I explain. He responds, "Why?" I explain another way. He gives the same response. After several incidents like this throughout the afternoon, he ends up in the school's time-out room. There, he antagonizes the school counselor, who keeps him in the room even longer. Today, Nathan got his fourth citation for misbehavior on the bus, so he has been kicked off the bus for the remainder of the year.

With Donnie, I have made the mistake of *allowing* him to be obnoxious and defiant, without consequence. I woke up at 4:30 this morning and lay in bed for two hours thinking about this student.

Any time I try to redirect him, he becomes defensive and argumentative. He is articulate and knows how to "push my buttons." His parents do not trust me and believe that I am out to get their child. Mistakenly, I respond passively to Donnie when he makes obnoxious comments or when he misbehaves. I am avoiding conflict. However, my neutral stance has empowered him to become more obnoxious and unpleasant, to me as well as other kids. Today, he said to me, "Ken, I just love seeing you get upset at me. I know how to push your buttons." His comment was like being hit over the head with a two-by-four.

Ah!!! I have created my own problem here, by allowing the boy to behave like this. I think the answer to the Donnie problem is for me to respond assertively to his aggressive behavior and treat him like I do the other kids: by challenging his errant behavior, sending him to time out, keeping him in for recess, not inviting him to the "active listener lunch bunch," etc. I realize that in my attempt to accommodate his needs and our fragile relationship, I have taken away any boundaries for the boy. *He* is in charge! Not me.

I realized that I need to (again) begin each afternoon with a review of behavioral expectations, but I also need to develop a set of consequences for appropriate and inappropriate behavior. Here is a set of expectations that I read to the class:

1. Enter the room quietly. Sit right down.
2. Be quiet when someone is speaking. Be an active listener.
3. During work time, keep voices low. No socializing.
4. Listen to adults' directions.
5. Raise hands. Do not call out.
6. Work hard. Have fun. Learn a lot.

Here are the consequences when students successfully meet expectations:

1. notes home to parents
2. extra recess
3. lunch in the room

Here are the consequences when students do not meet expectations:

1. loss of recess
2. time out
3. no invitation to lunch in the room

*Reflection: I spoke with Melinda about the possibility that our son might have attention deficit hyperactivity disorder (ADHD). We agreed that, if he does, we would homeschool him. We are both teachers, and we know how poorly trained and poorly supported teachers are in their work with special needs kids, especially ADHD kids. We don't know which one of us would stay home, but we are certain that it might be miseducative to send an ADHD kid to school, especially if he were our own child.*

*With Donnie, I am again failing to "play the adult." I am supposed to be the adult, and it seems that he is pushing me to assert my legitimate role. I worry about appeasing his parents, and I also think that we could achieve a working consensus by discussion, reasoning, and negotiation. He is not someone with whom I can negotiate. I have to resort to power, but I don't know how yet.*

Wanda has come back from break even more lost. She has a passive-aggressive orientation to dealing with problems. Abandoned by her father when she was two, she is wracked with orthopedic problems needing years of surgery. She has body odor again, so I need to speak to her and the mother. I looked over to her table group from a distance. I noticed that all the kids had their shirts pulled up over their noses. I walked over and was knocked over by a horrific whiff of human gas. Wanda's. During work time, she sits and plays with crayons and markers. When I sit with her and verbally manage her work, she will place pencil to paper and humor me with a bit of work. Otherwise, when I move away from her, she does nothing. And I always have to move away from her, since I have twenty-four other kids who need me. I am able to give her just a few short minutes each afternoon, when otherwise she does very little work. Compared to the first few months of the year, I am beginning to spend less time getting her to finish her work. Given the press of needs from the other twenty-four kids, I don't feel as though I have much choice.

At recess, she often lies on the ground, examining some toy soldiers, perhaps surrounded by some younger kids. She needs therapy, big time. In our last special education staffing, I thought that counseling was part of the plan. Maybe she's getting it and I just am not aware of it.

*Reflection: My reality with Wanda, Nathan, and other kids is reshaping my understandings of my teaching role. I am beginning to accept the fact that I cannot meet the needs of many of these kids. I can't do it alone. Given my current work conditions and the home conditions of these kids, the job of teaching them is, perhaps, insanely unrealistic and impossible. I don't know if we, as teachers, ever entertain the possibility that teaching may, at times, be an utterly insane endeavor.*

The new school superintendent addressed the staff at our weekly meeting on Wednesday. He described his efforts at balancing a three-million dollar deficit along with the plethora of his other challenges. I have no doubt that he is a busy and hard-working person.

I asked him one question. "Should our ideas about class size be mediated by the socioeconomic status of schools?" By this, I wondered if for Woodbridge, because it has so many high-needs students, the class-size formula that the district uses should take this into account. The superintendent dismissed this issue, first, by asserting that all schools were getting an increasing number of special-needs students and that many teachers all around town were under pressure. Second, he pointed out that Woodbridge gets the largest amount of supplemental funds of any school in town by way of Title 1 money, which allows us to employ six full-time aides, a full-time counselor, and a full-time family advocate specialist.

I became quietly angry as the superintendent's response rolled off his lips. He just "doesn't get it." The sheer numbers of special-needs kids at Woodbridge is overwhelming. I have a "normal" class size of twenty-five kids. My wonderful aide, Barbara, only helps to stem the tide of special-needs issues in the class. At best. Yesterday, she spent forty minutes helping two boys work out a problem. Interpersonal flare-ups between kids are endemic, especially during and just after recesses. Forget her role as an instructional aide. If I didn't have Barbara to help manage these problems, the academic program would be in shambles.

*Reflection: I sometimes wonder if our anger at the superintendent and other local bureaucrats is a distraction from at least two more elemental factors that influence our work conditions. First, society has never been willing to fund* public *education. A radical reduction in class size would require a serious redistribution of wealth, so the rich would have to bear more of the burden of assigning just ten to twenty students per teacher, as elitist private schools do.*

*Second, societal values have changed. Traditional sacred cows, such as respecting authority and elders, have given way to instant gratification, materialism, and individualism. When I was a kid, we would jump when the teacher said, "Jump!" I welcome the postmodern conception of teacher as collaborator and facilitator. However, this conception just doesn't work with large classes of kids in a context of intense teacher and school accountability, higher standards, and economically stressed families.*

On Friday, I did a craft activity with the kids at the end of the day. Each table group needed brushes, paints, water, and paper. I told each group to assign one group member to retrieve each of these things. Thoughtlessly, I placed all the objects on the same table.

Again, I thoughtlessly told the students to go get their assigned objects. The entire class moved at once, converging on one small area. It was pandemonium. One girl, dressed in a new silk blouse, was knocked down and drenched with a bowl of colored water.

If I were a student teacher being observed by my university supervisor, I would probably have a plan of assistance thrown at me for this blunder.

## January 7, 1999

A good day. I tried my new management system, and for the most part it kept the students calm and focused. Actually, I am referring to about seventeen kids who need this structure. There are eight kids who respond to my directions without the threat of teacher-imposed consequences. The others need the threat of time out, loss of recess, or not being able to eat in the room once a week.

We are doing a unit now on food chains and webs. I asked the kids to name animals that are at the top of food chains. The usual animals were mentioned, such as lions, hippopotamuses, and humans. With a big grin on his face, Nathan called out, "Skunks!" I wasn't sure. We both agreed that the skunk probably doesn't have many predators.

## January 12, 1999

Bad day. I had an out-of-body experience. Donnie's got my number and I've got to put a stop to it.

An assembly was to begin in a few minutes. The kids were not listening to directions. I lost my temper. I didn't shout at them, but my voice was tense, my pitch was a bit higher, and it was obvious that I was angry.

Donnie called out, in full voice, "You are shouting at us, and I don't think that kids should be shouted at. We don't deserve this, and you shouldn't do it. No one likes it, and stop it right now!" I looked around the room, and I noticed that kids didn't seem to be paying any attention to his comments. I ignored him and carried on with the lesson.

I was mortified. I agreed with everything he said. I need to control my emotions and not allow any more outbursts. On the other hand, his defiance was a challenge to my authority. Given the many behavioral issues, I needed to maintain the authority to direct kids without their questioning my authority. His comment clearly suggested that he has power, and I sensed that the other kids realized that he had power that they don't have.

He is smart, his father doesn't like me, and he knows this. I can't make any mistakes with him. I need to respond to his obnoxious or disrespectful statements head on and rationally. I can't lose my cool with him, particularly since he thinks he can manipulate my emotions by his actions. He has already admitted that he enjoys pushing my buttons.

*Reflection: I had to suppress many dark emotions here. I was made scared and anxious by Donnie's comments. I kept an expressionless face and voice as I continued with the lesson. Donnie's comments were especially painful, because they reflected my own guilt and discomfort about my conduct as a teacher. I always feel badly after I show anger, although Barbara affirmed my outburst by saying, "Well, this is what they are used to at home." Anger does not fit into my image as a teacher. Still, most teachers would defend the occasional use of anger to control children. I'm not sure. However, the reality of teaching is that teachers do become angry. In any relationship, anger is a natural response. I suspect that suppressing this emotion is probably unhealthy for the teacher. Anger is part of our everyday lives. Why shouldn't it be part of the teacher–student relationship. Of course, the teacher needs to show anger in a way that is in the best interest of children's psychological and social well-being.*

In April, my third graders take the state tests in math and reading. I am responsible for math. I looked at the test specifications, and the items on the test reflect the same kind of one-answer basic skills knowledge that has been tested since I entered education in 1977. The tests do address all of the NCTM Standards, such as numeration, estimation, probability, statistics, and measurement. Much of the test requires basic calculations, measurements, and estimations. I realized that the most efficient way to prepare the third graders for the test is to have them work their way through a traditional third grade math textbook.

I am introducing more strategy games to the class. This week, I am showing them how to play Mancala, an ancient African math strategy game. I need to broaden their experience of mathematics.

We've begun a unit on food chains and food webs. It's also Martin Luther King's birthday on Friday, so I want to do some activities that deal explicitly with racism and the civil rights movement. I want kids to consider the reality of racism now in America, and that the work of King was an on-going effort that began before him and continues to this day. I have a video of the children's book *Whitewash* (Shange, 1997). I will show it to the students on Friday. The book shows a blatant act of racism: the attack on several African-American children by skinheads. I also want to show kids more subtle kinds of racism. I'll read *Amazing Grace* (Hoffman, 1991) to them, which is a light examination of race and gender issues.

*Reflection: I feel some psychic space, at last, to begin planning some activities that reflect some deeply held beliefs about education. Multicultural strategy games are the kind of activity that reflects my image as a math teacher. Multicultural education is important to me, and educational experience that gets kids to develop broader understandings of the world around us does, indeed, support and affirm my teaching self.*

## January 13, 1999

Good day. No power struggles.

We examined crickets today, their physical characteristics. The students enjoyed this. After the activity, I led a discussion of their observations, and I had students write notes to include in their project folders. Today, we will do an experiment to determine the foods that crickets eat.

I read the third chapter from *Shiloh*, by Phyllis Naylor (1991). The students love this book so far.

*Reflection: I sense that "good days" are dependent on at least two related factors: first, how well I have planned and, second, my frame of mind. When I have planned well, I usually feel more confident and I worry less prior to teaching. Recently, however, I have planned well, but I have still been frustrated by the students. I need to be more conscious of how I respond emotionally when I get frustrated. I need to reframe feelings of anger. Somewhere in my life, I have learned to use this emotion to relieve, respond to, or resolve frustration.*

## January 14, 1999

Good day. No power struggles.

Today is Martin Luther King Jr.'s birthday. I have children's literature to read to the students, about King and about racial issues. I'll read a biography of King and then have the students do watercolors or drawings of an incident from his life.

## January 20, 1999

Yesterday was a nightmare. Barbara has been sick all week. I have a substitute aide, but she has no authority with the kids. They don't listen to her. I realized how indispensable a full-time aide is to me. I spent the entire afternoon working to maintain the students' attention. On January 19, Barbara's sub took her eight-student math group to the project room, as usual. However, they were so out of control she asked if she could keep the math group in with the whole group today. I was embarrassed, since she is the parent of a third grader in another class. So I had eight more squirrelly kids in the room during math.

Joey's mother got arrested, so he was agitated during the entire afternoon. Nathan taunted Wanda about her "ugliness." I had to send Billy to the school time-out room, since he did no work and was loud and disruptive at his table. I got locked into a power struggle with Donnie. Deacon and Sally did not stop talking. Timmy cried that Rob pinched him. Etc. Etc. Etc.

## January 21, 1999

Better day. Barbara is still sick, and I still have the substitute aide.

I called a meeting for Judy (the principal), Donnie, and me. For weeks, Judy has been offering to "lower the boom" on Donnie, but I didn't want to admit that I couldn't handle this problem alone. By now, I was desperate for any relief, even if it meant that someone needed to rescue me.

The meeting with the principal, in her office, really scared the boy. Donnie cried as he entered the office, and I realized how fragile he was under that tough blustery exterior. Judy and I calmly reminded him that I was, indeed, the teacher and in charge of the classroom and that he needed to listen to my directions without delay or argument. Otherwise, he would have to sit in the office. Donnie cried like it was the end of the world. The remainder of the day, he was the model conformist.

I had created a monster in this boy. I had acquiesced to the boy's need for power to the point where he had gradually taken control over our relationship. I am amazed at the simplicity of the solution to this problem: a meeting with the principal and then, from me, consistent directions and consequences.

**January 22, 1999**
Ugh. A day from hell. Even Dorothy noted, to the aide, that the kids were "in control" this morning.

*Reflection: The kids weren't "in control" in an organized manner, such as the counterhegemony described by Hargreaves (1972). When kids are in control, the teacher typically acquiesces and engages in a series of rationalizations to make sense of the fact that they are not in charge. In my case, I was in the midst of a struggle for control with the students. Like in a military standoff, my life in the class consisted of a series of skirmishes, some that I won and some that the students won, with the intermittent truce during which time the students and I were able to hammer out a working consensus. The great metaphor used by many teachers to characterize their life in classrooms, "in the trenches," was most real for me this week.*

A few factors at play. First, it's been a torrential downpour all week. The kids have been cooped up inside pretty much every recess this week. They need to run around outside and blow some steam.

*Reflection: I could have played more math games, done an additional art activity, and relaxed a bit more. I've got to be more flexible.*

Second, Barbara's been gone, so I have acquiesced to more student misbehavior than I do when she is able to support my enforcement. The substitute aide is able, but she doesn't have the experience with these kids to respond quickly and decisively to problems. Third, each table group has a terrarium on its table with a chameleon in it. For most of the kids, the presence of chameleons is almost a religious experience. Some of the kids fight almost continuously over who gets to hold the chameleons. When I give directions or instructions, some of the kids are unable to focus, since they can't keep their longing hands away from their chameleon.

*Reflection: The chameleons provided a relief from the tedium of school. I was responsible for this distraction.*

Fourth, the counselor has been out of the building all week. Minor surgery. So I haven't been able to send kids to the "alternative learning environment" and I haven't been able to use him as a mediator for some of the student conflict.

Finally, some of the students simply can't get along with each other. Seven of the students, particularly, are magnets for interpersonal conflict wherever they roam. Nathan (my impulsive and loud one), Joey (whose mother just got out of jail), Rob (kicked out of his home and now living with the grandparents), Justin (a former fetal alcohol kid living with grandma), Timmy (a former fetal alcohol baby living with grandma), Bonnie (a stubborn girl whose feet talk to each other), and Goldie (who behaves like a four-year-old). Almost continuously, these kids fight over everything: pencils, seats, time with the chameleon, whatever. One of the kids will burst out of his seat crying that Nathan is giving him a dirty look, or that Wanda called him stupid, or that Joey took his pencil away from him.

Today, Timmy was the victim of a series of incidents. He is the smallest kid and the least verbal, so he can't defend himself physically or verbally. A sociogram showed that no one wants to work with Timmy, nor do kids indicate him as someone with whom they want to work. He is a harmless kid, but for some reason he has become a punching bag for Rob, Justin, and Larry, who themselves are pariahs. The sociogram showed that most kids do not want to work with Rob, Justin, and Larry, either. Their social life at school is negative, for the most part, and so is their home life. I figure that they have to torture someone, to express their frustration and failure, so Timmy has become the target. Even Deacon, usually a mild-mannered kid, shows aggressive behavior toward Timmy. Deacon took a pair of scissors and stabbed a drawing Timmy made on their table's file folder.

Sometimes, the social problems among the kids are like a flood, and I can only address so many incidents. I fear that the students do not feel safe, and this is a recurring feeling I have had all year. When I am on overload, which is what happens when I am using all my psychic resources to keep the whole class in line, small flare-ups become totally distracting, for me and for the rest of the class.

*Reflection: Peer conflict is unavoidable, even among so-called normal kids. Perhaps the only way for me to reduce this conflict in a measurable way is to keep the kids separated and working alone on tasks, with talking prohibited. Of course, this is unrealistic. Besides, some conflict is important so kids can learn how to live together. My weakness as a beginning teacher is in teaching kids how to manage peer conflict. The obvious problem here for me is that the kids are bringing so much dysfunctional behavior to their classroom interactions that the problems are too frequent for me to handle alone. This is why Barbara and the counselor's absences this week are a problem.*

Our room is too small for our class size and the needs of these students. All but one of our tables has problematic groupings. There is one functional table where all five kids get along. The rest of the table groups have two to four kids who have problems. They fight or they can't sit still or they can't stop talking. Frankly, I would like to get individual desks and put these kids into rows. When I asked the students a few weeks ago about their preferred seating, almost all of them voted to have their own desks. It won't happen, at least this year. We don't have the desks in the building, and Dorothy is philosophically opposed to them. She believes that, with table group settings, the kids are under more pressure to learn how to get along. With desks, they wouldn't have this learning opportunity, an opportunity that these kids do, indeed, need. Desperately need! For me, desks are simply an expedient solution to an immediate problem of classroom order. I ask myself the question, "What is more important, that students learn to get along or that students learn from the explicit curriculum—here and now?" I should also ask, "What is more important: my sanity or students' opportunity to learn to get along?"

We have twenty-five students, and seventeen of them are socially challenging to the adults and to each other. The room is small. I sometimes feel like we are rats in a cage. Confine too many rats or any animal together, and they'll begin snipping at each other. I wonder if the Association for the Prevention of Cruelty to Animals has guidelines for how many dogs or cats can be put together in a confined space. Our class is twenty feet by thirty feet. It seems unnatural and even inhuman to have twenty-seven people confined to this space for six hours a day, every day, for nine months. Yes, there is some flexibility built into the system, since kids sometimes leave the space (they go to the resource room, lunch, outside breaks, etc.). But essentially, we are crammed together, and our movement is confined to a space that, except for prisons, is unnatural to most any other experience people have in everyday life.

I am coming to question the whole notion of mass public education. Is school nothing more than forced confinement of an adult with a group of young people around an agenda that is somewhat irrelevant to the youngers and often the adult!? We have children caught in a physical, intellectual, and social trap that, to an adult, would be inconceivable and intolerable. Besides prisons and mental hospitals, where else are people subjected to forced confinement for long periods of time? At least in prisons there is the chance of parole for good behavior. One redeeming virtue of most schools today is that corporal punishment has been banned. But still, the psychic punishment to children is real, and it continues. But it is perhaps class size alone that is the single most significant factor in the mental health of a class and school culture. Simply put, small classes allow teachers to seek out and develop fuller relationships with students. The imperative for teachers to develop relationships with their students becomes increasingly unrealistic as class size increases.

What I need to do:

1. Hold regular class meetings, where we talk about sharing and speaking nicely to each other. Do some teaching demonstration on how to share the chameleon, how to solve problems, how to give I-messages, etc.
2. Move Timmy from his table. He sits with Bonnie and Justin, and they do not get along. No one gets along with Justin and Larry. This is the table group from hell.
3. Take action on most conflict, immediately. Even if I have to stop class. Use the counselor, who has offered to help. Certainly, Barbara's return will help.
4. Implement punitive consequences for misbehavior. I have been lax in dispensing time outs and recess losses. It takes so

much mental energy to be punitive, so lately I have allowed more off-task behavior and talking and roaming than I did earlier in the year.

*Reflection: This is an eclectic set of strategies here. Item #4 represents a punitive approach that takes advantage of my greater power over the students. Item #1 reflects a social constructivist perspective whereby I serve as facilitator as the students learn to manage their own conflict. Item #3 recognizes the primacy of social issues in my thinking, in relation to academics. And item #2 is an expedient strategy that simply reduces the frequency of incidents for me to mediate.*

*This was a bad day, indeed. My rant about public education, I believe, has some truth value. However, this analysis alone of what is wrong with public education is limited and leaves out other germane explanations, such as school funding, poverty, my inexperience, my personality, and the school ethos.*

## January 29, 1999
Good day. In the first five minutes after the kids walked in from lunch break, I sent Nathan to the alternative learning room (time out), and I had nailed six kids for talking as I began the lesson. I sentenced them to a loss of afternoon recess. Basically, the group was subdued the rest of the afternoon whenever I talked or gave directions.

I have had a bad back all week, until today, so I haven't had the physical energy to manage the class. Today, I did it. I realize that *achieving order* really isn't rocket science. Students need boundaries, they want to know what our adult boundaries are, and most will respond positively to these boundaries. There also needs to be consequences that are reasonable and *consequential* to the kids, and the implementation of the consequences has to be fair, direct, consistent, and unambiguous.

## February 1, 1999 (morning)
I stayed home this morning. Claire was sick. She wants to begin planning her birthday party in April, so we sat and brainstormed ideas and attendees. We then practiced some arithmetic together, which

she loves. She then practiced her piano, and then we met again for conversation. What a lovely way to start the week. This morning, before I knew I was staying home this morning, I woke up at 4:30 a.m. with high anxiety about the week looming ahead. I couldn't fall back to sleep. I worried about my observation by Judy, the principal, tomorrow, a day without Barbara since she is going to a reading methods workshop. I worried about my next unit after the food chain, a social studies unit I have yet to plan. And I worried about facing my kids for another week. It's hard, after a weekend of relaxed nothingness. I have to get psyched to stay on top of everything, to stay "up," to stay vigilant and consistent and fair, and to maintain a positive persona.

Monday mornings are tough. Staying home this morning has been relaxing. I wonder if I could arrange this every Monday.

I ran into Mike, a friend who teaches high school social studies. He injured his knee playing basketball, so he is missing some days at work. He teaches advanced placement classes only, so he works with the top students. Mike acknowledged that he was enjoying the time off. He's relaxed and doing a lot of reading. He talked about the continuous psychic stress when someone is a teacher. Just under the surface most of the time. Sometimes, of course, the stress is way above the surface and visible. But most of the time, it's that just-under-the-surface angst about the next lesson, the next day, a recalcitrant student, an unwieldy class, planning the next week, the next term, staying cheerful, and so on. Only when I have a couple days off in a row or even three or four days without students can I truly relax. I can get work out of my mind and, instead, focus on my family, my kids, on my own recreational reading. Mike said that the time off has improved his quality time with his wife and kids. I understand what he means.

**February 1, 1999**
Good day. No power struggles, kids were on task most of the afternoon, and most kids listened to directions.

Yesterday, in math, I worked with one group of kids that was learning how to do the algorithm for carrying when doing two-digit addition. Several of the students did not understand the meaning underlying the algorithm. I am not concerned, since we'll keep hacking away at it until they do understand. Another group was beginning multiplication. Another group was doing an open-ended math problem. And one group was doing some practice of basic addition facts.

Two of my more well-behaved girls were caught writing dirty words in mud on the outside wall during recess. One of the mothers happened to be volunteering at the time, so she was able to deal with the problem in school. I called the other girl's father. I told him that she was sorry and that it wouldn't happen again. He responded brusquely, "She's not as sorry as she's going to be in a few minutes!" Click! I sensed that he was going to be physical with his kid. I know the father a bit, and I should have anticipated this reaction. I wonder if I could have avoided calling this girl's parents. If I know that certain kids receive corporal punishment at home, should I avoid sharing unpleasantness in order to spare these kids beatings that I believe only harm their fragile psyches?

Rob, a first grader, walks around with a cloud around his head. Almost every hour of every day, he has a personal crisis. For example, someone will stick out his tongue out at Rob, so he starts yelling and kicking. He will ask me if he can share some trinket from home, and I say, "Let's do it at the end of the afternoon." He'll storm off, sulking.

**February 2, 1999**
Good day.

I was observed, a formal observation, by Judy. It was a science activity. Worms. Students each received a live worm, and they conducted a series of observational tasks: measuring its weight and length, drawing and labeling, and observing its reactions to dirt, water, and light/darkness. After my quick overview of the tasks, I started to distribute the materials, but as usual I wasn't organized. There was a bit of confusion at first as students rushed to the front to get their worm, tray, and magnifying glass. I had to send them back to their seats. I looked up and Judy was busily taking notes. I was sure she noted this mess. Finally, everyone got their materials, and students noisily explored what happens when a pile of dirt is placed next to a worm. I passed out a worksheet for students to record their observations, and most of the kids (mostly olders) knew what to do. Nathan finished the tasks in ten minutes, so he started to work on some unrelated craft activity. I asked him to return to the worm; he said "no," and a power struggle ensued. I asked Judy to take him to the ALE. She did, which I am sure she jotted down in her observation notes.

Every time I tried to give the students additional directions, it was hard to get their attention for more than five seconds. I realized that these are six-, seven-, and eight-year-olds, and they have in their hands a bunch of worms, dirt, and water. The thirty minutes of student exploration was hectic, noisy, and a lot of fun for the kids. After the activity, I brought the kids together for a discussion of what they learned from their work. I was pleased that we were able to sustain a conversation for fifteen minutes.

I did struggle a bit with giving directions and getting the students' attention, but it wasn't a *bad* session. Still, I was extremely self-conscious about the observer sitting in the back taking notes, face impassive and obviously judgmental. I didn't have a good time being observed. I remember Mark, last week, was anxious about his observation. I laughed, since I told him that he (as a twenty-year veteran) had nothing to worry about. I, as a one-year short timer, should have had even less to worry about than Mark. I have known Judy as a professional friend for about ten years, and she was supportive of my coming to Woodbridge for the one-year sabbatical; she has been empathetic and supportive about my less-than-perfect experience in the classroom.

I wanted to *look good*. My professional self-concept is that of a successful teacher, years ago when I taught elementary school and more recently as a university teacher. Judy was doing a formal evaluation, and I know that my performance was not strong. As things appeared a bit haywire, I felt a little embarrassed that it wasn't going more smoothly. But these problematic teaching episodes have occurred enough that I have become used to things being "haywire" in the classroom. In spite of the messiness of the lesson, the kids had a great time and they learned some new information about earthworms.

**February 3, 1999**

Another good day. I'm on a roll!

I feel positive vibes from the kids. One girl has written in pen on her arm, "I like Ken." Kids want to talk to me, about life, throughout the afternoon. I like them, but sometimes our affinity doesn't necessarily translate into their learning or their productivity. Some of my most ardent admirers still try to do nothing. They have so much negative emotional baggage from their home lives, it is hard for them to focus on doing a page of math exercises of regrouping when adding. I realize that this kind of work isn't fun, but I feel that they need to know this algorithm. Tomorrow, I'll have them write original math story problems in which they have to incorporate this algorithm.

Today, I showed a movie about earthworms. It was funny to watch their eyes glued to the television monitor. Barbara suggested that I videotape some of my lessons and then play them back to the kids on the VCR. She suggested that I would get a more attentive audience if I did my lessons on videotape. We laughed.

Since I started being stricter about students talking when I am talking, the class has moderated considerably. I feel more *psychic space* when I give instruction, and this sense of order allows me to relax, speak more slowly and thoughtfully, and even show a sense of humor. My management gimmick of the moment is a simple one: time outs and loss of recess. Earlier in the week, I nailed a large group of kids, but now, as they're sensing that my boundaries have become tighter, fewer and fewer kids are joining me for break.

*Reflection: I'm not deluding myself into thinking that all the kids are attending to me. Often, they are just appearing to attend by the direction of their eye gaze. However, when the room is quiet as I talk and I have the impression of attentiveness, I feel more at ease and able to use humor. The use of humor and, in general, the expression of my personal self (warm, friendly, funny) allows for a bit of role distance, which then can effectively promote students' cognitive engagement. When I am more human, I find that students are more inclined to connect with my interests. The catch is that many students interpret my use of humor as an invitation to become silly and out of control.*

## February 4, 1999

After break, I was supposed to finish the reading of *Shiloh*. I couldn't find the book. I sent Nathan to the library to get its copy, and in the meantime I attempted to conduct a short discussion of one of the story's ideas: lying. When is it all right to lie, if at all? Is it ever all right to lie to your parents? Most of the kids couldn't generalize the question and, instead, stuck to the story: they said that lying is appropriate when a dog's life is at stake. Several olders argued that lying is appropriate when the lie will result in a better outcome than would telling the truth. About ten kids raised their hands, indicating that they would not have lied to their parents, as the protagonist did in the story. The kids said that they would have trusted their parents, unlike the protagonist.

After about five minutes, the outlier kids (the ones who were unengaged in the discussion) started getting antsy. They had trouble staying seated, trouble keeping their hands to themselves. Timmy started stabbing his table file folder with his pencil. Sally tried to get it away from him, so they began wrestling over the box. Joey got up, holding plastic drinking cups to his ears, and roamed across the room until he was intercepted by the intern. I caught Stevie sticking his tongue, with an eraser cupped to its tip, out at Justin, a harassing action that usually pushes Justin's buttons, causing him to start screaming. I sent Nathan to the classroom room across the hall.

Finally, the book arrived, and I continued reading the final chapters.

This morning, I imagined the last day of school, in four months. I got a bit maudlin. I laughed. The kids are growing on me. I like seeing them. I'm laughing a lot more, at school but also when I am not in school. Like when I'm driving the car or having dinner. I'll spontaneously picture one of the kids, usually doing something weird, and I'll laugh (e.g., during my observation by the principal, in the middle of my introductory lesson on worms to the class, Timmy ran to the front of the room with the non sequitur of proudly showing me some new baseball cards). It is funny. It has to be funny.

**February 5, 1999**
Another good day. The kids were challenging, as usual, but my attitude about it all seems to be changing. Finally, I accept the fact that it is natural for them to get tired in the afternoon, and it is natural for some of them to generate non sequiturs at the most inopportune times. Perhaps the biggest change is in my head. I have recognized my own limitations and those of the kids. I still have high expectations, for the students and me. But I *know* the students more now than I ever have, and this intimacy makes it easier for me to like them. I don't think you can fully like someone unless you know them. And when you like your students, it's more enjoyable to be with them. It's easier to discipline them, because they know you like them, and they are more apt to listen because of this.

**February 9, 1999**
Good day. An easy day.

I am getting anxious about the collection of student assessment data. Student-led conferences are in five weeks, and I don't have any samples of student work in science and social studies. We've done a lot of work, especially in science, but I have overlooked the collection of student work. Luckily, in math, I've saved everything, so I can go back and pull out samples of problem-solving sheets the kids have done since September.

It's funny. I've been overloaded with so many other issues, such as developing curriculum, classroom control and management, and student and parent relations. Science and social studies comes at the end of the day, and it's often a major accomplishment to have the kids staying in their seats, coherent and superficially focused on the task at hand. Still, I feel as if I've overlooked the collection of assessment data. Ironically, when I work with preservice teachers, I am most critical of them when they fail to collect adequate assessment information. Now, I am guilty of flubbing the same task.

We worked on close-ended problem solving. (E.g., I went to the store. I had $25. I bought $x$, $x$, and $x$. How much change did I get back?). Many kids tend to shut down the second they get stuck on a problem. I need to do some demonstrations of patience when I hit a block on math problem solving, and how I engage in strategies to work it out.

Today, the fifth grades administered the state math open-ended problem-solving test. The kids could choose from among three problems. The problems themselves were difficult, and it is unlikely that most of our fifth graders were able to understand the problems. If they understood a problem, they would have to then solve the problem, and once it was solved, they had to communicate, in writing, their thinking about the problem. The cognitive load of this task is appropriate for prep school kids, who had been trained for this genre of math task from the crib. Our teachers had been working vigilantly with their kids for months on open-ended problem solving. After school, the teachers looked anxious, dejected, and angry. The coup de grace, especially for one fifth-grade teacher, was a form that she had to sign promising that she would not cheat by inappropriately helping her students.

**February 10, 1999**
Easy day. Twelve kids were absent. Sick.

It's the second week of February, and I am only now feeling relaxed about being with the kids. I am not saying that the first five months were a waste of time for the kids, academically. I know much learning has transpired since September. But my focus has been on establishing a sense of order, a calm, a peace of mind . . . in *my* mind, about my experience every day of going in and being with an antsy group of kids. Now that I have this out of the way, I think I have the mental space to focus on the details of teaching and learning.

Yesterday, after school, we had a grade-level meeting: all of the primary classroom teachers. It was depressing. We had no agenda. I think that we were supposed to share work samples of student writing and score them. But only Mark brought samples. We got bogged down in the district's expectation that we send home to parents a form on which we circle the scores that their children achieve on their reading, writing, and math work samples. After much discussion, there was consensus among the seven of us that the parents wouldn't understand the form, or it would mistakenly reduce the large picture of their children's performance in school to a few checks on a form. Saul offered to write a letter to the district, arguing against this way of reporting to parents. We figured that the new report card, which indicates if the child is "working toward, meeting, or exceeding the standard" in all the subject areas, is an appropriate form with which to report to parents. At the meeting, there was a sense of exhausted stress about the demands on teachers, in terms of teaching, testing, documenting, and reporting students' work in a standards-based curriculum. And in a high-poverty school, where some kids have a slim chance of meeting the standard, teachers' stress is even greater. I went home bummed out.

I was also down in the dumps because Saul is leaving Woodbridge. After eight years teaching nongraded primary, he has developed an incredible expertise in this area. Along with Dorothy, he is our most forceful and articulate spokesperson for developmentally appropriate curriculum, and now he is leaving. He's moving to San Francisco. I'm concerned that Dorothy will also leave the school.

**February 12, 1999**
Fun day. Valentine's Day party. After math, the kids passed out valentines, and then we had treats. Quick afternoon.

**February 17, 1999**
A stressful day, but all in all, a good one.

I am emphasizing problem solving in math. I'm immersing the students in problems: open-ended problems, textbook-type problems, and student-written problems. I'm emphasizing the use of three strategies: making an organized list, making a table, and drawing a picture. There are some problems that require simple arithmetic to solve, such as making change problems.

Kathleen didn't sleep much last night, so she was obviously tired in the afternoon. In math and later in science, she didn't do much work. Neither did Joey, who does little work unless I am sitting with him.

In science, I had the students draw food chains, showing how their favorite foods were connected to plants and the sun (e.g., cheese, milk, cows, grass, sun). I asked that they write three chains and then illustrate. For the first graders, it was enough for them to do just one chain, and some of the third graders did five or six chains. Most of the students understood the idea of this task. Once students were done with their work, I have trouble keeping them in their seats. I am reminded how I feel after spending an entire day in an airplane, sitting in the steerage of coach class, crammed like a sardine between people invading my space. My body aches, so the second the plane lands and the door opens, it is no wonder that everyone rushes to get out. I think that kids are in the same situation. They sit in these hard seats all day. Especially at the end of the day, it seems hardly palatable for them when I ask them to remain seated after they've finished their tasks and they don't have anything else to do. I need to have secondary tasks, so the kids have some activity to transition to when they are done with the primary assignment. Today, I had kids wandering the room, stretching their legs, and generally getting into trouble. Tomorrow, I will set up clearer options for what to do when they are done with their work.

Staff meeting today. Judy talked of the budget woes, at the district and building levels. She intimated that money is running short, not only for supplies but also for substitutes and personal leave days. Inadvertently, she made people feel self-conscious about taking personal leave days.

The district does not have any money in reserve this year. The reserve was used to cover a $3 million shortfall last summer. The district's claims that it doesn't have any money in contingency are real. Some of the teachers now feel guilty about taking any time off in case of illness, when a substitute will have to be paid from a "fast-depleting building fund." I also worry about that one "mental health day" that many teachers sometimes take during the year, when they need just one day to get psychologically grounded after, perhaps, a difficult period. Teachers are prone to guilty feelings, naturally, in their work with students.

I spoke with Dorothy. We identified five more students in our class whom we're recommending be tested by our special education specialist. We are concerned that these kids are making little or no progress in reading, writing, or math. Stevie is experiencing a free fall behaviorally. He doesn't listen, and he has become defiant with adults. Most of his defiance is passive. He just ignores adult direction. This tends to be the coping strategy of choice among the kids.

I am learning that each student sometimes needs a unique and personal response when he or she misbehaves. When Donnie gets on my nerves or looks resistant to some adult directive, I find that humor works best with him, such as when he is trying to tell me what to do with the class: "Hey, I can get you into the teacher education program at the university. We have a budding elementary teacher right here!" Earlier in the year, I used to get "in his face" with fairly assertive responses. With this kid, this strategy was wrong. He needs the indirect, soft response. As Donnie is best served by humor, Billy is best served by a clear and assertive "No!" in his face. Kathleen needs a reassuring touch and a friendly, "Come on, help us out." When Justin becomes irrational and refuses to get up off the floor, I will say to him, "Hey, buddy, I have an important job for you. Would you turn off the lights for me in five minutes when I need to get the class's attention?" Justin will give me a look like I've just offered him a million dollars, jump to his feet, and stand at attention at the light switch for five minutes. With about eight or nine kids, I have to simply say, "Hey kids, I need active listeners now. Let's remember our classroom rules." And with eight or nine other kids, I need to have some more concrete punitive consequence, such as the loss of recess, time out, or a trip to the school's time-out room. For example, Joey covets his afternoon recess, so I just have to mention the possibility of him staying in for recess and he calms down. Eventually, I hope to transition the externally motivated kids to more social/ relational motivations; these include the kids who respond to directions because . . . actually, I don't understand why these kids acquiesce to my directions.

I am also learning that children respond to academic difficulties differently. Nathan, Joey, and Kathleen tend not to have much task persistence when they get confused by a problem, and they tend to act out when they do become confused. When confused, these three often encourage each other's dysfunctional behavior. The pair of Nick and William tend to persist when they get stuck, so they encourage their group mates to do the same. Some of the youngers will effectively seek out an older for help. Crystal tends to show effective teaching strategies, since she doesn't tell kids the answers but instead poses questions that lead the youngers to try to figure out the problem for herself. Donna tends to show decent understanding of problems, but she rushes through her work so she can play math games, which is what most kids do. I find myself sending kids back to redo their work when their writing is illegible and they've obviously rushed like madmen and madwomen to get it done.

Of course, the tasks that I develop for kids in math are becoming more and more appropriate to them individually. The ideal problem is one that is moderately challenging. Of course. And for a teacher to know what is *moderately challenging* for her students, it takes time to develop this knowledge. The value of knowing one's students is obvious to me, for both academic and behavioral aims. Certainly, the practice of keeping the same kids for at least two years is a sensible one. Dorothy and the other 1–3 blended teachers here at Woodbridge have the benefit of three years with students. And Waldorf teachers often spend as much as eight years with the same students!

*Reflection: I feel as though I am continually negotiating with Donnie in order to maintain the balance in our relationship, and I find this to be exhausting sometimes. I negotiate with everyone it seems. Not that this is a bad thing. I think we all negotiate at some level, in order to establish balance and reciprocity in any relationship. I assign two math "jobs" a day, and then the kids can have "free time" to play math strategy games. However, if a child has worked really hard on one job for most of the period and asks to play a game toward the end of the time, I will bend the rule about the two jobs and give the child permission to play. I have asked that the kids not use calculators when practicing double-digit addition with regrouping exercises. However, I noticed*

*Nathan using the calculator. He insisted that he couldn't do the problems with the calculator. I noticed that he had trouble doing the simple additions of the ones columns and then the tens columns. I negotiated and suggested that he use the calculator to add each individual column, and then he'd have to show how he carries the ten over to the tens column. He agreed.*

**February 18, 1999** (5:00 a.m.)
I woke up at 4:30 a.m. for the second morning in a row. I did not plan well for this day, so I woke up thinking thinking thinking. Obviously, I need to plan well before I leave the school. At least, I need to be done with it before I go to bed.

(after school)
It was a good day. I worked with Barbara's group in math. I've assigned her the youngest kids, developmentally, in math. I was surprised at how dependent the group is on adult direction. Especially Sarah. This group of kids is gifted when it comes to non sequiturs: generating comments that have nothing to do with what we are talking about. I will be showing geometric figures on the overhead, and Wilma will call out, "Can I hold the chameleon?" I will be reading a book on Harriet Tubman, and Timmy will blurt, "Do you know that my grandmother is married to my grandfather?"

We set up a worm bin in the room today. The kids are getting the idea of decomposition, and the role that decomposers, such as worms, play in the life of the food chain. Later, I had the kids copy some key ideas about worms from the board and then illustrate the ideas. I feel good when I've introduced and taught some science content.

Fran, our intern from last fall, is coming back on March 1, in just ten days. She'll be with us, full-time and all day, until the end of the year. I am excited about having "another body" in the room. In the past, I was always leery of prospective mentor teachers who were interested in interns only as "another body," someone who could help reduce the load of teaching a full class. Instead, we looked for mentors whose primary interest was teacher education: they liked working with adults and they enjoyed the task of teaching interns. Now, I understand the need to have more help.

**February 19, 1999**

I had two nightmares last night. In my sleep. First, I was walking around town, looking for a teacher in my school. Suddenly, a tornado appeared out of nowhere and began chasing me. Eventually, I found shelter in an ice cream parlor. I looked out the window at the devastation and noticed some kids trying to stay afloat in a pond nearby. I ran out to rescue them.

Later, in the predawn, I dreamed that my kids were out of control. Joey assaulted Nathan, so I had to send him home. I lost my temper with Stevie, and I hit him. He thought I was just playing, so he started wrestling with me. In the entire dream, we were wrestling. Meanwhile, the remainder of the class was out of control, hanging from the rafters, having a good old time.

**February 22, 1999**

The kids were difficult today. It was Monday, and the rains were torrential. Recess was indoors.

There are a few kids who are not doing well in math. I think it has less to do with their ability (whatever that means) than with their effort. Woody Allen once said, "Ninety percent of life is just showing up." It might be the same for school achievement. Effort means so much. Just making an effort to make sense. I know that this is not as easy as it sounds, especially for kids who have a negative self-concept as learners or as mathematicians. Kathleen, for example, does very little work. I called her parents last night, and unfortunately her father answered the phone. Unlike the mother, he is uncommunicative and tends to be harsh with the daughter. I told him that I was going to send her math folder home every night, so the mother and he could review it and help Kathleen finish her work. He muttered short answers like, "okay" and "yep." Kathleen and about five or six other kids need an adult sitting with them during work time, an adult who is ready to help, prod, and hold high expectations.

I believe that a vital role for teachers is to make sure that the kids do their work and do it with care. I call it the teacher's "bookkeeper function." If kids will not naturally do their work with care, the teacher needs to monitor this and insist that it be done. Otherwise, the kids who are most prone to do shoddy work will do shoddy work, since they know that the teacher is going to allow it.

But the task of "running kids down" when their work is sloppy is exhausting and unrelenting, especially with a class of high-needs students. And if the math curriculum contains a lot of problem solving, then the possibility for sloppiness increases. When solving problems, I want the kids to be explicit about their solution strategy and the thinking underlying their solutions. This takes work, and a lot of my high-needs students find this to be difficult. Naturally, some of them will attempt to do the minimum.

There are the kids who will do no or little work, unless I am sitting right on top of them. However, when I have *five or six* kids like this, it takes a lot of concentration and time to manage these kids. I have the entire class with whom to work, and I usually get overrun with the regular normal questions in the course of the math period: kids need help; kids need their work to be reviewed; they are off task; or two kids are having a fight over a chair.

At about 1:10 p.m., it is time for science and social studies, and I *have* to transition to this next subject area. Otherwise, if I gave the kids free time so I could review everyone's production for the day in math, we would *never* get to science. I use the 1:45 p.m. recess and keep kids in for fifteen minutes to finish up math, but this is not enough time for them.

What to do:

1. Identify parents who have the wherewithal to support their children at home in math, call them, and indicate that the math folder is coming home every night for their review.
2. Make sure that kids check in with me before they play math games. I let the kids play math games when they finish their assigned tasks. As I get snowed by kids needing help, I haven't

been monitoring some of the kids who rush off to play games before they finish their work.

*Reflection: To be a caring teacher, someone who cares about each student, it takes an inordinate amount of time. It requires total immersion in the job, which means staying late in the afternoon and bringing work home on most school nights, phone calls to parents in the evening, and spending one of the weekend days back at school, planning. Grace (1978) describes socialist teachers in England who resisted this immersion by working less in the classroom and instead channeling their intellectual energy and time into political activism. Many teachers who have no interest in politics simply refuse to immerse themselves completely in the job so they can have a personal life that is full and stimulating. They know that they could be doing more for their students, and that they could be "better" teachers. However, this is a trade-off that most teachers make at some point in their career. For the beginning teacher, I think the challenge is for her to understand the need for trade-offs, to have balance, and to still feel a sense of competence and caring for her students.*

I think that we need to *name* our days with our colleagues, who would truly understand the meaning behind the name. My day, you ask? The kids were crazy this afternoon. They wouldn't stop talking. My day, you ask? The kids wrote some compelling stories about their grandparents. My day, you ask? This kid just sat all day and did nothing. I got aggravated but this other kid worked until he had calluses for the first time this year. We, as teachers, have enormous, bigger-than-life experiences every day, but for the most part we don't share them, or reflect on them, or reexamine them. One day rolls into another and then another. I need my wife and children, when I come home, to say "How was your day?" and *really* want to hear about my day. I tell them. And then we reciprocate. This mutual obligation of caring is what makes my home life so cherished and nurturing.

I had the delusion that my professional life would be social–collaborative, or there would be more caring conversations led by the question, "How was your day? Tell me about it."

Recently, I have spent more time talking with Mark and Beatrice, two teachers who tend to share my point of view about life at Woodbridge. They show just the right balance between idealism and commitment and a slight case of cynicism—cynicism about the state reforms, about the school, the kids, the curriculum, everything!

The other night, I called Dorothy about some trivial question. Somehow, we started talking about our kids. We both know the kids so well, all we had to do was name someone—for example, I'd say, "Bonnie"—and then we'd both laugh, mostly nervous laughter, I think. Then she'd say, "How 'bout that Justin?!" I might relate a funny story about some bizarre incident with Justin, she'd do the same, and then we'd burst out into nervous laughter again for awhile. After a while, I had tears running down my face. I don't know if I was laughing or crying. Somehow, this particular phone call validated parts of my experience with the kids. In essence, Dorothy was saying that she was having a similar experience. I needed this. I need this from my colleagues. With Beatrice and Mark, I feel that I have reference points who I can trust and who share my point of view. When I nurtured these two relationships, I think I began to feel better about coming to school.

*Reflection: One way teachers cope with role strain is to have reference groups, in or out of school, who understand and see the world as they do (Nias, 1989). Obviously, colleagues are an important reference group. Teachers who don't have like-minded colleagues in their own building will sometimes find them in other buildings, in other districts, or in professional associations. The healthiest situation, perhaps, is when the teacher has reference groups of different kinds (colleagues, students, family, principal) and in many locations, even including reference groups that represent memories of key individuals in one's life, such as a mentor or parent or teacher of long ago.*

### February 23, 1999

Good day. We dissected owl pellets, a part of the unit on food webs. For some of the kids, this was almost a religious experience. We had posters of the skeletal anatomy of voles, moles, and mice. The kids worked with tweezers and carefully compared their discoveries with the poster examples. The most exciting part was their discovery of skulls and teeth. Tomorrow, I will have the kids wash the bones, and then they'll glue them on poster paper for a display.

*Reflection: The idea of the noisy room as being conducive to learning is problematic. Learning is essentially a social process (Vygotsky, 1978), but much of the research that examines this focuses on small social units, such as the mother–child relationship. There are many factors that impede or support learning in the context of social activity in classrooms with large numbers of students, and it is silly to simply equate noise and learning. In fact, I wonder if noise may tend to be an inhibiting factor, generally, in learning for most students. Kids need to talk, to each other and to more mature others. If they could just do it with "five-inch voices"!*

The good days have become more a regular feature of my life now. I can think of five contributing factors.

- We have established routines for behavior. The kids come into the room, sit down, and wait for the afternoon's opening procedures. I give an overview of the afternoon and then begin math with a whole-class minilesson of five to ten minutes. And then the afternoon continues. There are some routines I am still working out, such as how I want them to sit on the floor during circle time.
- I've gotten a handle on order. My techniques aimed at eliciting students' attention and compliance are adequate. I use a time-out desk in the room for kids who need to be separated, and I allow them to come back to the group when they are ready to comply. For three or four of the kids who don't care about in-the-room time outs, I use recess as the "carrot." None of the kids, except Donna, likes to stay in during recess. Usually, when I keep kids in for recess, I sit with them individually and talk to them about their behavior, and we talk of ways they could "make better decisions." Rarely do I have to keep a child in for the entire recess. Occasionally, I will use the school's time-out room as a management tool.
- My daily schedule is established, and I have developed my own routines for developing curriculum. It still takes a lot of time,

but planning the curriculum has become a bit more routinized. I still often wait until Sunday night to plan for the week, and this makes me very anxious during the weekend. But if I have planned well, my mental state at the start of each day is calmer.

- I know the kids. I know their personalities, their idiosyncrasies, their sounds, and even their smells. It's all becoming familiar and more predictable. I can almost predict Cesar each day at 12:15 p.m., coming in loud and excited with a tale of recess adventure. I can predict that Rob will have had some altercation with Timmy or with Nathan, and I am ready to respond. I can count on hugs from the same four or five kids. I know how Donna learns and what pushes Nathan's frustration button. I realize that one can teach only those whom we *know.* I am getting to know them and am able to enjoy them and their idiosyncrasies more. Even Donnie, even the incessantly bossy and opinionated Donnie, whom I now humor—and it works! The class has become almost like a family, of sorts. I find them endearing, irritable, often impossible to be around, loving, and almost never boring.

- I have a sense that the students are engaged in an academic agenda that makes sense to me, and that they are learning. And I am pleased with the progress most of the kids have made in their use of several problem-solving strategies. In science, the food-web unit went well, and I was able to collect interesting student assessment data.

**February 24, 1999**

I lost my voice, so I called in sick.

I woke up again this morning at 5:00 a.m. Sam came in, thinking it was time to get up. I put him back in his bed, but I wasn't able to fall back to sleep. It is ironic. I have been having almost consistently good days, but I am again having trouble sleeping. Earlier in the year, when I was really struggling, the insomnia made sense. Now the insomnia doesn't make as much sense.

Perhaps the occasional insomnia is the bane of teaching. I lie in bed and run through the catalog of all the things I have to do, or I ruminate on all the things that I *should* be doing and haven't, or I think about the previous day:

- I need to be firmer with Timmy and Deacon when they socialize too much in math.
- Deacon cried yesterday when he got confused by a math problem; he ran to the bathroom in tears, and I got diverted by other problems and didn't get to talk to him.
- The next staff meeting will address the issue of reporting test scores to parents and how to do it.
- I haven't been teaching my kids how to use the scoring guides to assess their performance as math problem solvers. I still have three months to do it. Whew!
- I am meeting with a friend who is a member of the local chapter of the NAACP, and we'll talk about my upcoming unit on black history and racism. I want her to come and do a guest performance.
- The students need to wash their owl pellet bones and then mount them on poster board. How should I organize the movement of twenty-five kids as they do this?
- Nathan scratched in the wall outside, "Ken is supid (stupid)."
- Fran, our intern, is coming back on Monday. She is pregnant.
- Timmy had a bad day. He engaged in a series of disturbances with peers and adults, all afternoon. He is six-years-old and very at risk, and I don't know what to do to help him.
- I read an article in *New Yorker* about Ritalin and ADHD. I run through my head all the kids whom I suspect are ADHD. I would love to have them tested, but the special education team is now backlogged with months of referrals.

The job is working out, and I feel good that "I can do this." I *actually* enjoy going to work and opening the door to let my kids in. The question "Can I teach elementary school?" has probably been the quintessential question that I needed to answer this year. It's late February, and I am now confident that I could do this job and, if I did it a second year or more, I could again develop into a good teacher.

Still . . . still, the work of teaching, even when things are going well, permeates my conscious and subconscious mind. I can't get away from it. I dream about it. I wake up in the early hours and dwell on it. I have a vague memory that this is what life was like when I taught fifteen years ago as an everyday teacher. I was a successful teacher, but it still invaded my private life, after hours. Much of this is probably a function of my personality, and I know that there are teachers who are able to "turn it off" and not dwell on work. However, I know many teachers who, like me, find it difficult to turn it off.

> Teaching but half day.
> 2:35 and kids
> blow out and play.
> Take a breath
> by walking halls
> hello to you and
> hello to you
> how was your day?
> Thank you very much!
> Then back.
> Take a broom
> pick up room.
> Review kids' work.
> Plan math for groups.
> Thinking of state's hoops
> and next week.
> Find wood for
> science project.
> Meet with principal.
> Call three parents.
> Run papers off
> derailed by talking custodian.
> Check on chameleons
> and worm bin.
> Go home by five
> and dinner, kids, and wife.

Kids in bed and
gather papers and thoughts
for lessons tomorrow
barely time to think
about my teams, friends and
ailing mother.
At last bed, book, sleep.
And up at 5 a.m.
mind racing
heart pounding
already thinking
about kids sounding,
and I'm only half time!

**February 26, 1999**

Hard day and hard week. It rained every day, so kids' outside recesses were curtailed. A lot of pent-up energy, expressing itself in disruptive behavior in the classroom.

We had a whole-group circle meeting at 2:00. The focus was on "kindnesses observed." I wanted the kids to share kindnesses they'd observed being performed by their peers during the week. There was a bowl of pretzels in the middle of the circle, and the doer of the good deed, once identified by a peer, could take a pretzel. This was a follow-up activity to a circle meeting two weeks ago when the group generated a set of strategies to make our class a more caring place. Some strategies that we had generated were things like (a) including everyone, (b) including everyone when it might even be inconvenient, and (c) helping someone in need, in the class or on the playground.

Today, the kids finished gluing their owl pellet bones onto poster-board displays. Some of the kids did quality work. They carefully organized their bones into groups based on appearance. With some other kids, I had to cajole them to finish their work, and these kids tended to produce more sloppy displays.

There is an inherent frustration in teaching in that kids will never all do exactly what I, as teacher, imagine or envision them doing.

There is always going to be a gap between the ideal and the real. And with this group, given the number of kids who are so easily distracted, the amount of psychic energy that I have to expend to lead some of the kids to completion is enormous. I have become inured to the gap between my intention for what students produce and what they actually produce. It is getting better. In the beginning of the year, they often didn't produce *anything*. Later on, the kids were generating some paper product, such as a solution to a problem or a research report, but the products often defied convention for what I considered normal for the work of six-, seven-, and eight-year-olds. Now, it's getting closer, on my good days. More kids are more often generating solutions that approximate my ideas about math problem solving. Their work in science is now getting completed with more punctuality and coherence. But there are days and weeks when it seems that we have regressed to September, when nothing I did made any sense.

After lunch in the room, math, owl pellets, circle time, and *Shiloh Summer*, I came home today tired, drained, and ready for a funny video in the evening after the kids went to be bed.

**March 1, 1999**
Good day. Fran, our student teacher, came back today. She will be with us every day for the remainder of the year.

**March 2, 1999**
It wasn't a good day, nor was it a bad day, either. But I came home frazzled.

We played a food-chain game. In this game, the students were divided up into three groups: owls, chameleons, and crickets. Popcorn was spread out across the floor, and the crickets ran around and collected the popcorn in plastic baggies. The chameleons then tried to eat by tagging the crickets. The owls pursued the chameleons. The game went on for about ten minutes, and then the kids traded roles and the game was played a second time. The game was intended to provide an explicit demonstration of the food chain.

The playing of the game was a series of catastrophes. I went into the gym and threw about eight cups of popped popcorn on the gym floor. Unbeknownst to me, the janitor had just mopped the floor, so half of the floor was slightly wet. When the kids began running around, many of them fell and hurt themselves. The janitor came out, saw crunched popcorn beaten down on his newly cleaned and still wet floor. His face turn beet red. He looked at me. I looked at him and asked, "What do ya' drink? It's on me." He smiled, and I knew that I had dodged a bullet.

The game depends on a sense of fair play by the students that when a peer tags them, they turn over their popcorn bag to their predator and then leave the game. However, too many kids refused to leave the game, or they claimed that they hadn't been tagged or were in the safe zone. The game of tag became more important than the demonstration of the food chain. Some of the kids walked off the playing area, angry that some of their peers were not playing fairly. Making matters worse, there were some accidents: kids crashing into each other. There were some tears as well as hurt egos and bodies. When we lined up to return to the room, Nathan intentionally crashed into Rob, so he spent the last part of the day problem solving his actions with the counselor. By the time we got back to the room, everyone was fed up and tired. I attempted a discussion of the main ideas underlying the game, and this went better than I expected. If I had been a university supervisor doing an observation of a student teacher who'd done what I had done with this lesson, I would be very concerned about the student teacher's future in the program.

I was a little embarrassed and worried by the food-chain game fiasco. Fran is going to be with me during the afternoon for the duration of the year. So far, in the two days she has been back, she has observed me doing bad teaching, and she has had her own difficulties with one small math group. I want her to be successful. Some ideas:

1. Work with her as she plans her lessons. Give her feedback *before* she gives the lesson.
2. Encourage her to accept no silliness from students. She needs to set clear and limited boundaries and, then, clear consequences.
3. During spring quarter, when Fran is doing solo teaching, I need to make sure that she has some adult support in the

room, especially during math period. I'll find some under-graduate preservice teachers who need to do a field experience in the spring.

*Reflection: The working consensus is situation specific. A teacher and students can have a consensus about behavior in the room, but when the venue changes, then it means that a new consensus has to be forged that is relevant to that venue. Besides my own teaching miscues when doing this particular simulation, this was such a radically different venue and activity than what the kids were familiar with. The absence of a fully developed working consensus between the kids and me did not bode well for the activity. Actually, any kind of extremely open-ended activity, such as a simulation in a gymnasium, makes it imperative for teachers to plan ahead and anticipate the unanticipated.*

**March 3, 1999**
Good day. The kids were squirrelly, but there weren't any power struggles; students tended to engage wholeheartedly on tasks, and I collected some interesting assessment data.

I have been focusing on problem solving in math. Most kids are showing persistence when they experience the initial confusion after reading the problem. However, Nathan tends to shut down before he even reads the problem. He has a really negative self-concept as a learner of school knowledge. He gets really angry with me if I sit down with him and insist that he engage with the problem. When I walked away from him, several kids reported to me that he muttered, "Ken sucks." This kid has so much negative emotional baggage, it is a wonder that he is able to function as well as he does. I sense that he needs a large dose of discipline, a highly structured environment that is nonnegotiable, such as a Boys Town or the marines. In our classroom, there is simply too much freedom, too many choices, too much room for him to maneuver. For most kids, they have the metacognitive knowledge necessary to make intelligent decisions about how to manage both body and mind. Nathan doesn't have this kind of metacognitive knowledge.

I gave a final assessment of the kids' learning from the food-web unit. I asked the kids to draw a series of food webs and chains, and then I asked them to respond, in writing, to several questions. With twelve first graders, Barbara and I had to move quickly from student to student, helping them read and write their responses. It felt good to collect some solid assessment information.

## March 4, 1999

Good day. I read a short book about Harriet Tubman. I read for about forty-five minutes, and the kids sat still and listened. Tubman's life was a dramatic one, and the book was a good read.

I then put on the board the names of men who are honored with major national or local holidays: Presidents Day (Lincoln and Washington), Martin Luther King Jr., Columbus, St. Patrick, Dr. Seuss (whose birthday we celebrate on March 2). I asked the kids to figure out what these names had in common. They had trouble seeing that they were all men. I then asked them to generate names of famous women. The kids mentioned about ten television, film, or musical performers. One girl mentioned Rosa Parks and another named "Clinton's wife."

Obviously, the kids are not sensitive to gender issues. I feel that this is an important issue, and I want to influence the kids to recognize a bit of gender inequity on this topic.

## March 6–7, 1999

Melinda, Claire, Sam, and I are spending a few days on the coast. I'm walking this pristine and deserted beach, and some of my students keep flying into my head. I worry about Wanda, with whom I've basically lost touch since the resource room increased her time in the afternoon. She is in school maybe four days out of five. She sometimes is pulled out of school early by her mother, or she shows up in the late morning. I am so busy with the other twenty-four kids, I sometimes don't have the mental space to check up on what she is doing, why she isn't in school, why she is getting pulled out. I feel guilty, and I wonder what else I could do for this kid, who is a psychological and physical wreck. Her needs are beyond my skills. She needs much more than I can offer, like a new home, an activist father and mother, a new body, therapy.

**March 8, 1999**

Student-led conferences (SLCs) can work, and this is a potentially powerful way for students to organize and synthesize their year's learning. However, if the teacher has not adequately prepared the students, or if the teacher has not saved representative samples of student work, then student-led conferences are more difficult to implement successfully. The key factor in the SLC is the student's ability to reflect on their work, their ability to evaluate their work using some set of developmentally appropriate criteria.

Yesterday in math, I passed out to each student folders of collected work in math for the year. Each student had between thirty and fifty pages of work to review. I wanted them to identify five "favorite pieces," work that they felt was "their best." I had done several minilessons on "identifying good work," but there wasn't much more preparation. The inevitable chaos ensued. First, it was just too much paperwork for the youngers. Papers were flying everywhere—across tables, on the floor, and even in the air. Some kids indicated that they couldn't omit any work, so they would present all fifty-odd pieces to their parents. Other kids didn't have *any* favorite pieces. Some kids randomly picked pieces that, in my eyes, probably represented their worst work.

The entire session was a fiasco for several reasons. First, the kids had too much work to review. It was overwhelming. Second, they didn't know any criteria with which to evaluate their work. In retrospect, this is a type of learning that ought to be going on all year, in which we use selected criteria to assess or evaluate their work, maybe on a weekly or biweekly basis. I hadn't done this. Now, at the end of the year, I am expecting the kids to do this and, naturally, they can't. And third, about fourteen of my kids can't write independently, so the completion of the cover sheet is best done cooperatively, with an adult or a capable older student. To have all the students do this task at the same time puts the adult support system in the room on overload. There just aren't enough adults in the room to do this.

After school, I reviewed the five or so pieces that each student identified. For about half the students, I removed several pieces that were ill-advised choices and added one or two that were more representative of their best work. After school, I sorted and filed piles of student work, so the parents could also take home a large file of their children's work this year, work not included in the SLC. I sat in school until around 5:00 p.m., filing and fretting about the SLC. I know that the students will be ready for these, but I am worried. I haven't done them before. I also noticed that, for some kids, such as Wilma and Rob, there is an alarming paucity of collected work for the year. Where have they been all year? They've done work, but I don't know where it is. What will their parents think? That I've done nothing with their child!

Fran is doing her action research project on how we prepare the students for student-led conferences. I am embarrassed that she observed some flawed teaching by me.

What is influencing me to more thoroughly "think through" my lessons is my memory of what happens when I do not do this. Pandemonium! Early in the year, I had a cavalier approach to planning, so when activities went awry, I gradually learned to improve the planning so as to increase the chances of effective implementation and to avoid chaos. Still, I need to be more conscious of my natural tendency to teach by the seat of my pants, as it appeared I did today.

**March 9, 1999**
A stressful day. This afternoon we helped kids identify and describe their best work for the math component of the SLC. Several kids showed passive resistance to this activity. The basic problem is that some of these kids do not enjoy math, so they don't have any "favorite" pieces or work samples that they find, in any way, interesting. This gives me high anxiety, especially as I imagine the parents parading into the room for the next three days. I sat with Kathleen, miserable beyond words about having to engage in this task, and cajoled

her to complete her cover sheets. She didn't know or *want* to know what to write, so I basically told her what to scribe. Other kids wrote meaningless words on the cover sheets. For example, in response to the prompt, "I learned . . . .", Bonnie penned, "I learned math."

Nathan's behavior is deteriorating. He mutters to himself continuously. He calls out or shouts out at will, and he seems to be impervious to time outs or removal from the room. Sometimes, he becomes completely rigid, like when I ask him to give me a stapler he shouldn't be using. He refuses, and I have to work consciously to not fall down the fatal slope of the power struggle. Today, he became so disruptive I had to send him out of the room. I realize that sending him out of the room will not improve his behavior. Since Fran was teaching a lesson just after I sent him out, I went to the time-out room and took him to the counselor's office. In this quiet space, I offered to read him a story. He was interested. I read the story, we talked about the story and a bit about his life, and then he went back to the room, a little more relaxed than he was an hour before. This kid needs time with a caring adult having quality conversations and experiences. I know he has them with the father, but he needs more. A few weeks ago, I brought my two-year old son, Sam, to the class. Nathan and Sam became fast friends, and they walked about the room hand in hand. I saw a different side to Nathan when he was with Sam. It was a nurturing and caring side. I need to get him lined up as a volunteer in the preschool based at Woodbridge. Maybe get him in there as a volunteer each afternoon for twenty to thirty minutes.

*Reflection: How we behave is driven by situations. I am coming to the realization that it is harmful to draw attention to kids' "deficiencies." As David Elkind once put it, a more appropriate descriptor for most schoolchildren who fail is "curriculum disabled."*

## March 10, 1999

There was a grade-level meeting after school. My primary teacher colleagues are angry about the workload of state reforms. For each student, we have to collect a gargantuan amount of work samples, in reading, writing, math, and public speaking. The samples have to be scored and then reported to the district and to parents. In addition, we need to teach the students to use scoring guides so they can score or assess their own work. In theory, this is quite rational and educationally important. However, the implementation of the entire performance-based curriculum is extremely onerous, especially the evaluation/accountability component. On paper, it makes sense, so I suppose that the policy makers who've concocted this scheme believe it is all a good idea. However, everything we do with kids always, always, takes more time than can ever be imagined by those who are distant from the classroom.

A good day with the kids. Barbara, Fran, and I sat with most of the kids individually and helped them write cover sheets for their work samples in math, work they will share with parents at the SLC. Everyone has "seat work" (drill and practice), so we had the time to get to most of the class. After math, there was an Audubon Society presentation in the library, which the kids loved. I took them out for a break, and then we came and I taught them the song "If I had a Hammer." Barbara and I, both in our forties, led the singing. We laughed when Fran, twenty-four, said she didn't know the song. It showed our age!

*Reflection: What made the day so much fun? Some high-interest activities, some structured activities, some song, a recess, and perhaps most important, three competent adults managing the class.*

Tonight, before bed, I surreptitiously (in my head) went to Kinko's to do some copying. I didn't tell anyone what I was doing, not Melinda, Dorothy, or anyone else. I made copies of basic fact sheets—drill and practice. I do more of this than I am comfortable with, and I am slightly embarrassed that I've resorted to this. I am concerned that my students will not be facile with basic number operations by the end of the year. But I also rely on paper–pencil arithmetic as a management device. When I am trying to coordinate several math groups, I need the groups with whom I am not working at the moment to be engaged in work that can be accomplished without my help.

Today, a friend who is the director of the local Montessori school walked in and saw the copies of the drill and practice. I leaned over and tried to cover the copies. To my horror, I left one pile of papers uncovered, and he picked them up and immediately rolled his eyes as if to say, "You've *got* to be kidding." He offered to loan me a book on teaching math developmentally. I sheepishly accepted his offer, as I lamely tried to reassure him that skill drill is not the emphasis of my math program.

Kinko's is open twenty-four hours a day. Next time, I will copy this stuff between midnight and 6:00 a.m. Under the cover of night.

*Reflection: I avoided printing many of these worksheets at school, so no one would see how much I relied on skill drilling. I figured that I would be able to manage people's impressions somewhat by printing the worksheets away from their judgmental eyes, such as at Kinko's.*

*I was embarrassed when my director friend saw through my "front" as a developmentally appropriate teacher. His condescending and sneering response put a kink in my teaching self-concept. I had always had reservations about my approach to the teaching of math, but at least it wasn't public knowledge. Public disclosure of my performance as a teacher, particularly as I myself had misgivings about what I was doing, really stung.*

## March 11, 1999

The meeting after school addressed the budget cuts for next year. The legislature, as usual, is underfunding K-12 public education. The district is looking at a $2 million cut, and our little school is facing a shortfall of about $40,000.

Judy gave the group of teachers and parents three choices: (a) cut a teacher and increase class sizes; (b) cut one or more specialist (counselor, family advocate specialist, music, or physical education); and (c) move the building's Title 1 money to the general operating fund. The last option would mean that our aide support would be cut. All of the options are unacceptable. Any of the options would intensify the working conditions of teachers and students. People at the meeting seemed to have a fatalistic stance toward this situation. Opponents of increased funding tend to represent the rural areas of the state, areas that experienced increased funding recently when a plan was implemented that equalized the historically poorer districts with the better-funded suburban and urban districts. Compounding the problem of school funding is a current initiative to build a new generation of prisons in the state, which is going to cost the state hundreds of millions of dollars.

Ironically, as the legislature is squeezing more districts with unrealistic budgets, the state's expectations that teachers move ahead with curriculum reform remain full steam ahead, uninterrupted. The state board of education has announced a slowdown of the targeted reform schedule. However, the reform agenda that has been implemented is still considerable and stressful for almost all teachers with whom I talk.

### March 12, 1999

After school, Fran was upset that she performed so "badly" in front of me. I told her that I felt the same way. I was often embarrassed when I performed poorly in front of her. I gave her some suggestions about improving things for Monday. We put on happy faces as we said goodbye, but I knew that we were both hurting as we drove out of the parking lot.

I had plans to meet Mark and Arthur at a local pub. I got there early. Alone, I went in and sat way in the back and ordered a pint. Suddenly, I noticed Fran standing in front of me. She said, "I saw you walk in a few minutes ago. (pause) So *this* is how you cope!" We laughed. I tried to explain that I was meeting Mark and Arthur, but she walked out thinking, perhaps, that every day after school I sit in the back of this pub and drink away my troubles.

### March 16, 1999

A wild day. It's two days before spring vacation. I wasn't counting the days until today, which is a good sign of my emerging confidence and comfort with teaching. However, today was déjà vu to last September and early January. Wild!

This morning, Fran asked Stevie to get off the floor and return to his seat. He ignored her as she repeated this directive three or four times. Dorothy got involved, and she finally took his arm to escort him out of the room. As she pulled his arm up, he turned to her and vomited all over her. Another occupational hazard. Getting puked on by a kid.

This afternoon, I had trouble getting Justin to return to his seat. He fell to the floor in a Ghandian pose of passive resistance. He sat almost in a Buddha position, with his head tilted down. I needed to get the rest of the class going, so I asked Fran to "get him out of the room." I didn't mean for her to pick him up, but she did. She grabbed him from behind by the armpits. His body froze, and he kept the Buddha pose. It looked quite funny as she carried him off. The class, which I was working ineffectively to calm down, burst out laughing at the sight of Fran, a tall pregnant woman, carrying off a little Buddha screaming like a siren on a desperate police car.

*Reflection: Even given the small size of these kids and their inability to physically defend themselves from adults, they are able to show symbolic (and sometimes poetic) expressions of resistance.*

After school, we had student-led conferences. Students shared a large portfolio of work with their parents in conferences that lasted about one hour each. We had half the class tonight and will have the other half tomorrow night. We scheduled five students for each hour, so the "concurrent sessions" caused quite a hubbub of activity in the room: parents, siblings, and students all huddled around portfolios, talking, questioning, visiting the owl pellet display, worm bin, and chameleons and, for the most part, the kids sharing visible signs of progress with their parents.

I made an observation after the SLCs. For kids whose home lives are ordered and stable, parents take time for read-alouds and civil conversations and there are somewhat traditional lines of authority between adults and kids . . . kids who came from these homes tended to show real progress in their portfolios. On the other hand, for kids whose home lives are disordered and unstable, parents don't have the time for conversations and there isn't strong discipline and authority from the parents . . . kids who came from these homes tended to show no progress. Now this is just a *tendency*, since there are other factors that affect student learning (e.g., the relevance of the curriculum, teacher competence, student learning style, and the constraints of a traditional classroom of twenty-five kids in a 25' by 30' space).

*Reflection: I realize that my observation about family background and student achievement is unremarkable, since research has long pointed to this relationship. My reminder of the relationship suggests that the technical emphasis of teacher professional development is, perhaps, a mistake. Millions of dollars devoted to developing teachers' skill at implementing performance-based assessment, for example, is going to have a marginal effect on the academic destiny of kids from poor backgrounds. Instead, we should be channeling available resources into helping teachers build relationships with families, support struggling families, and support family literacy. Still, I am leery of putting too much onus of responsibility on the these "dysfunctional" families without also considering the socioeconomic conditions that make it very difficult for these parents to have the time (or wherewithal) to have civil conversations with their children. So is it appropriate for teachers to take a more explicit political role in the legislative arena, for example?*

I experienced a small success with Nathan today. A month ago, I brought my two-year-old, Sam, to class. When Nathan saw him, he was transformed into a nurturing and kindly older. He held Sam by the hand and gently led him out and about. His demeanor was calm for the entire time Sam was with him. He spoke softly to Sam.

Today, I arranged with the preschool facility, housed at Woodbridge, to have Nathan come at 2:00 p.m. for half an hour to work with the young children. The staff reported that he behaved beautifully. Just like he did with Sam, he was nurturing and loving. I want to continue to have him visit Little Beavers, and gradually, I want him to plan and lead activities for the little ones, like read-alouds. I would love for him to find a volunteer position this summer in a program for preschoolers.

Stevie is another one who needs an alternative experience. He is such a *young* first grader. Recently, he appears to have regressed emotionally. He is using baby talk more frequently, and he is unable to sit still in his chair for more than a minute. Kathleen is another case. She always has something in hand, especially when she isn't supposed to, like a stick that she is whittling with the scissors or a bag of marbles or some dried markers that she is resurrecting from death by dipping them in water.

So much of what I do seems to be inappropriate for these kids. I am so caught up in academics, teaching the skills. Most of the time,

I expect kids to sit and listen, sit and discuss, sit and write or draw. When we do a movement activity in the room, about five or six of the kids tend to lose all self-control, so I've tended to avoid physical activities with the kids. I wanted to do more creative drama and creative movement. I had a difficult time managing the kids last fall. This past month, with our "dramatist in residence" Kimberly, the kids were wild during the drama sessions.

I remember last fall, when I was skeptical about having the large cache of blocks and Legos in the room, for the kids to use during "choice time" each morning. I suggested to Dorothy that we remove these hands-on materials and, instead, develop writing and reading centers for choice time. She argued that these kids "needed" the materials. For a large number of our students, how wrong I was. I now watch them as they build and manipulate their structures. They seem to go into a *flow state*, where they appear to lose consciousness and become deeply engrossed in the activity and are aware of nothing else. I don't know exactly what, but I am certain that there is *something* in it for them to be engaged in this kinetic and nonacademic activity.

### March 18–19, 1999
No school. Teacher work days. It's also the start of our spring break. No school again until March 29.

### March 29–30, 1999
Good days.

On Tuesday, I introduced the idea of segregation laws, typical in the southern United States before 1970. We did a simulated bus in which the whites and blacks sat separately and showed how the black passengers had to give up their seats to the whites if the white section filled up. I read the story of Rosa Parks and the Montgomery bus boycott. We had a coherent discussion of these topics, and then I had the kids illustrate and caption some image from the boycott.

I am working with the third graders to get them ready for the state math tests on April 12 and 13. The teachers in the building are really frazzled by these tests. I sense a lot of bad emotions and feelings from teachers: inadequacy, anger, frustration, anxiety, resignation, and fatigue. Most of our kids are simply not ready, and they are not going to "pass" the tests. To make matters worse, the test results are published, by school and grade level, in local and state newspapers.

I find it demoralizing that this is the essential measure, for much of the educational community, of our effectiveness as schools and as teachers. What is most disheartening is that the low tests scores will imply that teachers in high-poverty schools like mine don't work hard and don't work smart. It's funny. I know that the teachers in my building feel overwhelmed by the demands of our students—the emotional, social, and academic demands. And each day, we show up for work and invest our emotional and intellectual *selves* to serve these kids.

**March 31, 1999**

Staff meeting after school today. I feel that as the year continues, I have become more and more cynical about any reform initiatives that come from the state or, for that matter, from anyone outside my classroom. It seems that the outsider-based reforms are out of touch with my everyday concerns. The state tests that we are giving in a few weeks are out of the realm of most of our students, especially in reading. Our collective teacher anxiety is raised at the specter of the results of the state test that are reported to the public, and the results are broken down to performance of schools and also the performance of individual teachers. So, for the world to see, a document will read something like, "Ken Winograd's math class: 60% of the students did not pass the test, 20% passed, and 20% were exempted because of special learning needs."

I worked with the third graders in math today to prepare them for the state tests in ten days. The tests make me feel anxious. Early on, Donnie began to badger Bonnie about her intelligence, her wardrobe, her hair, etc. I asked Donnie to stop. He continued badgering Bonnie. I pulled Donnie to the side of the room for a private conversation.

"Is there something bugging you today?" I asked.

"I think it was my trip to \*\*\*\*. I'm still excited."

"You have to stop hurting Bonnie's feelings. If you don't stop, you'll have to leave the room," I said.

Donnie nodded, understanding. However, within a minute, he started harassing Bonnie again. I tersely directed Donnie to leave the room. He asked for a second chance. My voice got taut but it stayed even. "No, you need to go." He again appealed.

"Then go sit in the principal's office." He now relented and walked off back to the classroom. On his way out, he complained that I hadn't used my sense of humor with him in this situation and, therefore, I had handled it badly.

His comment is revealing. I wonder if each child requires a unique approach to how we relate to them and how we "manage" them. In Donnie's case, he needs a humorous response when he needs to be redirected by the teacher. Since I figured this out in late January, I had been doing very well with him. Virtually no problems in two months. Today, I used an interpersonal tack that was direct and unequivocal: I told him that he was acting improperly and that he needed to leave the room. He was surprised by how I handled the situation. Still, as I have become more knowledgeable about my students, and I take the time to think as I respond to student issues, I am more effective when my response is customized to the child. There are some students that I have not yet figured out.

**April 2, 1999**
Bad day.

Today was "active listener lunch bunch," and the whole class made it. The kids sometimes acted silly, and sometimes their behavior was inappropriate. I warned them that they needed to stop, or else this would be the last lunch bunch event for a while. Justin had a fight with Crystal over nothingness. He started screaming, his normal modus operandi when he does not get his way. Barbara escorted him to the alternative learning environment. A few of the kids left messes. I went off to the playground to have Kathleen come back to clean up a chocolate milk mess, which was the third time I'd asked her to clean up. Already, I hadn't yet begun my official day, and I'd generated a nice dose of negative emotion.

In math, I took Barbara's group. Four of the seven kids in this group show behaviors typical of attention deficit disorder. Justin missed his medication today, so he was way off the wall. The whole period, I continuously responded to off-task behavior. Meanwhile, in the room in which we are working, the sewing club volunteer had set up her operations, and the gardening person was working with kids to repot plants in another part of the room. My kids were naturally distracted by all this hubbub. My group met for forty minutes, and I enjoyed probably just five minutes of this time.

The transition between art and recess was a disaster. The kids did not respond to our directions to clean up. Fran was in charge, and Barbara and I were assisting. As we gave them directions, it was obvious that our adult voices were invisible. I have loosened my grip on the kids. Previously, up until a week ago, I would walk around with a clipboard and write down names of kids who did not listen. These kids would stay in for recess and would not eat lunch in the room. I've reduced the punitive edge of how I relate to the kids. This transition drained me.

After recess, I had the kids sit in a circle on the rug. I wanted them to reflect on and share "the favorite thing they did today."

They had little to say. Half the class said "Nothing," about a quarter of the students talked about some playground experience, and then there were about eight kids whom I sent to time out. I reviewed the circle rule, that in order to speak, one had to have the talking stick. When kids talked out of turn, I asked them to go to time out. Five minutes into the activity, I had unwittingly destroyed my circle by removing a large chunk of the class. The kids who remained in the circle continued to utter off-task comments, whisper among themselves, or look terribly bored. After ten minutes, I realized that the lesson had been poorly conceived and implemented, especially for 2:00 p.m. on a Friday afternoon, so I bailed out. I sent everyone back to their tables for quiet time for the last ten minutes of the day. Like lunch, math, and the transition between art and recess, this activity was a downer. Today, it seemed that the kids were in charge, and I was just along for the ride. It concerned me when so many kids said that the whole day was boring and that the rest of them could focus on only the interpersonal dimension (which does make sense to me).

After school, Fran and I drove out to Wanda's house. She wasn't in school today. We drove out just to say hello and give her some moral support. Her situation is getting worse: her mother is not taking her to her speech therapist, we suspect abuse, her depression seems to be getting worse, and there may be weapons in the house. We knocked at the door, but no answer. After five minutes, her mother's face appeared at the window. She wouldn't let us in. She said that Wanda was sick with the flu. We walked away, feeling badly for a kid whose suffering was out of our control.

Later, at home, I was depressed at dinner and didn't talk. I yelled at Claire for something that didn't matter. I guess that I felt this accumulated frustration of year-long struggle with these kids, and sometime after dinner I lost it. I went outside in the cool April evening and cried. I cried as I thought about how we had failed these kids, how the system had failed their parents, how their parents had failed them, as had the school system and teachers. I blame my own novicedom and my own tendency to take the expedient strategy when faced with difficult teaching or social problems with the kids. I cried because I was weary of my relationship with them, which is characterized by subordination and power, and the incredible strain it causes as I regularly impose this kind of Stalinist regime. And I cried because of a feeling of hopelessness, that there are too many kids in my room who have not made progress. I feel discouraged that I can't make a difference in their lives. Their lives are much bigger than me.

I haven't felt this way since late January. I know that today was an exceptionally difficult day. But even with my string of good days since January, there has been the inescapable latent stress of coping with these kids, everyday, day in and day out. Often, I'm not aware of the stress until I have a day like today, and the dam of pent-up emotions simply bursts.

*Reflection: The working consensus between the students and me has been effective, but fundamentally it has always been fragile. It is diffi-*

*cult for them to make the transition from Fran to me. I imagine that Dorothy (in the morning) and Barbara have similar problems. Perhaps we have just too many adults working with this class, adults who all have slightly different rule systems and interpersonal styles.*

*I am beginning to use the vernacular of special education in naming my students (e.g., attention deficit disorder). This marks the beginning of my use of the special education frame, which will continue to the end of the school year.*

## April 6, 1999

Good day for me. Bad day for Fran.

I went home feeling a little guilty. I wondered if I could do more for Fran. Maybe I could take this second-grade group and leave her with the first and third graders, who are much easier. Maybe I could set up a rotation, so Barbara, Fran, and I rotate the groups we lead. The second graders are so challenging. Still, she needs to work her way through this struggle, find some strategies to cope with this group, because in ten days she is going to begin four weeks of solo teaching. Eventually, she is going to have to make sense of this group's energy.

## April 7, 1999

I played a video of Martin Luther King Jr.'s "mountaintop" speech, the one he gave the night before he was assassinated. The kids were riveted, and they were focused when we discussed the video. Earlier, I had read a biography of Phyllis Wheaton, the first African-American poet. During my reading of her experience on a slave ship, again the kids were interested. During the passage about her owner teaching Phyllis how to read, I asked the class why they thought that it was against the law in most states to teach slaves to read. The kids understood the relationship between literacy and power. It was crystal clear to them, even to most of the first graders.

Kids *want* to be interested. They want to be engaged wholeheartedly in activity that matters. Of course. I am planning a month-long unit on ecology to end the year. I want to make this unit provocative.

## April 13, 1999

Good day. I read the book *Teammates* to the class. It's about the friendship between Jackie Robinson and Pee Wee Reese. The book describes an incident in which Pee Wee shows his support of Jackie in front of thousands of hostile fans in Cincinnati. The kids understood the courage demonstrated by both men. When I asked them how they felt about the book, the class applauded. This has become the class's way of giving a group response to a book.

*Reflection: Why a good day? Endearing personal relations with students. An academic focus in which students were engaged. Curriculum that reflected my beliefs about the role of education. And three adults working their fannies off.*

## April 14, 1999

Good day.

We planted cucumber seeds in potting containers and will begin using the garden outside to grow flowers and vegetables. It's exciting to have Tracy, a part-time gardener who's been hired with money the school got from a grant.

Joke from Goldie:

> Goldie: Knock, knock.
> Class: Who's there?
> Goldie: Ah.
> Class: Ah hoo?
> Goldie: Oh, God bless you!

We ended today with sharing, singing, and joke telling. Today, I taught the class "We Shall Overcome." It was a bit slow for them, so I don't think they like it as much as "If I had a Hammer" or (Pete Seeger's) "If We Could Consider Each Other."

Today was the last day of state testing. I looked over the kids' shoulders as they worked, and I was pleased that the six third graders from my class got most of the test items correct. Occasionally, I had to restrain myself from squealing with horror when I noticed a wrong answer when I knew the kid understood the problem and was making a minor mental error. There are so many ways for teachers to overinvolve themselves and bias students' response to test items. When I am alone with the kids when they take the test, there isn't anyone there to watch what I do. I was allowed to read the math test items to kids who had trouble reading, and I wonder if there was a certain inflection or stress in my voice that subtly suggested a solution path or a particular answer. I didn't do anything consciously to help the kids, but who knows what I may have done unconsciously. I do think it'd be interesting to include one final test question for the kids that reads, "Did an adult help you in any way on this examination?"

Now, with the test over, I can get back to open-ended problem solving.

## April 15, 1999
Good day.

I introduced jazz to the kids. I read some children's literature, a story about a boy who loved to play jazz on his trumpet. We watched a *Reading Rainbow* video about jazz. Then we discussed the idea of improvisation and its application to artistic domains besides music. I improvised a story, and then I talked about dance as improvisation. I played a tape of Thelonious Monk. The kids came to the front in pairs or alone and did improvisational dancing. The kids had a great time, learning about improvisation and jazz.

Tomorrow is lunch bunch Friday. Three kids are going to be excluded from the lunch. I have mixed feelings about this. Basically, I feel that kids' disruptive behavior in school is actually a quite sane response to the insane condition of sitting in school all day. I am sensitive to the fact that my students who talk incessantly when I am trying to give directions, or kids who do not listen to directions, or kids who do what they want to do . . . these kids have needs that are at variance with my need to control and direct large number of kids through an adult-generated agenda. I also wonder if the inability of these kids to acquiesce to my notions of classroom etiquette simply reflects their stormy home lives, over which the kids fundamentally have no control. So, if it is my curriculum that is dysfunctional or irrational and these kids are only acting rationally in their resistance to my shtick, do I add insult upon injury by excluding them from the active listener lunch bunch? Maybe I should call it "compliant student lunch bunch," because this is my bottom line. I want kids to obey me. Certainly, it is all a matter of survival (mine) and the education of these kids (or is it miseducation?). I feel funny about excluding these three kids tomorrow. But I know that if I don't exclude them the lunch bunch incentive will become meaningless, and I will lose one of my more effective classroom management tools.

*Reflection: I notice the contradictions and ironies of my regime. With the structural and material constraints of my teaching, I have to teach as I do. Otherwise, I might have anarchy on my hands. However, the resistance of students to the system is a sane response, reflecting an unwillingness to subordinate themselves entirely to my domination.*

**April 19, 1999**

Fran has begun solo teaching. For four weeks. I look at this as a respite from the grind of everyday planning and whole-class management. Still, I am taking our most challenging math group. Fran does the opening, plans for four math groups, teaches two of the groups (Barbara and I each have groups), teaches science and social studies, and then leads the last thirty-five minutes.

I have a friend who just took the national test to get her psychologist's license. We were talking about my students, and as I described them she began *naming* them as attention deficit disordered (ADD) and attention deficit hyperactivity disordered. When ***** came into our conversation, she named him as oppositional defiant disordered (ODD). She showed me the *Diagnostic and Statistical Manual of Mental Disorders* (DSM-IV), and I read the criteria for these disorders. It suddenly made sense to me. I went through my class list and figured that at least fifteen of my students showed behaviors typical of ADD, ADHD, or ODD. Carol told me that these disorders tend to be inherited, usually from the father, and do not have strong environmental causes (with the exception of prenatal alcohol and drug use by the mother). So the incidence of these disorders is no higher at my (high-poverty) school than it is at the high-income schools across town. The difference is that when ADHD kids are subjected to parental neglect or family stress, then the children's tendency toward a particular exceptional behavior becomes exacerbated.

I've been vaguely characterizing my class all year as "special needs" or "high needs," but I've never been clear about what this meant exactly. Without an understanding of these kids' needs, I haven't been making conscious and planned adjustments in my teaching based on those needs. My adjustments have been intuitive and nonsystematic. And until now, I have been trying to fit square pegs into round holes. I have tended to blame the students and have wanted to change them so they conform to my model or standard for behavior. The kids who can't stay in their chairs, all the fidgeting, their angst when faced with dittoed math worksheets, the inattentiveness, the spaciness . . . it makes more sense to me now.

I went to the library last night. I watched a video on ADHD and how teachers can accommodate kids with this disorder. The recommended "interventions" reflect an extreme behavior modification approach, which includes tight structure, immediate feedback, and frequent consequences, rewards, and punishments. I then began reading a book edited by Constance Weaver on a whole-language approach to ADHD. This approach also suggests tight structure, but it recommends that the interests of the child be used as a starting point for all curricular initiatives.

As I read and think about this issue, I am aghast at how little I addressed special needs in my methods classes for preservice teachers over the years. No wonder preservice teachers often accused us teacher educators of being out of touch. So much of what we present in methods classes works well in ideal situations, with students who are able to consistently sit quietly and acquiesce to teacher commands. Teachers have so little training in special education. Ironically, we are increasingly spending more time reacting to our special needs students, often in miseducative ways.

**April 20, 1999**

Fran was in charge again, and I took Nathan's math group. I had the group of six around the table, and they were to use strips of paper, each divided into different fractional parts to answer questions on a worksheet. The table was a mess, with folders, papers, paper strips strewn everywhere. For these students, it was difficult to focus on the task. The kids had made these paper strips, called fraction kits, yesterday, to use on fraction tasks. Hayley had lost hers already. The kids were very distracted, by the noise in the room, by the table mess, and by each other's side comments. The kids gave a cursory glance at the task and noticed that it was not routine, and most of them said that they couldn't or wouldn't do it.

There were too many distractions. First, I need to clean off the work area for them before they come to the table.

Second, these students have trouble attending to my directions. They play off each other conversationally, and it becomes difficult for me to maintain a sustained instructional conversation with them. If the task is nonroutine, requiring explanation, I think that I'll break the group up and simply do multiple explanations.

Third, I should have done a demonstration of the use of fraction kits on the overhead for the entire class. Everyone is using them, and this demo would have given my group a minimal schema for this operation.

I thought that it was going to be much more relaxing when Fran did her solo. It hasn't been so far. I have taken the Nathan math group, and this is an intense group with whom to work. Today, I made some tactical mistakes with them.

## April 22, 1999

I have become increasingly interested in looking at mental disorders as a way of understanding the kids. By naming certain students as attention deficit disordered, or attention deficit hyperactivity disordered, it gives me a theory to understand the behavior of these kids. The literature that I am reading about ADHD suggests that this is a real biological phenomenon. But I also believe that the normally rigid constraints of traditional schools and classrooms place extraordinary demands on the patience and capacities of ADHD-type kids.

We just have too many of these kids. I compared my class list to the characteristics of ADD and ADHD, and I figured that at least fifteen of my students show behaviors for one or both of these conditions. In addition, at least three of my students were fetal-drug babies. I am reading that these kinds of children tend to be upset by unnecessary distractions, and they need space to walk around and engage in peripatetic processing of information. Emotionally, these kids are edgy and ready to snap at the smallest provocation. I think of Sam's table group, along with Felice, Goldie, and Emily. Except for Emily, these students all show attention and/or hyperactivity behaviors. Goldie and Felice can never sit in their seats without tipping back, lying across the chairs, sitting backwards and tipping forward and backwards, or simply falling out. Their arms and bodies are in perpetual motion. Often, they will be poking each other with pencils, passing notes, or playing with objects in the pencil box situated in the middle of the table. School seems to be so uncomfortable for Goldie that she claims to be sick on many afternoons, hoping to be sent home. This group, lately, has pegged Sam as a victim, so the three girls have been taunting him by switching his chair whenever he gets up to go to the bathroom or to sharpen his pencil. He'd get up, and one of the girls would be sitting in his chair when he got back.

At Chris's table, I will catch him out of the corner of my eye slapping Brittany, for no apparent reason. Cesar and Crystal, at their table, sit facing away from the front of the room. They never turn around when I stand in the front leading some activity, unless I make a concerted effort to have them do so. Instead, they sit hunched down engaged in some doodling activity. Michael, at Edgar's table, sits and jabs his pencil into the writing folder on the table. The cardboard folders on all the tables have the abused look of a graffiti-filled wall of a collapsing tenement building. Wanda's favorite game is to line pencils and crayons on the table and blow them off onto the floor.

Bonnie is in perpetual motion (never sits still, plays with pencils, talks, writes, and draws whenever there is down time) and Nathan has Herculean troubles staying in his seat. He is up out of his seat once every few minutes. Justin's table is a continuous powder keg that erupts at least once every afternoon. Justin is on medication, but even so, he is volatile and careens into a screaming fit if someone

looks at him the wrong way. During every transition, I can count on
Justin to cause a fracas over a chair. Meanwhile, Nathan and Sam
know how to push Justin's button, so they will make hand motions to
him from across the room, signaling the word "loser," which causes
Justin to scream out.

Sarah is gifted at the non sequitur; she too can't stop her body
from moving, and she can't stop the subvocalizations.

Last week, we gave Nathan's group a worksheet of double-digit
addition problems with a dot-to-dot task, in which the kids were to
draw lines from each of the answers to make, eventually, a face.
Nathan couldn't handle the task. His face went into pained contortions, and he plaintively asked, "Why are you making me do this?
Why did they have to put these dots in here? It doesn't make sense!"
I'd explained it to him twice and even began the task with him. However, the extraneous visual information (the dots) was too much for
him. A few days later, I read that this type of extraneous information creates an excessive perceptual load on some children. The page
of exercises and dots appears to be a wild and often indecipherable
page of mishmash for these children.

Transitions are very difficult for this class. In retrospect, I realize
that I haven't provided nearly enough structure for the kids. When
I do, the transitions tend to be easier.

*Reflection: I suspect that I was overreacting to students' resistance
and nonconforming behavior by focusing blame on students' "mental
disorders." I fear that my blaming the in-the-head disorder of individual
students marginalized many other explanations for the low-level chaos,
such as my poor skills at classroom management, immature students,
and a developmentally inappropriate environment.*

### April 26, 1999

Today, I visited the intermediate class. She has the kids sitting at
desks. The desks are arranged in groups of four, in square shapes.
Sitting in desks, the kids have considerably more space between
them and the next student than do my kids who sit at tables. Tomorrow, I am going to measure the relative distance between kids in

the intermediate class and my rooms. Even if my kids didn't sit in rows, desks would provide some extra space that might mitigate many of the interpersonal skirmishes that ignite throughout the day.

*Reflection: There is something contradictory about a philosophy that insists that everyone must sit at table groups but, at the same time, argues for an individualized approach to curriculum. The goal of having kids learn to cooperate and become a community conflicts with the goal of treating our students as if they have individual needs and learning styles.*

## April 27, 1999

Esther, the counselor/family advocate, gave me information on reactive attachment disorder and fetal-drug disorder. Last week, I read more about ADD and ADHD. As Fran has taken over the class, I have more time to sit back and watch the students. It's disconcerting. The kids are incredibly fidgety, and their hands and legs are in perpetual motion, even when they are supposed to be sitting quietly listening to directions. When Fran talks, I watch the kids' eyes and rarely does she have a majority of their eyes on her at one time. Instead of their focusing on the speaker, I observe the kids engaging in a steady stream of furtive communicative glances, playing with pencils, whispering, and sometime blatant calling out.

I would love to get desks and put my kids in rows. I would like to find some credible textbooks and get the kids focused on this work. I would like to implement a tight behavior modification program for the kids who need it. I would like to enforce a rule that all classrooms are quiet places where the student's job is to generate hard copy. I would like to have students working alone more than they are now. I would like to give students their own desks, so they can learn to take care of their own place. And then, when there is some calm and quiet and focus, only then must we begin teaching the kids how to cooperate, how to make decisions over an increasingly complex number of choices, how to find the answers to their own questions, how to work cooperatively, how to solve their own problems, and yes, how to think critically both of text as well as their social lives.

But I am scared about making these suggestions. In the 1990s, this school was renowned in the region for its implementation of developmentally appropriate practice and nongraded. I fear that we are like flies in a bottle. The universe we know is that of developmentally appropriate practice (i.e., child-centered education), and we are not considering alternative universes.

## April 28, 1999

Fran began her science lesson today, and the kids were uncooperative. She began to explain a planet study project that the kids were going to do in small groups. After every sentence she uttered, another student acted out or talked out. Calmly, she directed these students to time out, different areas along the back perimeter of the room. After about five minutes, there were six kids sitting in time out! Then, for about fifteen seconds, there was a flurry of off-task student noise and movement. The fifteen seconds seemed like fifteen minutes. I was standing in the back corner of the room, as inconspicuous as possible. I became tense at what appeared to be an impending total loss of control. Outwardly, Fran appeared completely calm and unflustered. I could see her mind working, trying to figure out what to do to get the lesson back on track. She looked at several kids who *were* sitting quietly. She acknowledged them by saying, "I like the way Martha is sitting. I like the way Eileen is sitting. I like the way. . . ." This quick affirmation of the "active listeners" seemed to turn the momentum in her favor. Then, two more students made silly noises and, without batting an eyelash, Fran sent them to time out. The room settled down and she proceeded with the lesson.

Afterward, I told her that her demeanor and presence were an inspiration to me. Getting uptight or flustered has a counterproductive effect on student behavior. It is normal for an intelligent person to become anxious when he or she is out of control. I sense that Fran has quite a bit of inner control, so in a sense she is always in control, even if the kids are not. She appears to have a strong sense of self, and this self-knowledge guides her. I suppose that Fran passes the essential first measure of a teacher: a healthy ego.

## April 29, 1999

It's 4:00 a.m. I can't sleep. Things are on my mind.

Stevie's having a hard time at recesses. He's having altercations with peers, almost every recess. Esther has invited him to spend time with her in the ALE during recess for a while. Just to have some nonconfrontational quiet time.

Justin just left us. No goodbyes. He'd been with Dorothy since the first grade. Two years and eight months and, without a whisper, his grandmother moved him to the next town. He is the ultimate challenge for the teacher in the regular classroom. He is eight years old and should be working as an apprentice in a machine shop. Already. He has a knack for things mechanical. The time spent in school doing a conventional curriculum, I believe, is a waste of time. He gets nothing out of it.

Lately, Davey doesn't seem to have any self-control. I will be sitting next to him in math group. He will make a silly noise, and I'll ask him to stop. He continues. I threaten him with the loss of a recess. He continues. When I tell him he's lost recess, he stops the silliness. Later, during recess, he cries when he sits in the room when his mates go out to play. Earlier in the year, when I worked with him every day and there was consistency about his behavior and my consequences, he was more able to control himself.

## April 29, 1999 (evening)

Bonnie climbed *up* the slide, in violation of a playground rule. The aide on duty directed her to not do it again. Bonnie vehemently objected and continued to climb up the slide. At this point, the aide sent Bonnie to the wall to sit and cool down. Later, I asked her about it. She said, "But I am the cat lady. Look at my hands. It's safe. I have these claws that hold on real tight. There's no way the cat lady is gonna fall off." Bonnie believes that she *is* the cat lady. Still, I reminded her of the rules, which apply to both kids and cats.

We just wrote a behavior plan for Nathan. Three times a day, he is scored for his active listening, not shouting, and not making putdowns. He can get a maximum of twelve points. If he gets twelve points in a day, his dad will take him to Dairy Queen. And the rewards decrease in scope down to eight points. Below eight points, there are no rewards. Today, he scored six points. We keep the scoring form on a chart that is out of his sight. I wonder if he needs to be visually in touch with the chart and the feedback needs to be more regular. Fran reviewed his point total only at the end of the day. Perhaps he needs feedback after every time period.

I want to develop behavior plans for Sam and David. This means sitting down with the parents and devising incentives that are some combination of home and school based.

I read that three out of four children with attention deficit disorder are boys. What I find interesting and of concern are those ADD kids who are not behavior problems, but instead, whose attention deficit is hidden by their silence or passivity.

*Reflection: The teacher needs to be well versed in special education: assessment and appropriate pedagogy. This, perhaps, is one of the largest gaps in my knowledge this year.*

The special education teacher is overloaded with referrals. According to some formula, there should be one special education teacher for every twenty-six kids in a school who receive services. We now have over sixty kids who receive services or are or waiting to be tested. Dorothy and I are anxious about Sam, but it has been months since we've referred him.

## May 1, 1999

I was sitting in a coffee shop, reading a chapter by Peter Woods (1990b) entitled, "Establishing Order in the Classroom." I noticed Arthur and his wife across the room. They walked over, and as usual, the conversation immediately turned to Woodbridge. Arthur, as the counselor, experiences all the negative cases that the school has to offer, since this *is* his job. Esther (our family advocate) and he had just gone to a conference that focused on very behaviorist approaches to working with high-needs students, like ours, who have extreme emotional and social problems. Esther and Arthur are convinced that the school needs to change its approach to meet our high-needs population. I tend to agree with them. I wonder if we are still holding on to an approach to teaching that reflects middle-class interests and a middle-class experience.

**May 5, 1999**

Yesterday, I started a girls' group at the school. One girl from each class. I want them to develop a name to propose to the site council and faculty as someone the school could honor with a special day each year. I figured that we already celebrate days for Woodbridge, Washington, King, Columbus, Seuss, and da Vinci. One girl mentioned that we also honor St. Patrick and Jesus. The group of eight was enthusiastic to work on this project. I had the girls brainstorm famous women, and it was the stereotypical list: Joan of Arc, Harriet Tubman, Ruby Bridges, Rosa Parks, Eleanor Roosevelt, Hillary, Rosy O'Donnell, Princess Di, and Queen Elizabeth. One Latina girl struggled to generate a name, but she couldn't think of one. Later, her teacher reported that she returned to her classroom intent on finding a female from her group.

I would love to decide on a female of color. I know that I could influence the group to pick Tubman or some other woman of color. If I leave it up to the girls entirely, the outcome is unpredictable: what if they pick Princess Di? I don't think the faculty would ever approve Di, and neither would I. Today, I'll flood the group with books of women who fit my criteria. And I'll lay out the criteria, too.

Today, I was going to go observe another teacher in the school district. Yesterday, the kids were very unruly, so I think I will just stick around and support Fran. As difficult a time as she is having with classroom management, I don't think I would be doing much better (well, maybe a little). Certainly, Fran is calmer than I am. This is one essential lesson I am getting from her.

I watched more videotapes about ADD and ADHD last night. The bottom line is *structure*. These kids need structure, predictability, quiet, and order. They also need hands-on experiences, kinesthetic experiences, and cooperative experiences (which are not quiet). The longer I stand in front and talk at them, the more likely these kids are to lose patience and veer off task. Everyone talks about "structure." I am not sure what this means, since I don't envision a heavy-duty behaviorist model but, instead, one that incorporates social constructivist teaching. We are still welded to our history, so this is keeping us from seeing the options more clearly.

I am going to give these tapes to Fran, Barbara, and Dorothy.

## May 13, 1999

My girls' group met today, and we debated the final names: Susan B. Anthony, Eleanor Roosevelt, Helen Keller, and Harriet Tubman. Keller and Tubman received the most support.

The group was in favor of having the school celebrate the birthdays of both women. One girl suggested that we make the women's birthdays state holidays, and I talked about the possibility of eventually making a proposal to the state legislature. On Wednesday, I will present the committee's work to the faculty at a staff meeting. We would like the whole school to vote on the question of Keller (who was a socialist!) and Tubman (who spied for the North during the Civil War).

## May 16, 1999

The kids each receive three tickets when they come in the room after lunch recess. If they fail to listen to directions, at any time, they lose one ticket. They need to have at least one ticket to participate in the 2:00–2:30 p.m. center/choice time. Center time quickly has become the favorite time of day for the kids. They choose among a menu of hands-on activities, such as clay, pastel drawing, weaving, Play-Doh, and working in the preschool at the other end of the school. I realize that most of the kids need and will benefit from these activities. However, I am tying participation to their behavior. I am concerned, particularly, about eight or nine kids who simply do not have the wherewithal to remain calm and attentive from 12:15 to 1:45. It is only ninety minutes, and they do get two strikes before they are out. I will walk around the room with a clipboard, recording those students who lose tickets. At 2:00 p.m., those kids who've lost three tickets will do math worksheets, sitting in other classrooms. Already, after three days of this schedule last week, it has been the same kids who've missed out on centers.

I am excited about this new center schedule. I have been fighting the idea of using the 2:00–2:30 p.m. time period for open-ended activity. For most of the year, I have used this time to pursue conventional academic objectives, such as the completion of science or social studies activities or storytelling. By 2:00 p.m., however, the kids are tired and ready to play. Other primary teachers in town tend to stop direct teaching at this time and invite kids to engage in more student-directed activity. Especially with my kids, who need intensely tactile/kinesthetic experience, 2:00 p.m. is the appropriate time to *not* do routine paper–pencil/sit-and-listen activity.

## May 17, 1999

I'm back leading the class. It was tiring, stressful, and unenjoyable.

Michael, a counselor–educator–professor from my college, visited the class this afternoon and did a presentation on poetry. He is a poet, and he performs his work with great élan and drama. His work reflects themes of multiculturalism and racism. Michael gave a wonderful presentation, but only about ten kids were attentive. Most of the class didn't understand the meaning of his poems, or they simply had trouble sitting quietly in their seats. A lot of kids had things in their hands, and there was much fidgeting.

Michael performed a poem about how reality can push down one's dreams. He asked the class how this can happen. He anticipated answers such as, "Mean people can push down my dreams" or "When people don't work cooperatively, then we get pushed down."

Instead, he received responses such as, "Reality is pushed down because of gravity. It pushes us all down."

"I had a dream last night about my mother sledding down a mountain."

After about ten minutes, he looked at me, smiled, and said, "This is one tough audience." Overall, the class was quiet, and Michael praised me for my ability to keep them quiet. I winced as if he'd just thrown salt in my eyes. I keep them quiet, but at what cost? I feel like a drill sergeant, and the kids do not have sustained opportunities to engage in grand conversations with each other and adults about academic content, conversations that require a common focus from most of the kids in the class.

**May 18, 1999**

Sarah, a first grader, has been absent nearly three weeks now. She is in the hospital with a rare and very serious virus. At first, the doctors thought she had leukemia, but the disease that she may have is more serious than leukemia. Her immune system is failing, and so are her organs. I called her hospital room. She was asleep, and I talked to her mother. The mother and I went through some self-recriminations as we recalled Sarah complaining that she didn't feel well at school, for months, and we interpreted this merely as an antipathy toward school. I felt guilty about dismissing her when she would complain that she was sick, and I felt guilty that I hadn't worked more quickly to organize the class to support her as she lay in the hospital. I was upset when I got off the phone with the mother. I thought of little Sarah, lying in pain in the hospital, a girl who I barely got to know this year. And I thought of my own kids, and how fragile our lives are, together for such a short time.

I went to a presentation for teachers by a local psychologist on re-active attachment disorder. The information helped me understand several students. I realize that I'd been making some mistakes with these kids, and my blunders have only exacerbated their dysfunc-tional behavior. I am convinced that teachers ought to study special needs, and that this study should be integrated throughout the teacher education curriculum.

Good day today. Centers are going well. Today, Ralph, the custo-dian, offered himself as a center. He will take two kids each day at 2:00 p.m., and they will shadow him and help him do his job. Crys-tal and Edgar went today. She asked Ralph how much he made. He said, "$11 an hour." He asked her to figure out how much he makes in a year, given his forty-hour week and fifty weeks a year. Ralph is cool!

**May 19, 1999**

A day from hell. I walked in at about 11:15 and Fran told me to ex-pect a bad afternoon. I was surprised by her comment, since she is rarely outwardly pessimistic. In my unusually haughty manner, I replied, "No sweat. We don't have to *let* it be a bad afternoon. Don't worry." But Fran was right and I was wrong.

In math, I worked with three groups, and Fran took one group to another room. I worked with the gang of five in math. I introduced multiplication to the group. Whenever this group sits together in a circle, it is always challenging, and today it was especially challenging. Nathan was in a bad mood. He engaged in a steady stream of peer conflict, with any peer sitting near him. Usually, as the conflict erupted, it appeared that both kids were at fault, or it was unclear who'd started the fracas. After the umpteenth altercation, I told Nathan to leave the room. He refused and ran off to the side and sat down against the wall. He took a marker and proceeded to jab his paints, painting them black. I started bargaining with him.

"If you stay quiet, you could stay in the room," I'd say.

"But I didn't start it. Sam started it this morning when he called me an idiot," he said.

"Nathan, let's deal with the here and now. If you can sit quietly and finish your work, you can come back into the room."

"But I'm not leaving. I didn't do anything wrong. Why is everybody picking on me?'" He started to cry. He wouldn't leave, and I didn't push it. I could have called the counselor to come and remove him.

When I tell Nathan to leave the room with an aggressive voice, he goes. However, recently, if I am calm and affectless, he doesn't listen to me. I hate using the aggressive voice, but it works. And when he is wired and destroying any semblance of order in the room, I need to get him out ASAP. Today, he won.

Emily lost three tickets for not listening to directions, so she missed out on centers. I told her to go to Julie's room, but when she left she proceeded to the library to do the math busywork I gave her. I am conscious that I am punishing my students with math worksheets when they have to stay in for recess or when they lose center time. Using these sheets as punishment is probably ruining these kids' relationship with mathematics.

Between Nathan and Emily, I did ad hoc crisis management the entire math period. He was like a black cloud of negativism, and wherever he wandered, peer conflict ensued. I could never quite see the transcript of the altercation, and Nathan always had a reason why the other person was at fault. I should have removed him from the room after the second or third altercation, but I didn't. Perhaps I didn't want to deal with the stress of removing him, which would have required me to become outwardly aggressive and tense. Emily's disruption was less overt but, still, it consumed my time. She did none of the assigned work and, instead, interrupted the kids who sat nearby. I should have separated Emily.

**May 20, 1999**
Good day.

Sarah is sick but getting better. I read "Sadako and the Thousand Paper Cranes" to the kids. It's about a Japanese girl who develops leukemia nine years after the Hiroshima atomic bomb blast. She is nine years old. In the story, she begins making 1,000 paper cranes, in the hope that the cranes will make her better. She dies before she is able to finish this task, but her classmates finish the 1,000 cranes. It's a beautiful story about hope, relationships, and courage.

**May 21, 1999**
Great day. Math went well. Everyone was engaged. Then, Beatrice's fourth and fifth graders came in and taught my kids how to make paper cranes. It was beautiful to watch her kids sitting one on one with my kids, teaching them how to make a fairly complicated origami design. After break, some kids continued making cranes while the others chose to work in their usual centers. Periodically, during center time, the kids broke out in spontaneous singing of some of the songs we'd taught them this year, like "Lean on Me." I felt that the kids and adults, for a few fleeting minutes, were truly on the same page; we shared the same "definition of the situation." Singing together, making cranes together, adults and kids laughing together and sharing a common activity that both wholeheartedly enjoyed. After we string together 1,000 cranes, we will box them up and send them to Sarah.

**May 24, 1999**
Today, I sent home a homework packet with the second graders. In the packet, there is math homework for the last two weeks of the school year. When I send home a sheet of homework on a daily basis, I am finding that this system is too difficult for me to manage. Sometimes, I forget to pass out homework. Sometimes, the kids forget to bring it home. In two weeks, I will make summer homework "packets" for all the students.

**May 25, 1999**
Easy day. I worked with the young first graders in math.

I needed to tighten up my relationship with Nathan. He's started to ignore my directions, and he's getting more difficult to manage. I decided to respond to his every indiscretion today, even when he was talking quietly to a neighbor when I asked for active listeners. In an hour, he'd lost his three tickets, so he lost the privilege of center time.

Before center time, I escorted one of the students, whose father is a colleague of mine at the university, to his dad's retirement party. I would return to Woodbridge an hour later. Nathan saw me walk out the door to the parking lot. He opened the door and shouted at me (about one hundred feet away), "Hey, this is what you can do with your tickets!" He proceeded to rip up the tickets and dramatically throw them in the air. I called back, "I'll see you in the ALE at 2:00 p.m. Bring your pencil and eraser. You'll have some math to do." (Ugh. Again, I'm using math as punishment.)

Nathan screamed back, "Not on your life, buddy!"

Driving to the university, I asked Tommy what he thought of Nathan. He said, "I like him because he's honest."

"Yes," I thought, "Honest . . . he *is*."

**May 26, 1999**
I introduced gender equity to the students today. I read them "William's Doll" (Zolotow, 1972). Midway through the story, I posed the question, "Why would it be important or useful for boys to play

with dolls?" Only my girls responded to this question, and the first five responses were, "Because its fun." Finally, Bonnie said, "So when the boys are fathers, they will know how to take care of their children." I went over and low-fived her.

I posed the question, "Why is it that girls can do just about every-thing boys can do, but boys can't do much of what girls do, like play with dolls, do ballet, wear pink?" Edgar said that boys *couldn't* wear bras, and everyone roared in laughter. I will stay with the gender theme until the end of school.

**May 27, 1999**
Great day. I wrote math tasks that were more or less appropriate, *and* we had five adults in the room. Fran, Barbara, two preservice teachers from OSU, and me. Whew. If I had five adults in the room all the time, working with twenty-four kids, this would be transfor-mational. Forget pedagogic orientation. Small teacher–student ratio. That's it! Ah, the beauty of common sense.

I read "Oliver Button is a Sissy," a story about a boy who wants to do ballet and is persecuted by the other boys in his school. I brain-stormed with the kids a list of activities and interests that are typi-cal of girls and then activities and interests that are typical of boys. Everyone agreed that girls should have an opportunity to do every-thing on the boy list, including wearing "boy" clothes and colors. However, some of the boys balked at doing activities that are typi-cally associated with girls (like sewing, knitting, cooking).

Sarah came back to school, just to visit. She'd been near death in the hospital for the past month, and thank goodness she's back and healthy again. She was never big but now she is a bag of bones. Tues-day, she'll be back and the kids are going to present her with the 1,000 cranes.

Emily finished her math work today. It was something she was able to do. Very often, I realize that I am giving this kid tasks that are just too obtuse. Her antisocial behavior in the face of overly difficult tasks makes sense. Lately, when she gets bogged down in math, she misbehaves and interrupts other kids sitting nearby, and I sit down and attempt to work with her; she still doesn't understand, we both get frustrated, she writes notes that read, "I hate meth, I haet Ken, I hat skool!" When she finished her work, I gave her a "caught in the act" slip, which goes into a big jar in the main office. The counselor picks out names the next day and kids win a prize.

## May 28, 1999

The staff took the morning to discuss their ideas about the problems faced by the school and solutions.

Questions and problems to ponder:

- When we say that some kids need different structures than others, what does this mean? Most teachers agree with this idea, but its meaning in practice is fuzzy and ill defined.
- The lives of our students are discombobulated. To what extent do we devote our attention to the social–emotional needs of the kids and to the academic needs? Many of our kids may need to meet in sharing circle three times a day and experience antiviolence curriculum as well as other formal curricular experiences that addresses social learning. However, there is a trade-off, since we would spend less time on the academics. What is the right balance?
- What is the best class organization for these kids: straight graded classrooms or multiage classrooms?
- How much special education training do our teachers need?
- *Is* there a problem?

## June 1, 1999

Easy day. The kids did work on multiplication and basic word problems. Not much new ground. The task was doable, especially by the three or four kids who tend to lose it when they don't understand. Emily wasn't in school today. A dilemma for me is that she needs to be in school every day, but her presence is disruptive, especially for Hayley. I'm going to recommend that Hayley and Emily not be in the same class next year. Sam wasn't in school, either, and his absence reduced the number of interpersonal squabbles that I had to address today.

# June 10, 1999

Last day.
Relief and sadness.
Swimming, picnic, park.
Sweaty walk back
to school
along highway.
Drivers blaring horns,
trucks weaving.
Kids dodging cars
in the street.
Sarah comes back
after brain operation
and picks up 1,000 cranes
that saved her life.
Awards assembly:
fifth graders leave
with pomp and body odor.
At last, last day,
all year, ambivalence
and ambiguity.
Did I really matter??
Now last day,
feeling calm and sure
it was good
for them and me.
Singing *Lean on Me*
and if we could consider
each other a neighbor
a friend or a brother.
Awards to all.
Felice gets hot
sense of humor.
Wanda is storyteller
extraordinaire.

Crystal presents
"teacher of year" certificates
to me fran dorothy and barbara.
I cry to say bye
to nathan and
he cracks,
yeah, see ya around, bub.
Sarah holds onto me
for five minutes.
Won't let go.
Give bonnie pep talk.
You're so bright,
creative, interesting,
and wonderful.
Her mouth quivers.
Ready to cry.
Instead, she says
Ken, do you know
your beard smells
like an orange.
Stevie still doesn't
understand that he
doesn't come to school
tomorrow.
Never thought I could
do this, the whole year.
I showed up
everyday!!!
Goodbye smelly stuffy room
goodbye lovely smelly kids
goodbye lovely tired colleagues
who laugh and smile
in spite of the shakes
in heart and hand.

**II**

# DIMENSIONS OF TEACHING—THREE STUDIES

# 2

# THE NEGOTIATIVE DIMENSION OF TEACHING: TEACHERS SHARING POWER WITH THE LESS POWERFUL

The struggle to establish and maintain order in the class was continuous and perplexing. During the year, I came to appreciate the negotiative work that must be done in teachers' relations with their students. Here is an entry from my journal, February 17, 1999.

I negotiate with everyone it seems. Not that this is a bad thing. I think we all negotiate at some level, in order to establish balance and reciprocity in any relationship. I assign two math "jobs" a day, and then the kids can have "free time" to play math strategy games. However, if a child has worked really hard on one job for most of the period and asks to play a game toward the end of the time, I will bend the rule about the two jobs and give the child permission to play. I have asked that the kids not use calculators when practicing double-digit addition with regrouping exercises. However, I noticed Nathan using the calculator. He insisted that he couldn't do the problems without the calculator. I noticed that he had trouble doing the simple additions of the ones columns and then the tens columns. I negotiated and suggested that he use the calculator to add each individual column, and then he'd have to show how he carries the ten over to the tens column. He agreed.

The negotiation I do is most explicit with the high-needs kids, since it is these kids with whom I have the most frequent interactions and who need the most accommodation if they are to remain orderly and coherent and engaged. Still, negotiation goes on with everyone and even the class as a whole. During end-of-day read-aloud, I ask that everyone sit on the rug with nothing in their hands and listen to the story. Well, Jeff needs to sit in a chair because of his physical problems. The other day, I noticed Kathleen sitting at the table drawing quietly as I read. I let it slide, so she continued as I continued reading. Angelica hates sitting on the floor at the end of the day, so I've begun to look the other way when she stays in her seat as I read the story. The other kids notice, I am sure, but they all appear happy sitting on the rug as I've directed, so no one makes a stink about the nonconformists. If more kids resisted my directive, I would either force everyone to sit on the floor (which I find no reason to do) or I'd engage the class in discussion (negotiation) about how we can do the read-aloud and meet everyone's needs.

This is a journal entry that explicitly illustrates the negotiative nature of teaching. In this chapter, I suggest that teacher–student relations have to do with power relations and the negotiation that goes on between the teacher, students, and parents as well as larger institutional and structural forces. This process involves the construction and reconstruction of relationships, between the teacher and a large number of students, in the context of a huge variety of situations and activities, in the context of the physical space of the classroom and school and the historical political–economic context of teachers and school districts. These reconstructions of power relations are unrelentingly subject to continuous negotiation between the participants. Although teachers have more power due to their adult status and teacher status, students do engage in resistance and struggle to maintain their dignity or pursue their interests as they are forced to sit each day in situations that are essentially not of their own making. In this structural/relational context, it is simplistic to view the teachers simply as more powerful players who control student behavior and learning. It is also a misconception to view the teacher–student relationship as primarily a collaborative endeavor, which is an oft-cited romantic view of teacher–student relations, in which the two parties unproblematically work together for the purpose of constructing goals that meet each others' needs.

The goal of this research was for me to understand more deeply the complexity of teacher–student relations and, then, to use these ideas in my work as a teacher educator. My thesis is that teacher–student relations are characterized essentially by a negotiative process that reflects the idiosyncratic and situational nature of the teacher–student relationship in the larger political, historical, and structural contexts of teaching.

## CONCEPTUAL FRAMEWORK

### Power and Resistance: Situational and Shifting

I refer to power as a relative and ever-changing aspect of relations. Foucault argued that power is dynamic and relational. He argued against its reification and any notions of power as an absolute possession of the dominant.

> Power is dispersed across complicated and heterogeneous social networks marked by on-going struggle. Power is not something present at specific locations within those networks, but is instead always at issue in on-going attempts to (re)produce effective social alignments, and conversely to avoid or erode their effects, often by producing various counter-alignments. (Rouse, 1994, 109–10)

From this perspective, power is not simply held by the dominant agent in relation to the subordinated. Instead, it is present in social alignments, represented in the interaction of the dominant, the subordinated, other interested individuals, and the historical and physical reality of the encounter. These power alignments include people, but they also include the "instruments of power (buildings, documents, tools, etc.) and the practices and rituals through which it is deployed" (Rouse, 1994, 106).

A teacher's power over students, then, reflects the broad structure surrounding situations, and this includes other people who are present in the lives of the teacher or students. For example, the power of the dominant agent, such as a teacher, is constrained by the presence of others. Even when one person appears to have more power than another, power depends on "other persons or groups acting in concert with what the first person does" (Rouse, 1994, 106). There is also a structural limitation on the dominant actor, since he or she can treat the subordinate only according to the rules of the situation. Conversely, the subordinated agent is never completely powerless, since "countering alignments are a means through which the power of a dominated agent within a power relation can be constrained" (Wartenberg, 1990, 174), and these "alternative alignments decrease the hierarchical structure of power that a given power relation has" (176). So how the teacher and student behave is "transformed into a set of social realities" that reflect the presence and influence of others, such as parents, the principal, and the teacher's colleagues.

Furthermore, Foucault (1978) argues that power and resistance are inextricably linked; with power always comes resistance:

> [T]his resistance is never in a position of exteriority to power. . . . Their existence depends upon a multiplicity of points of resistance: These play the role of adversary, target, support, or handle in power relations. These points of resistance are everywhere in the power network. (Foucault, 1978, 95)

Occasionally, there are what Foucault called massive "binary ruptures" (e.g., open rebellion), but he observed that most resistance consists of slightly shifting and momentary "cleavages." Scott (1990) studied how subordinated groups engage in resistance, and he described some elementary forms of *disguised* resistance, which is what subordinated groups do when direct confrontation with the dominant is too risky. Some common interactional strategies include disguised messengers (i.e., the anonymous note), disguised messages (use of polite words but with a hostile tone), gossip, or grumbling (communicated through a "sigh, a moan, a chuckle, a well-timed silence, a wink or a stare") (Scott, 1990, 155). Collective protest is often safer than individual actions, such as the protest of prisoners who rhythmically rap the bars of their cells with tin cups. In situations in which the "structure of domination is viewed as inevitable and irreversible, then all 'rational' opposition will take the form of infrapolitics: resistance that avoids any open declaration of its intentions" (Scott, 1990, 220).

## Why Negotiate?

There are structural and cultural factors that give life to the negotiative dimension of teachers' work. Students and teachers have different interests or goals for time spent in classrooms (Hammersley & Woods, 1984; Waller,

1965). John Holt (1964/1982) described the reality of competing *definitions of the situation* held by students and teachers.

It has become clear . . . that these children see school almost entirely in terms of the day-to-day and hour-to-hour tasks that we impose on them. This is not at all the way the teacher thinks of it. The conscientious teacher thinks of himself as taking his students . . . on a journey to some glorious destination, well worth the pains of the trip. If he teaches history, he thinks how interesting, how exciting, how useful it is to know history, and how fortunate his students will be when they begin to share his knowledge. If he teaches French, he thinks of the glories of French literature, or the beauty of spoken French, or the delights of French cooking and how he is helping to make these joys available to his students. And so for all the subjects.

For children, the central business of school is not learning, whatever this vague word means; it is getting these daily tasks done, or at least out of the way, with a minimum of effort and unpleasantness. Each task is an end in itself. The children don't care how they dispose of it. If they can get it out of the way by doing it, they will do it; if experience has taught them that this does not work very well, they will turn to other means, illegitimate means, that wholly defeat whatever purpose the task giver may have had in mind. (37–39)

Related to conflicting goals for school is the notion of self-interest. Self-interests are needs that must be met in order for one's sense of self and dignity to be maintained or supported (Hewitt, 1976). For teachers, there tend to be two central needs: an orderly classroom and learning (e.g., Lortie, 1975). For students, peer group membership and mental stimulation appear to be of central importance (Everhart, 1983; Montandon & Osiek, 1998; Pollard, 1985). When the curriculum and teaching is interesting to the students and some learning is happening, then the needs of both the teacher and the students are being met. However, when the curriculum is boring to students, they may seek mental stimulation in ways that subvert the teacher's intention, and the teachers' interactional response is a negotiating maneuver to get the students to do what they would not have done, naturally, without teacher action.

Power is the second factor in our understanding of negotiation (Hewitt, 1976). School attendance *is* compulsory. As involuntary participants in school, students are subjected to a curricular agenda that is usually not of their making or, worse, not interesting. From a larger politicostructural per-spective, Collins (1975) argues that all organizations are "best understood as arenas for conflicting interests" (289) in which people pursue their own in-terests, sanctions are used by the dominant to gain compliance, and particu-lar tasks shape the nature of the conflicts. Classrooms and schools are orga-nizations like any other, and the fundamental task of teachers is to influence or control students to behave in a manner that will lead to their learning and, ideally, and as Wartenberg (1990) suggests, their eventual transformation and independence from the teacher and school.

The problem for teachers is that the *kind* of control one wields with stu-dents can support only particular types of teaching (Collins, 1975). For exam-ple, normative control occurs when teachers try to get their students to iden-tify with teacher and school goals; the students are given more control; and students are co-opted into positions of responsibility in the class. Normative control is required if the members of the organization are going to engage in nonroutine, problem-solving, and creative tasks. "The more initiative required in a task, and the less predictable or visible the outcomes, the more its suc-cessful accomplishment depends on strong normative control" (Collins, 1975, 314). When the control of students depends on material incentives or, worse, coercion, then "the tasks that can be carried out under these controls are lim-ited to ones of low initiative" (313). Material rewards, or external incentive pro-grams, work best when the outcomes or tasks by students are well-defined, standardized, and require only "lower-order thinking."

Some degree of normative control in classrooms appears to be imperative if students are going to engage effectively in creative, problem-solving types of activity. Effectively implemented, normative control tends to diminish the hierarchical structure of organizations, since it gives more power to the sub-ordinated and fosters egalitarianism. Normative control encourages students to question and critique the existing structure and organization of class-rooms. It gives students license to politic for more control over curriculum and the culture of classroom life. However, the contradiction here for teach-ers is that in the dominant culture of classrooms, teachers are supposed to be "in charge" of students; and at a macrolevel, the state (and *not* teachers and students) is increasing its control over the goals and content of the curricu-lum. In the interaction of teacher–student relations and the larger structure of schooling, there is the conflict between teachers' interest to engage in reason and dialogue with students and the cultural and structural dimensions of school that position the teacher as dominant and the representative of state interests.

The historically situated conception of an appropriate teacher–student ratio in the regular classroom, which in the United States hovers between twenty and thirty students per class (Glass, Cahen, Smith, & Filby, 1982), further complicates teachers' lives with contradictions. The present state of diminished funding for public education tends to put more pressure on school districts to *increase* class size. It appears that larger classes restrict teachers' ability to meet the interest or learning needs of individual students (Glass, Cahen, Smith, & Filby, 1982; Zahorik, 1999). Teachers are then forced to direct their instruction to the general group. However, this reduces opportunities for teachers to implement a more "normative control" in their relations with students whereby students freely participate in the co-construction of curricular experience.

The contradictions apparent here could be very confusing, especially for the beginning teacher. The ideal of student agency and student control is a central dimension of teaching and teacher education today (e.g., Atwell, 1987; Lensmire, 1994). Typically, there are always aspects of the curriculum that require problem-solving behavior, such as in many states where students are required to engage in complex mathematics problem solving, and to generate large interdisciplinary projects. However, the culture and structure of public schools essentially requires the subordination of students, which may tend to depress student motivation to engage in these sorts of open-ended problem-solving activity (cf., Collins, 1975).

## Teacher–Student Negotiations

A dictionary definition of *negotiate* is to "confer with another so as to arrive at the settlement of some matter" (*Merriam-Webster's New Collegiate Dictionary*, 1965, 566). For the teacher, the "matter" is students' interaction with and learning from the curriculum. For students, who are (structurally) in a disadvantageous power position in relationship to the teacher, the "matter" is how to manage the teachers' initiatives toward them and, concurrently, how to maintain their dignity and some sense of enjoyment or interest (Pollard, 1985).

While students do not hold structural power, they can still wield power if the situational factors support it: if the teacher is inexperienced or weak; if the parents do not support the teacher; if the students are particularly cohesive and nonconforming; or if the teacher is skilled and able to manage a democratically governed class effectively. Students may have power as individuals and as collectives. Particularly as collectives, students can have enormous power in relation to a teacher who they deem to be unfair or boring. But except for when working with the most conformist of students, teachers need to engage in some give and take with most students, particularly if teachers are going to come close to reaching their learning goals for students (Pollard, 1985). However, using brute power in order to get their way and to control students is not a viable option for most teachers, particularly those (like many elementary teachers) who have a sense of self that values warm personal relations and rapport with students (Nias, 1989).

There are two broad types of negotiation: open and closed (Pollard, 1985; Woods, 1984). Open negotiation occurs when the teacher and student are able to reason together about their interests, and both sides are willing and able to meet each other's needs by engaging in a voluntary give and take. When open negotiation takes place, teachers and students engage in "joint activity, based on a certain amount of good will towards each other, recognition of the value of cooperation, and belief in the possibility of consensus" (Woods, 1984). Closed negotiation occurs when the students are not able to reason and understand the teacher's position, and both parties make concessions only if they have to; in closed negotiation, it is usually the students who are forced to make the concessions (Woods, 1984).

The outcome of negotiation, when successful, is a working consensus. The students get some work done and some learning occurs, and hopefully, for the teacher, this learning can be demonstrated to parents, supervisors, or the district on state tests. The working consensus allows for some student deviance along with the mild and predictable censure from teachers; the type of censure is consistent with the school culture and what the students consider to be reasonable. Hargreaves (1972) believed that there is almost never true consensus between teachers and students in their respective definitions of the situation. Goffman (1959) also maintains that real consensus, in the context of everyday interactions, is rare. The agreement that the participants construct reflects less a real consensus but, instead, an agreement as to whose claims about certain issues are going to dominate. Rarely are teacher and students totally in sync. Consensus understandings are both rare and fleeting. At best, after much negotiation, teachers and students reach what Hargreaves calls "pseudo-concord," in which the negotiated *working consensus* only partly meets the goals of teachers and students. He identifies three types of pseudo-concord:

1. *(Working) Compromise.* This is probably the common type of pseudo-concord, when conflict does exist regarding the definition of the situation but some compromise is met. When compromising, the

   power differential between the teacher and pupils is small . . . where the teacher does not feel that a compromise would involve a fundamental neglect of his duties; where the teacher knows that an attempted use of power to impose his own definition of the situation would be perceived as illegitimate . . . and this would lead to more student opposition. (Hargreaves, 1972, 170)

2. *Hegemony.* This is when the teacher and student definitions of the situation conflict, so the teacher simply imposes his or her own.

3. *Counterhegemony.* This occurs when the teacher and student definitions conflict, the teacher is unskilled, and the students are particularly savvy politically. The students' definition prevails, since they possess dominant power. In this situation, the teachers "yield as if they were granting privileges rather than rights to the pupils" (Hargreaves, 1972, 170). Teachers really fear counterhegemony, particularly when colleagues and parents become aware of the situation, since it means they are incompetent.

There is a fourth state of affairs, not addressed by Hargreaves (1972), a situation in which control is contested by the teacher and students. There is a struggle for control. There is a problem; neither party is able to work out a resolution with the other party, so there is an impasse. This is called the "power struggle" in everyday teacher vernacular. A teacher may have a power struggle with an individual, a small group, or the entire class. The teacher does not really have control of the class, but neither do the students! The power struggle may be characterized by chaos in the classroom, or it could resemble a more civil state of argument and unresolved discussion.

Most students fall somewhere in the middle of a continuum between complete conformism and open rebellion, and it is with these students that teachers do most of their negotiations. (Cooperation doesn't mean that students see the world as teachers see the world. Rather, it means that a process of negotiation has occurred and a truce has resulted from the give and take of negotiation.) In negotiations, teachers and students may engage in a variety of strategies, such as bargaining, flattery, cooperation, promises, cajoling, and emotional and social manipulation (Martin, 1976). Given the natural differences between teachers' and students' goals for school experience, the steady and unrelenting give and take of negotiation is an essential part of teachers' working conditions. According to Woods (1990b), "Schools are . . . trading places" (ix).

## A NOTE ON RESEARCH METHOD

Along with the concepts of consensus and the power struggle, I used Hargreaves' three categories for pseudo-concord to code and organize the data. I read and reread each journal entry and asked the question, "How would I characterize my interactions with students here?" There were times that there were various types of negotiative outcomes within a single teaching event (e.g., in one lesson, I would move fluidly among teacher hegemony, dialogue with students, power struggle, and maybe working consensus). For the purposes of this study, I focused on those teaching events that were somewhat unambiguously one category or another. I used social interactionist theory (e.g. Pollard, 1985; Rosser & Harre, 1984) as well as criticalist theory (e.g., Collins, 1975; Foucault, 1978; Wartenberg, 1990) to inform my analysis and interpretation of the data.

In the next section, I report data from the journal that illustrate the five categories, or types, of relations with the students. The goal of this research is to generate theory that explains a more complex, interactive, and negotiative dimension in teacher–student relations. Theoretical memos follow each journal excerpt. The memos were written in the year after I completed the journal and the sabbatical.

## THE NEGOTIATIVE DIMENSION: CATEGORIES, STORIES, AND REFLECTIONS

### Consensus

**February 23, 1999**

Good day. We dissected owl pellets, a part of the unit on food webs. For some of the kids, this was almost a religious experience. We had posters of the skeletal anatomy of voles, moles, and mice. The kids worked with tweezers and carefully compared their discoveries with the poster examples. The most exciting part was their discovery of skulls and teeth.

*Reflection: Some other conditions that may support consensus between teacher and students, as reflected in the last three entries, are the following: compelling subject matter (jazz, gender equity, owl pellets), opportunities to move around in a playful way, the opportunity to express some silliness or humor, discovery science, and open-ended discussion.*

**April 15, 1999**

Good day. I introduced jazz to the kids. I read some children's literature, a story about a boy who loved to play jazz on his trumpet. We watched a *Reading Rainbow* video about jazz. Then we discussed the idea of improvisation and its application to other artistic domains besides music. I improvised a story, and then I talked about dance as improvisation. I then played a tape of Felonious Monk. The kids came to the front in pairs or alone and did improvisational dancing. The kids had a great time, learning about improvisation and jazz.

**May 21, 1999**

Great day. Math went well. Everyone was engaged. Then Beatrice's fourth and fifth graders came in and taught my kids how to make paper cranes. It was beautiful to watch her kids sitting one on one, with my kids, teaching them how to make a fairly complicated origami design. After break, some kids continued making cranes while the others chose to work in their usual centers. Periodically, during center time, the kids broke out in spontaneous singing of some of the songs we'd taught them this year, like "Lean on Me." I felt that the kids and adults, for a few fleeting minutes, were truly on the same page; we shared the same "definition of the situation." Singing together, making cranes together, laughing . . . adults and kids sharing a common activity that both wholeheartedly enjoyed. After we string together 1,000 cranes, we will box them up and send them to Sarah.

*Reflection: Both the students' needs and my needs were being met here. For the students, they engaged in enjoyable peer relations around a pleasant activity. The activity was voluntary, so only those students who wanted to make cranes did so. For me, the students enjoyed the activity, the activity was "educational" in my view, and everyone got along. This activity was "teaching" students to develop a sense of responsibility to others, especially those who are sick.*

## May 26, 1999

I introduced gender equity to the students today. I read them *William's Doll* (Zolotow, 1972). Midway through the story, I posed the question, "Why would it be important or useful for boys to play with dolls?" Only my girls responded to this question, and the first five responses were, "Because its fun." Finally, one of the girls said, "So when the boys are fathers, they will know how to take care of their children." I went over and low-fived her.

I posed the question, "Why is it that girls can do just about everything boys can do, but boys can't do much of what girls do . . . like play with dolls, do ballet, wear pink?" One of the boys said that boys *couldn't* wear bras, and everyone roared in laughter. I will stay with the gender theme until the end of school.

## Working Consensus

### February 17, 1999

I am learning that each student sometimes needs a unique and personal response when he or she misbehaves. When Donnie gets on my nerves or looks resistant to some adult directive, I find that humor works best with him, such as when he is trying to tell me what to do with the class: "Hey, I can get you into the teacher education program at the university. We have a budding elementary teacher right here!" Earlier in the year, I used to get "in his face" with fairly assertive responses. With this kid, this strategy was wrong. He needs the indirect, soft response. As Donnie is best served by humor, Billy is best served by a clear and assertive "No!" in his face. Kathleen needs a reassuring touch and a friendly, "Come on, help us out." When Justin becomes irrational and refuses to get up off the floor, I will say to him, "Hey, buddy, I have an important job for you. Would you turn off the lights for me in five minutes when I need to get the class's attention?" Justin will give me a look like I've just offered him a million dollars, jump to his feet, and stand at attention at the light switch for five minutes. With about eight or nine kids, I have to simply say, "Hey kids, I need active listeners now. Let's remember our classroom rules." And with eight or nine other kids, I need to have some more concrete punitive consequence, such as the loss of recess, time out, or a trip to the school's time-out room. For example, Joey covets his afternoon recess, so I just have to mention the possibility of him staying in for recess and he calms down.

Of course, the tasks that I develop for kids in math are becoming more and more appropriate to them individually. The ideal problem is one that is moderately challenging, of course. And for a teacher to know what is *moderately challenging* for her students, it takes time to develop this knowledge. The value of knowing one's students is obvious to me, for both academic and behavioral aims. Certainly, the practice of keeping the same kids for at least two years is a sensible one. Dorothy and the other 1–3 blended teachers here at Woodbridge have the benefit of three years with students.

*Reflection: I think that the working consensus depends on the teacher knowing his or her students, having a wide repertoire of strategies that can address a whole range of student needs, and then being flexible and adaptable in responding to individuals and particular situations (Hargreaves, 1972). Teacher knowledge (of the students and parents and of pedagogy and curriculum that fit those students and parents) is a crucial factor in the power teachers may wield in their work with students.*

## September 16, 1998

Today was a hard day. I introduced a math center on tessellations. I gave a five-minute explanation and then invited students to work at this center. The six students who worked on tessellations really didn't get it. One girl just wanted to fill in the tessellation worksheet with random colors. Other kids thought that I wanted them to make simple patterns on the worksheet. I realized that this topic is more complex than I'd originally thought. I need to reteach tessellations. Tomorrow.

*Reflection: The kids found the activity either too easy (and boring) or too difficult. The students redefined the task in a way that made sense to them, maybe even in a way that was interesting, and in a way that would keep me off their backs since they were doing* something. *It is common for teachers to ignore minor deviant behavior if it is not disrupting the general order of the class. In this case, students generally missed the point of the lesson and were engaged in some activity that was working for them. The students and I generated a working consensus in that I did not force them to redo their tessellations (since this would have been inappropriate from a cognitive–developmental perspective), and they appeared to engage wholeheartedly in the task, although they missed "my" point in the activity.*

## October 22, 1998

We went to Colleen's room next door so my students could tell this week's story ("How the Boy Turned into a Peanut") to her students. It went well. My students paired up with students in Colleen's class. So one student sat with one other student and told a thirty- to sixty-second story. Most of my students accomplished the storytelling task quite well. Even students who struggle with the rest of the curriculum excelled today. I allowed shy students to tell the story collaboratively, with a peer. One or two students still did not want to do the activity (too shy), so they were allowed to watch. Tomorrow, we do it again in the kindergarten.

*Reflection: The activity worked since the students and I were able to forge a working consensus about the activity. Storytelling did appeal to their interest to engage in enjoyable activity. The story was simple and short, so the task was manageable to all students, even first graders and special-needs kids. They were telling the story to same-age peers in the next classroom. Some of the kids were too self-conscious or insecure to do this in front of unfamiliar peers, so I allowed them to modify the task (do it collaboratively or just watch) so they could still participate. And pairs of kids sometimes acted silly during or before the storytelling, and I tolerated this behavior. Power seemed to "circulate" among students and me in this particular situation.*

*If I had forced everyone to do the storytelling, some of the recalcitrants might have simply refused or, if they could have been coerced into doing it, they might have become angry or cynical about me and our relationship. Of course, there is the possibility that some recalcitrants, once they had tried their hand at storytelling, would've done a good job, discovered some confidence about the task, and in the end, really enjoyed it! I chose the open-negotiative style because of my respect for individual differences, particularly the needs of introverts to have some control over when and how they take public speaking risks.*

## November 30, 1998

Today I announced a new lunch program, called the Active Listener Lunch Bunch. Students who consistently exhibit positive behavior will be invited to eat lunch with me in the classroom. The students generally hate eating in the cafeteria since it is loud and impersonal. During the afternoon, as I taught, I held a clipboard in my hand and wrote the names of students who did not follow directions. At the end of the day, I read the list of students whose names I had not written down. These nine students were invited to have lunch with me tomorrow. Most of the 14 students who weren't invited to eat in the room tomorrow either disagreed with me or they simply didn't understand why they couldn't have lunch with me.

*Reflection: Clearly, Lunch Bunch was a bargaining chip. I was in effect saying to the students, if you moderate your behavior and comply with my rules, then you can come and eat with me in the classroom. For the most part, this bargain was effective in helping me maintain the working consensus.*

## The Power Struggle

### October 21, 1998

Today was the trip to the public library. The students pretty much behaved as they do in school. I asked Barbara what she thought of their behavior, and she answered, "They were all right. It was pretty normal for a class trip like this."

Since we were in a public place, my awareness of their behavior was heightened. The librarian gave a twenty-minute presentation to them. For the entire time, I had to remove kids, give dirty looks, remind the class about active listening, etc. After the presentation, the kids had an opportunity to peruse the shelves and check out books. Four or five kids could not control themselves. They fought with each other over the water fountain. They ran through the aisles. They raised their voices. One parent volunteer had to physically remove a boy who was disruptive. I had to drag Nathan by the arm away from an altercation with a peer. While most of the students behaved appropriately and had a great time, my focus was on the errant children. According to my tunnel vision, the trip was a bomb, stressful, and not fun. When I surveyed the class later, all but one of the children asserted that they'd behaved appropriately, and that they had had a good time.

I think it's hard for some children, especially from homes that are not calm, to understand my middle-class (and middle-aged) notion of *calm*. Perhaps they *do* understand what it means to be calm. However, they are lacking in the metacognitive strategic knowledge to monitor and regulate their behavior. My common sense tells me that it is home environment. Homes that are calm and environments that support civil conversations . . . children who come from these homes will come to school able to be calm and engage in civil conversations.

*Reflection: I blamed kids' home environment for the debacle at the library. I now sense that this explanation is too easy and a bit simplistic. I know of many instances when "good" classes (and kids from "good" homes) went berserk for a substitute teacher. Home experiences certainly do influence kids to behave only in general ways much of the time. However, I sense now that it* isn't *the disorder of kids' home lives that makes*

*for particularly stressful class trips. Rather, I think teachers have to ex-
amine the presence of a negotiated order (or disorder) that is situated in
specific school settings (cf., Rosser & Harre, 1984).*

*The working consensus I have with the students is very tenuous, and
it is situated in the classroom. When students are in the room, there are
a set of rules, both explicit and tacit, for what needs to happen. In our
particular classroom, the rules are related to movement, sharing of space
around tables, taking turns, manipulating materials, and doing work.
Besides, the consequences for deviant behavior were all tied to the classroom: for example, be deviant and go to the time-out table and do a worksheet. The space and design of the classroom and the school facilitate my
ability to monitor and control the students. Gore (1998) notes this monitoring function, or surveillance, as one essential technique of teacher
power. Students are put in small, crowded classrooms, with little privacy,
perhaps in rows of individual desks, all facing the teacher at the front,
and it is easier to monitor them. Scott (1990) observed that the real feelings of the subordinated are least inhibited when the "control, surveillance, and repression of the dominant are least able to reach" (120), and
when the site is composed of close confidants. Both conditions were present on this class trip: hence, there was a virtual open rebellion.*

*There is a third condition that contributed to the chaotic class trip. I
hadn't worked out a definition of the situation with the students on how
to go on a class trip to the library (and on a city bus!!). We haven't yet
constructed rules, such as for walking to the bus stop, standing and
waiting for the bus, entering the library, or walking around the library
and looking for a book. I realize now that it is impossible to work out
rules for behavior before an experience, especially if the experience is in
any way complex (like a class trip). Sure, I can lay out the rules about
walking, raising a hand to speak, not shouting, and so forth. But, except
for the extreme conformists in the class, most rules have to be negotiated
and constructed in the context of the experience. I was nervous because
of the public nature of the trip and my kids' behavior. The public (in the
library) along with my nine adult volunteers will be watching and judg-
ing my competence as a teacher (i.e., my ability to keep order).*

*In retrospect, I could have been much more controlling and domi-
nating in how I managed the trip. For example, I could have asked each*

*of my eight adult volunteers to physically attach themselves to one of my eight most unpredictable students, and then I would have had the adult physically restrain or remove the student if he or she acted out. I didn't resort to this power strategy since (a) I didn't think it was necessary, and (b) this strategy is in opposition to my core beliefs. In the absence of a "socially constructed order," especially with the nonconformists, kids will act quite naturally: by running, talking, fighting, and shouting—mostly at inappropriate times. Not surprisingly, without a clear set of rules (implicit and explicit) for behavior, the students will have no way to evaluate their behavior in a way that makes sense to the teacher. It is no wonder that my students thought that they actually behaved well during the trip!*

## October 21, 1998

I have heard students putting down other students, often from a distance, but I haven't been responding to this problem. In the rush to manage math and the rush to just keep students working on tasks, I again realize that I am ignoring the plethora of "penny ante" interpersonal problems that crop up in the course of the day. I think that the students may realize that I sometimes take a laissez-faire attitude toward this interpersonal dimension, and my stance may give some of them license to really act out. So I sit here now and plan how I can teach more proactively to reduce put-downs and then more actively respond when put-downs occur. If I let put-downs happen with impunity, the class is going to become unsafe very quickly for all students.

*Reflection: There are at least two dimensions of influence that are a focus of the working consensus between teacher and students. The first is the negotiation that goes on in establishing the rules for teacher–student relations. This includes how students and teachers talk to each other, how students and teachers respond to each other's initiatives, and so forth. The second dimension is student–student relations. In this area, the teacher strives to influence how kids treat each other and work together. However, I think that teachers have less power in influencing the definition of the situation among children than they do between the students and themselves.*

*Certainly, a teacher skilled at "building community" could effectively influence kids to be more interpersonally adept, responsible, kind, and caring. But when out of the purview of adults, kids are prone to exhibit their natural (and developmentally normal) behavior when interacting with peers, and teachers have relatively little control over student peer relations (Geer, 1971; Scott, 1990). Particularly with kids who have emotional/social issues that are unusually harsh, the likelihood of their appropriating the teacher's worldview when alone with peers on the playground, perhaps, is remote. Besides, even among kids who share the teacher's worldview, it is normal for them to behave like kids when the adult isn't around, which means they may act in a mean-spirited or aggressive way toward others. This is why recess duty is often an unpleasant experience for many teachers (and kids): the already fragile working consensus, operational in the classroom, regarding student–student relations is really lost in the absence of the mediating adult. Hence, recesses result in the inevitable rash of fights, tears, confusion, and friendship breakups, many of which land in the duty teacher's lap for adjudication.*

## November 6, 1998

During math, the power in the building went out, and so did the lights. The bathroom lights, especially, were intriguing for the kids, since the bathroom has no windows. Suddenly, *everyone* had bathroom emergencies. Everyone wanted to run to the bathroom or the darkened hallway. I foolishly tried to maintain an orderly, on-task math period. It was a struggle, and I let my stomach turn to knots. This is when I started dispensing "loss of recess" consequences on students who did not comply with my directives. Then, at the end of math, I learned that my "ace in the hole" was lost. I was going to show a Bill Nye video on flight, but the teacher next door hadn't been able to finish her video because of the power outage. Her aide came in and said, "Do you *really* need the video?" I knew that Eileen needed it as much as I did, so how could I take it from her? I didn't have a contingency plan for science, so I ended up giving the students a free choice time during this period.

*Reflection: Power alignments are situated in the immediate situation, which includes the architecture of spaces. The social–physical situation changed, but I persisted in my definition of the situation in viewing this as a learning situation: kids will continue working on their math. When the lights went out, the kids' definition changed radically: the building is dark and the bathroom is black . . . now, the task is to experience this change in the visual routine. I tried reasoning and cajoling to get kids to stay in their seats and get back to work. It didn't work, so I reverted to domination and explicit use of power through the imposition of loss of recess penalties. In retrospect, I should have respected the children's natural curiosity. By not modifying my definition of the situation, when the actual situation changed dramatically, I unnecessarily subjected myself to a cacophony of negative emotions, which worked effectively to ruin my day.*

*I also think that our definitions and power relations have an essential temporal dimension. How teachers think about situations has to be placed in some time context: end of day, beginning of day, before lunch, and so forth. I haven't sensibly defined the 2:00–2:35 p.m. time period. Obviously, the kids are tired, especially the first graders and low-attention students.*

## November 6, 1998

A difficult day. I got sucked into a power struggle with Donnie regarding his math assignments. The assignment was to write an original math problem, solve it, and then share it with a same-age peer. He said that he didn't want to do it since he had already done two math tasks. (In the math class, the general rule is that once kids have done two tasks, they can play a math game.) I argued that one of the tasks he claimed to have done was completed yesterday. He argued that he had done most of it today.

When he and I reached an impasse in the power struggle, I wasn't able to distance myself from the situation, so my behavior toward him was angry and histrionic. I need to distance myself from these problems and, instead, respond dispassionately—and with a pleasant face.

*Reflection: My negotiating strategy was an open one, in which I tried reasoning and logic. He also tried to use reasoning and logic with me, reflecting his nine-year-old framework for reason and logic. Neither of us was willing to compromise, so we were at an impasse. I was frus-*

*trated with my inability to resolve the problem using my preferred strategy (an open negotiating style fits my teaching self), so I responded with dark emotions. I used anger to intimidate the boy, but this didn't work. He simply withdrew and refused to talk. His response to my emotional outburst was a sane one, and one that I use in my everyday life. (If someone won't talk to me calmly, I often refuse to engage them in further discussion.) Donnie doesn't respect me as a teacher, so he doesn't care to do the negotiation necessary to forge a working consensus.*

*The problem in using force to engage him in a task that was creative and open ended is obvious: under this coercive condition, it is unlikely that he would perform the task with interest and with wholeheartedness, which is a fatal stance for the learner. When I gravitated to a more normative control strategy by attempting to reason with him, our dysfunctional relationship got in the way of a negotiated agreement.*

*A more fundamental problem was that the social alignment surrounding our relationship reduced the power I had with Donnie. The father was critical of me, and the son most likely picked up on this criticism. He knew his father and I were not allies, so I had little leverage in my control of this student. I had to find a counteralignment if I was going to have any success with this student (which is what I did later in the year by successfully enlisting the principal's power in managing the boy's behavior).*

## Teacher Hegemony

### November 6, 1998

I started using recess as a negative consequence of disruptive behavior. It worked. I'd hold up a clipboard, signaling that I was about to write down kids' names who had to stay in for recess. When students failed to respond to a warning, I would tap them quietly on the shoulder and then write their name on the clipboard. Today, it had a calming effect on behavior. I'll continue it for the time being. The trick in implementing this technique is to do it discreetly: don't embarrass the kids who stay in but, at the same time, make it clear that this consequence is going to be implemented.

*Reflection: I am resorting to domination and my adult power here to control students' behavior. I use recess as a bargaining chip in return for their compliance. It seems that I have unquestioned power to control the movement of their bodies, and my use of this power is well defined, direct, and effective! I tell students to stand up, line up, leave the room, sit in a particular chair, have them come to the classroom after lunch instead of outside for recess, and for the most part, they do it. This structural feature of teacher power is an unquestioned assumption for teachers and most students. However, my power to control their thinking and to have all (or most) students meet the benchmarks is utterly ill defined, indirect, and normative. It requires a complex and often fleeting alignment of the teacher's goals with the goals and interests of the students, parents, colleagues, the state, and of course available resources. The disconnect between the expectations that the state and the public have for teachers and the reality of classroom life makes me anxious.*

## March 16, 1999

A wild day. It's two days before spring vacation. I wasn't counting the days until today, which is a good sign of my emerging confidence and comfort with teaching. However, today was déjà vu to last September and early January. Wild!

This morning, Fran (the intern) asked Stevie to get off the floor and return to his seat. He ignored her as she repeated this directive three or four times. Dorothy got involved, and she finally took his arm to escort him out of the room. As she pulled his arm up, he turned and vomited all over her. Another occupational hazard. Getting puked on by a kid.

This afternoon, I had trouble getting Justin to return to his seat. He fell to the floor in a Ghandian pose of passive resistance. He sat almost in a Buddha position, with his head tilted down. I needed to get the rest of the class going, so I asked Fran to "get him out of the room." I didn't mean for her to pick him up, but she did. She grabbed him from behind by the armpits. His body froze, and he kept the Buddha pose. It looked quite funny as she carried him off. The class, which I was working ineffectively to calm down, burst out laughing at the sight of Fran, a tall pregnant woman, carrying off a little Buddha screaming like a siren on a desperate police car.

*Reflection: These two kids' definitions of the situation are so at variance with the teachers' definitions that the use of force and physical power by the teacher is the only recourse. Still, even given the small size of these kids and their inability to physically defend themselves from adults, they are able to express symbolic (and sometimes poetic) expressions of resistance.*

## March 31, 1999

I worked with the third graders in math today to prepare them for the state tests in ten days. The tests make me feel anxious. Early on, Donnie began to badger Bonnie about her intelligence, her wardrobe, her hair, etc. I asked Donnie to stop. He continued badgering Bonnie. I pulled Donnie to the side of the room for a private conversation.

"Is there something bugging you today?" I asked.

"I think it was my trip to ****. I'm still excited."

"You have to stop hurting Bonnie's feelings. If you don't stop, you'll have to leave the room," I said.

Donnie nodded, understanding. However, within a minute, he started harassing Bonnie again. I tersely directed Donnie to leave the room. He asked for a second chance. My voice got taut but it stayed even. "No, you need to go." He again appealed.

"Donnie, then go sit in the principal's office." He now relented and walked off back to the classroom. On his way out, he complained that I hadn't used my sense of humor in this situation and, therefore, I had handled it badly.

His comment is revealing. I wonder if each child requires a unique approach . . . to how we relate to them and how we "manage" them. In Donnie's case, he needs a humorous response when he needs to be redirected by the teacher. Since I figured this out in late January, I had been doing very well with him. Virtually no problems in two months. Today, I used an interpersonal tactic that was direct and unequivocal: I told him he was acting improperly and that he needed to leave the room. He was surprised by how I handled the situation. Still, as I have become more knowledgeable about my students, and I take the time to think as I respond to student issues, I am more effective when my response is customized to the child. There are some students whom I have not yet figured out.

*Reflection: In my working consensus with Donnie, we had constructed and used "rules" to govern our relationship, as I did in some way with all the students. I broke one of our interactional rules, and he drew it to my attention. Besides, the state tests had me on edge, so I was less patient and thoughtful in my work with Donnie.*

## Student Counterhegemony

### September 16, 1998

It sometimes feels as though Nathan is taking over the class. He is only eight years old, but his stubborn and volatile responses to teacher directions have me on the defensive. He gets emotional when he is asked to do something that he doesn't want to do. He'll storm around the room, raise his voice, pout, and sometimes cry. Today, when he started crying and running around the room, I followed him, asking sympathetically, "What are you feeling? What's the problem? What can we do about it?" I am taking a therapeutic approach with the kid, but this strategy just seems to give him license to simply continue his theatrical-hysterical behavior.

*Reflection: Nathan appears to be "taking over the class" because I am engaging him in open negotiations when he is a kid who doesn't have the interpersonal knowledge necessary to engage in open negotiations: he can't appreciate or recognize my position and is not willing to compromise. I failed to appropriately assess the situation, so it enabled counterhegemony by the student.*

*In the absence of a working consensus between students and teacher, order is achieved in one of two ways: domination or negotiation (Pollard, 1985). Martin (1976) found that teachers typically engaged in domination with students such as Nathan since these kids did not have the skills or psychological disposition to negotiate. But I wonder if I am again foolishly blaming the student for the breakdown. Perhaps it was the negotiated order (or disorder) among the participants that was at fault. Or maybe it had to do with the larger structural dilemma of having twenty-six high-needs kids in one room who tend to "play off" each other and engage in all sorts of interpersonal squabbles, sometimes intended to just disrupt the class and sometimes reflecting angry passions among the combatants. It is hard for me to unpack the reasons, exactly, that I am unable to engage in a more open-negotiations style with this kid.*

*Back to demands of the immediate situation, the strategy that I fell back on, essentially to expel students if they persist in disruptive behavior, relied on power and force. While this tactic violated my self-image as a teacher, I realized that my (personal) long-term goals as a teacher were seriously jeopardized if I didn't manage Nathan more effectively.*

## January 12, 1999

Bad day. I had an out-of-body experience. Donnie's got my number and I've got to put a stop to it.

An assembly was to begin in a few minutes. The kids were not listening to directions. I lost my temper. I didn't shout at them, but my voice was tense, my pitch was a bit higher, and it was obvious that I was angry.

Donnie called out, in full voice, "You are shouting at us, and I don't think that kids should be shouted at. We don't deserve this, and you shouldn't do it. No one likes it, and stop it right now!" I looked around the room, and I noticed that kids didn't seem to be paying any attention to his comments. I ignored him and carried on with the lesson.

I was mortified. I agreed with everything he said. I need to control my emotions and simply not allow any more outbursts. On the other hand, his act of defiance was a challenge to my authority. Given the plethora of behavioral issues in the class, I needed to maintain the authority to direct kids without their having any license to question my authority. His comment clearly suggested that he has power, and I sensed that the other kids realized that he has power that they don't have.

He is smart, his father doesn't like me, and he knows that I don't have much leverage with him or the father. I can't make any mistakes

with him. I need to respond to his obnoxious or disrespectful statements head on and rationally. I can't lose my cool with him, particularly since he thinks he can manipulate my emotions by his actions.
He has already admitted that he enjoys pushing my buttons.

*Reflection: I had to suppress many dark emotions here. I was made
scared and anxious by Donnie's comments. I kept an expressionless face
and voice as I continued with the lesson. Donnie's comments were especially painful because they described my own sense of guilt and discomfort about my conduct as a teacher. I always feel badly after I show
anger, although Barbara affirmed my outbursts by saying, "Well, this is
what they are used to at home." Anger does not fit into my image as a
teacher, nor do I think that this reaction was educational for the kids.
Still, most teachers would defend the occasional use of anger to control
children. I'm not sure. However, the reality of teaching is that teachers
do become angry. In any relationship, anger is a natural emotional response. I suspect that suppressing this emotion is probably unhealthy for
the teacher. Anger is part of our everyday lives. Why shouldn't it be part
of the teacher–student relationship? Of course, the teacher needs to show
anger in a way that is in the best interest of children's psychological and
social well-being.*

*The essential issue here, however, is the counterhegemony exercised
by Donnie. Because of my own passivity in our relationship, his intel-
lectual/emotional autonomy, and the support he had from his father, he
wielded power and, in effect, threatened my authority status with the
other students.*

## DISCUSSION AND IMPLICATIONS

I returned to the classroom with a slightly romantic conception of student–teacher relations, not unlike how many beginning teachers enter their
first full-time student teaching experience. After years of reading the *unproblematic* literature in readers and writers workshops (e.g., Atwell, 1987;
Graves, 1983), it was easy to become lulled into thinking that curriculum is
the *central* factor in how students behave. As a language arts educator, I am
familiar with the Heinemann catalogue, which is dominated by books for

teachers that promote important ideas such as teacher–student collaboration, cooperation, co-construction of curriculum, and inquiry-based classrooms. In fact, most of my early research presented student-centered ideas about the teaching of mathematics (e.g., Winograd & Higgins, 1994) with a similarly unproblematic and tacit assumption: if the curriculum draws on student interest, oppositional behavior by students will disappear, or at least it will be a minor phenomenon in the classroom.

Interesting curricular experience is certainly one condition for student engagement and learning. In terms of curriculum, the quintessential task for me as teacher is to conceptualize academic tasks in ways that have multiple entry points for students to find personal and cognitive meaning. Teachers need to design curricular structures that intentionally incorporate students' voices. Otherwise, students will engage in resistance to the teacher's agenda, which then requires more negotiation by both parties. The more consensus that teachers and students can achieve, the less time is wasted and the fewer compromises are struck in the negotiation process. Woods (1984) suggests that the most meaningful activities for students are those that reflect the students' culture, "in keeping with the private sphere" (234), for example, activities such as child care, social crafts, sports, and games. Still, as Dudley-Marling (1997) and Dyson (1993) point out, students always will find spaces within the official curriculum in order to express their identities, whether or not teachers facilitate this.

Strauss (1978) argues that negotiation is essential to social order, and I would argue similarly that negotiation is essential to social order in classrooms. The nature of negotiation that marks teacher–student relations is complex, and any model or scheme for successfully negotiating with students is fraught with caveats. There are many factors that influence the negotiative process and product, factors that reflect an interaction of both micro- and macropolitical factors. The microfactors include the personality of the teacher and students; the teacher's understanding of students; teacher's confidence and ability to articulate (to students) his or her own definition of the classroom culture; the willingness or ability of students to make sense or agree with teacher's reality; and the teacher's and students' willingness or ability to see the other's point of view.

For me, this study makes explicit the notion that students do wield power when, for example, the teacher is a novice (as I was) and has not yet clearly articulated his vision for the classroom culture, or the teacher does not have parental support (as I didn't) and the students are sensitive to this parental cynicism about the school or the teacher. Occasionally, there were "binary ruptures" in my class, as in the case of Donnie (January 12) and Nathan (September 16) or the day we went to the library (October 21). In the cases of Donnie and Nathan, these children had very dominant personalities and were unafraid of confrontation with a more powerful other, especially when they knew that they had alliances (with parents) that blunted the power of the school to affect their behavior. However, most student resistance was of a disguised and relatively passive nature, which included quintessential student behaviors such as social talk during work time and ignoring teacher directives. This passive behavior is quite "rational," since most students, as members of a subordinate group, would not even entertain the idea of open rebellion, since they do not have the structural support or alliances to make this happen (cf. Scott, 1990).

But in a powerful way, factors external to the teacher–student interaction also influence the nature and outcome of negotiations. These larger structural macrofactors include the demands made on teachers from the outside, such as by the state legislature or a school district; state-imposed curricular and assessment structures; the number of students that teachers need to manage in classrooms; the presence of allies for teachers, including special educator resources and parents; and the socioeconomic and emotional health of the students in the teacher's classroom. Class size, in particular, poses dire consequences for teacher–student relations. Large class size is rooted in the long history of public education as a way to educate large numbers of working-class children cheaply (Hogan, 1989). Bearing some similarity to the Lancastrian classrooms of nineteenth-century England (Hogan, 1989), large classes of today mean that teachers need to standardize curriculum, reduce student movement and initiative, and keep things quiet. Obviously, as class size goes up, the number of negotiative conversations with students also increases. The outcome of this intensification of work for teachers is that it leaves them no time or psychic space to engage in critical analysis of their working conditions, to engage in meaningful collaborations with parents and peers, and to engage in organized political activity (e.g., see *Rethinking Schools* journal). Large classes, increased expectations for schools, reduced budgets, and the concomitant negotiation that permeates teacher–student relations makes it a truly Herculean task for teachers to simply help students learn what the state has mandated. And the state *is* watching.

Obviously, the skilled and caring teacher can more effectively manage the competing and contradictory forces that interact with teacher–student relations. Many teachers are able to construct spaces within the official curriculum that are safe and interesting to students (Calkins, 1986; Dyson, 1993). However, even in the student-centered spaces of the whole-language classroom, student resistance and miseducative behavior do occur and are probably inevitable (Lensmire, 1994). Student resistance and the negotiative demands on teachers is an inevitability even in the best of teaching situations. However, it is the macrostructural forces that make the negotiative demand on teachers increasingly wearing. The demands of teaching large groups of students, in a compulsory system of education, with curricular mandates generated by a state legislature along with rigorous time deadlines and the pressures of testing, make it virtually impossible to meet the individual needs of all or most students. Inevitably, in most classrooms at most times, there will be students who are disaffected, bored, resistant, or outwardly rebellious. It is important to note that the data from my journal show that I was increasingly able to negotiate a working consensus as the year wore on into the spring, and that instances of power struggle decreased. Still, the negotiative dimension in my relations with students was inexorable and constant.

There are several lessons in this study that I can now bring to my work as a teacher educator. These implications are especially apropos for my work with beginning teachers.

1. With preservice teachers, I have begun to examine the negotiative dimensions of teaching and the factors that influence its nature and direction. New teachers are well served to engage in the explicit study of the negotiative dimension of teaching, so when it inevitably happens in their first years in the classroom, they have conceptual handles to make sense of and learn from this experience. Especially for beginning teachers, power does circulate more freely between their students and them. Beginning teachers are particularly vulnerable to power struggles and the other types of pseudo-concord described in this chapter, and especially the (sometimes unintentional) sharing of power with students and the negotiation that goes along with it. These experiences can depress the

personal satisfaction of beginning teachers to the point that they leave the profession prematurely. In teacher education, the study of the negotiative and power dimensions of teacher–student relations is warranted.

2. I have become more tentative in my presentation of methods to preservice teachers. When presenting methods, I need to raise both the micro- and macropolitical difficulties of these methods, such as the inevitability of student opposition to any curricular experience, even so-called student-centered curriculum; the problem of doing more authentic forms of assessment with huge numbers of students; or the use of democratic approaches to classroom management when faced with large numbers of special needs students. I now also explicitly raise the dilemmas of meeting the needs of individual students when faced with large class sizes, and the challenges presented by students who are understandably bored, underchallenged, or overchallenged. The presentation of teaching methods ought to recognize and even embed the reality of student opposition and resistance, so preservice teachers can early on in their education learn to develop the dispositional trait of flexibility as part of their teacher identity.

3. There tends to be a certain fatalism that spending on public education will never be what it ought to be and that class sizes in public schools will never be what they are in many private schools. Notions about class size were constructed early in the history of public education, and having classrooms with twenty to thirty students is now taken for granted by most teachers and the public. I believe teacher education ought to spend more time with preservice teachers unpacking the origins of class size and its implications for curriculum and teaching (e.g., how large classes pressure teachers to standardize the curriculum and reduce time available for teacher reflection). An understanding of the historic and economic reasons for class size can only support teachers' ability to critique school funding policy and, perhaps, enhance teachers' capacity for or interest in participating in the political process. Certainly, reducing class sizes would ameliorate the negotiative demands on teachers and, hopefully, support more consensual relations between teachers and students.

# 3

# THE FUNCTIONS OF TEACHER EMOTIONS: THE GOOD, THE BAD, AND THE UGLY

An interesting dimension of my return as an elementary teacher related to my emotional response to my work with students, colleagues, and parents. Not surprisingly, I found that teaching was a profoundly, all encompassing *emotional* endeavor. Just as in emotional life outside school, I emoted it all as a teacher: guilt, joy, embarrassment, sadness, anxiety, depression, satisfaction, and anger. Because I kept a daily journal throughout the year, I was certainly more aware of emotional responses to my work than I would have been if I had not done this self-study.

The topic of emotional labor has been an important topic in sociology for some time (e.g., Hochschild, 1983), and recently it has received more attention in the educational literature (Connell, 1985; Hargreaves, 1994a, 1994b, 1998; Kelchtermans, 1996; Nias, 1989, 1996). This chapter explores the emotional dimensions of teaching from feminist and sociological perspectives. I will show how I engaged in both functional and dysfunctional uses of emotion in my teaching. The functional uses of emotion tended to alert me to problems in my work, which is the first step in my effectively taking action to address those problems. The dysfunctional uses of emotion reflected situations in which my emotions (especially dark emotions such as anger and disgust) did not lead to positive action but, instead, led to the blaming of self, students, parents, or the system.

My interpretation of the data reflects a feminist perspective that considers the public school to be a gendered institution (Boler, 1999). Because most elementary teachers are women, cultural expectations of women tend to become normalized in elementary school culture, and these expectations carry over to the men who work there. The rules for emotion inhibit the free expression of emotion, particularly anger expressions that might be aimed at hierarchical/patriarchal structural arrangements or at larger economic and political structures. In this case, emotions are what Boler (1999) calls sites of social control, in which the culture of elementary teaching tends to suppress the free expression of anger, which in turn inhibits teachers' potential to critique their working conditions and then work to effect social change.

In my recent teaching experience, I found myself suppressing much emotion, reflecting the feeling rules of the elementary school, by engaging in "emotional labor" (Hochschild, 1983). For much of the time, I worked at suppressing or changing my emotional response to teaching problems. I also experienced feelings of inadequacy when experiencing other emotions, such as embarrassment, shame, and guilt. I suggest that the self-accusatory stance of teachers diverts teachers' attention from structural problems in their working conditions and, instead, focuses attention on the inadequacies of teachers as individuals. Furthermore, I argue that it is from the collective naming and examination of emotions that teachers may be able to learn to accept and understand the darker emotions of teaching, to understand the relationship between emotions and social structure, as well as learn to use these emotions as catalysts for social activism and change.

## CONCEPTUAL FRAMEWORK

### What Are Emotions and Why Do We Have Them?

Kemper (1978) defines emotion as "a relatively short-term evaluative response essentially positive or negative involving distinct somatic (and often cognitive) components" (47). "Somatic" refers to bodily changes that result from emotions, such as increased blood pressure, breathing, and pulse; bodily flush; and perspiration. The cognitive component of emotion refers to one's actual verbal reflection that identifies the emotion, such as when one thinks or says, "I am happy. . . ."

There are two fundamental ways of looking at the origin of emotions. A traditional view, reflected in the work of Darwin and Freud, conceptualizes emotions as rooted in or driven by our biology (i.e., instinct) or psychology. From this perspective, emotions basically exist in our biology or psyche independent of social situations. Social or environmental factors set off biological reactions that lead to an emotional response.

A second perspective on emotions considers the interaction of the person and the environment. The emotional response, then, reflects the individual's personality and motivations, as well as the social structure and culture (Lazarus, 1991, 2001). Lazarus's view of emotions (1999, 2001) attributes agency to individuals who are constantly making appraisals based on their goals for the activity, including decisions on how to cope with and behave emotionally in different situations. Although social structure, culture, and roles play a part in Lazarus's theory, these factors are more prominent in other theories in social psychology and sociology on emotions (e.g., Goffman, 1959; Hochschild, 1983; Kemper, 1978). From this perspective, social factors have a significant effect on how people develop, manage, and show emotions. Gerth and Mills (1953) maintain that institutions and emotions are inextricably linked. In large part, the emotions that people use reflect the needs of institutions and the roles that people serve in those institutions. Although social interactionists recognize the biological and psychological origins of emotion, they give weight to the social: "Social factors enter not simply before and after but interactively during the expression of emotion" (Hochschild, 1983, 211).

From a social-interactionist perspective, expressions of emotion serve to defend social norms and beliefs. Armon-Jones (1986) believes that emotions have a sociofunctional purpose. Emotions are "functional in that they are constituted and prescribed in such a way as to sustain and endorse systems of belief and value" (Armon-Jones, 1986, 57). Reflecting the idea that emotion and personality reflect social structure and role, Sarbin (1986) maintains that emotions and how we respond emotionally are "tied to values, to conditions that involve one's identity" (91).

# A Feminist Perspective on Emotions

Feminist perspectives, like other social interactionist theories, consider emotions to be a social construction, and one's experience and display of emotions reflects the totality of a person's experience, which includes organizational culture, gender, race, class, education, and personality. Although not ignoring or discounting the possibility that women and men have emotions that are biologically based on their sex, feminists focus instead on questions of how the experience and display of emotion may be a site of social control *or* a site of political transformation, and on how emotions may serve to maintain the status quo of dominant patriarchal, hierarchical capitalist systems *or* be used to disrupt these systems. Harrison (1985), for example, argues that anger can be a vehicle for social change:

> All serious human moral activity, especially activity for social change, takes its bearings from the rising power of human anger. Anger can be a signal that change is called for, that transformation in relationships is required. (15)

Jaggar (1989) termed *outlaw emotions* to be unconventionally unacceptable emotions. Like Boler (1999) and Campbell (1994), she found a strong relationship between emotions and power:

> [Outlaw emotions] may provide the first indications that something is wrong with the way alleged facts have been construed, with accepted understandings of how things are.... Only when we reflect on our initial puzzling, irritability, revulsion, anger, or fear may we bring to consciousness our "gut level" awareness that we are in a situation of coercion, cruelty, injustice, or danger. (Jaggar, 1989, 161)

Jaggar maintains that outlaw emotions can lead to change only when feminists (women and men) share their experience, by naming this experience as particularly cruel, unjust, and so on and then by forming alternative subcultures within the dominant (male) stream. When outlaw emotions are the expression of a collective, then these emotions may be "politically and epistemologically subversive" (160). Barrows (1996) defines "outrage" as anger that "takes a leap into the arena of injustice" (53). She also argues that anger, fully realized, can lead to action, resistance, and social change.

Campbell (1994) notes that the association of women with feelings has been the "long-standing historical ground on which to dismiss women" (49). Although women's sentimentality is seen as virtuous in the private sphere, the expression of emotion in the public sphere (i.e., the workplace) is seen as a defect in character and as a reason to not take them seriously. According to Campbell (1994), the dilemma for women is that if they do not show emotion, they are viewed as cold; however, when they do display emotions, women may be characterized "as out of control." Women's free expression of emotion (such as anger and impatience) in the public sphere, then, is often considered inappropriate by the male stream.

Organizations tend to reflect hierarchical and bureaucratic systems that value rationality and dispassionate discourse and, in effect, marginalize the free expression of emotion (Ferguson, 1984). Open displays of emotions in modern organizations, in general, emphasize rationality over emotionality. "The prevailing view of emotions in organizations . . . is rooted in a 'myth of rationality'" (Putnam & Mumby, 1997, 36), in which rationality is good and emotionality is bad. "Bureaucracy is intertwined with the system of dualisms that privileges rationality and marginalizes emotional experience" (41).

Certainly, schools are organizations, and they reflect organizational culture regarding its rules for the expression of emotion. Schools as a gendered culture, dominated by women, also inform the rules here for emotions. The rules for the expression of emotion for female elementary teachers historically have reflected expectations that women show emotional restraint and self-control (Boler, 1999; Grumet, 1988; Weiler, 1988). The ideal of womanhood in the nineteenth century exemplified the notion of woman as self-sacrificing, restrained, morally upright, and uncomplaining. Female teachers were supposed to express the image of the ideal woman (nurturing, restrained, patient) in their work with children. At the same time, they were expected to conform to the expectations of the emerging school bureaucracy, with its demands for rationality and the control of students and teachers (Boler, 1999). The ideal woman was well suited for classroom teaching and the needs of society to domesticate and socialize the impulses of the new immigrant populations, particularly in the cities, as well as the need of the system to control teachers. For teachers in this situation, there are two contradictions. The first is what Rousmaniere (1994) called "the idealized image of the gentle, nurturing teacher, and the realities of the cold and confusing working conditions of city schools" (49). Teachers needed to be both nurturing and caring but, at the same time, strict and in charge of oftentimes large and unruly classes of children. The second contradiction is that, though they needed to dominate the will of their twenty to thirty students, female teachers also needed to be acquiescent to principals and supervisors, at least to their faces:

> The cult of maternal nurturance prohibited those who stayed behind the desk from confessing their rage, frustration, and disappointment to each other. The moralistic and impossible demand that women, without expressing anger or aggression, control children who were resisting a tightly repressive and tedious regime encouraged teachers to confuse the logical consequences of these harsh conditions for the failure of their own discipline, intelligence, and inspiration. (Grumet, 1988, 52)

Conway (1987) noted the economic and patriarchal reasons that women were recruited for teaching beginning in the late nineteenth century. With large numbers of students due to compulsory education, public education became expensive, and women were a cheap form of labor. The relation between the needs of teaching and some idealized notions of women also were raised, since women typically are considered more nurturing and caring than men. However, "some of the arguments used for opening up teaching to women were at the expense of reproducing ideological elements that had been part of the root causes of patriarchal control in the first place" (Apple, 1989, 63; also see Boler, 1999). Women tend to be viewed as more self-restrained, patient, nonaggressive, caring, nurturing, and passive, and these traits tend to be considered as virtuous in a teacher. However, these discourses led to the control of women's emotions and enhanced their status as subordinate in patriarchal culture.

> Women's "natural" skills in teaching moral virtues reflect on the increasing modes of pastoral care. Women are conscripted as the agents of this power: required to enforce patriarchal values and laws, to instill virtues which are gendered. Not only do women assist in strategies of individualization, urging children to self-control, they also participate in their own subjugation by reinforcing the control of emotions and gendered rules of emotions. (Boler, 1999, 40)

It is important to note, particularly since I am a man, that male elementary teachers are privileged by their gender position to express outlaw emotions more freely than women (Williams, 1993). However, given the dominance of elementary school faculty by women and the historical position of women in society and organizations, the culture of elementary schools and the rules for emotional expression tend to apply to both male and female teachers. As a male teacher, I felt subject to many of the same rules for my display of emotion as my colleagues, most of whom were women. Later in this chapter, I suggest that the suppression of emotion leads to the subversion of professional communities for teachers (Harrison, 1985). This results in the maintenance of a politically conservative position by teachers as it relates to the control of curriculum and school budgets.

## Feeling Rules and Emotional Labor

There are certain feeling rules, historically determined and locally redefined, that influence how teachers experience as well as display emotion. When teachers do not display or feel emotions that they are *supposed* to have, they do what is known as emotional labor or emotion work. Hochschild (1983) developed the idea of "emotional labor," which is the work of inhibiting, generating, or displaying an emotion to elicit an emotional response in someone else. Hochschild proposed three criteria for work that requires emotional labor. First, it requires face-to-face contact with the public; second, it requires that the worker produce an emotional state in another person; and third, there is a degree of external control over the emotional labor of the employee.

Teaching obviously fulfills the first two criteria. The third criterion for teachers, external control, comes in the form of cultural expectations. The external control for teachers is usually subtle and indirect. The profession does have generalized notions about how teachers, good teachers, emote. For teachers, however, the rules about emotional behavior are reflected in particular schools as well as the general culture of teaching. For example, teachers generally are supposed to enjoy children, enjoy their work, maintain a patient and kind front, become angry with children infrequently, and so on. These rules are not necessarily taught formally to teachers, but they are collaboratively constructed in the everyday work of teachers, students, principals, parents, and teacher educators.

Hochschild (1983) goes on to distinguish two types of emotional display, surface acting and deep acting. In deep acting, the person gets into the role, almost like method actors, and there is no disconnect between their outward appearance and generally how they feel. When doing deep acting, emotions don't just happen. Rather, the actor has actively manipulated her mind. For example, a teacher who is grumpy just before school may purposefully remember wonderful past images of her students, her reasons for going into teaching, and her love of her students. Through this purposeful "exhorting (of) feeling" or making use of her imagination, the teacher is able to both appear and feel happy when the students come through the door. This is deep acting. Hochschild identified two strategies for doing deep acting: by using a trained imagination (e.g., method acting) and by exhorting one's self to reframe an emotion. (This is similar to what Lazarus, 2001, termed "emotion-focused coping.") Ashforth (1993) pointed out a third way: when the person feels the "genuine experience and expression of the expected emotion" (94). In this last case, the teacher has internalized the emotion rules of a particular culture and situation, and she actually feels what the situation dictates.

However, if the teacher is unable to draw on imagery or experience to exhort feeling that is appropriate to the situation, then she may simply look the part without the accompanying feeling. The surface effects associated with emotions, such as smiling, frowning, sighing, and laughing, are a put-on and do not reflect how the individual is really feeling. Hochschild warns of the dangers of surface acting: it can lead to alienation between our working lives and our more natural selves. We become alienated from the part of ourselves that does the work.

I view emotional labor as an act of impression management because the person tries to form behavior "towards others in order to foster both certain social perceptions of himself or herself and a certain interpersonal climate" (Ashforth, 1993, 90; also Goffman, 1959). Instead of being simply an alienating experience, emotional labor can be a satisfying or even liberating experience, since it can lead the worker to enhance his involvement in activity that is fundamentally meaningful and satisfying. For example, Yanay and Shahar (1998) found that the emotional labor in a therapeutic setting led to increased empathy and caring by the therapist. In a study of food market clerks, Tolich (1993) distinguished emotional labor regulated by another person, such as an employer or supervisor, from emotional labor that is regulated by the worker. Tolich maintained that emotional labor led to deeper feelings of satisfaction regarding work when the emotion work was controlled by the employee. Rafaeli and Sutton (1987) similarly distinguished faking in good faith and faking in bad faith. When doing emotional labor in bad faith, the worker does not entirely agree that the emotion ought to be part of the job, and he or she has not internalized the feeling rules for that role. When doing emotional labor in good faith, the worker agrees that the emotion ought to be part of the job, and he or she has internalized those feeling rules.

It appears that the effects of emotional labor are significantly mediated by the individual's personal or social identity: the more the norms or values inherent in the work role have been internalized by the worker, the more likely emotional labor will lead to a sense of personal well-being (Ashforth, 1993). Emotional labor can become dysfunctional in at least two ways: when the expectation of a particular emotion display cannot happen because of a structural constraint (due to physical or resource limitations) and when the worker simply does not feel the emotions that the situation requires be displayed. Dysfunctional emotional labor can lead to work-related maladjustment, such as depression, poor self-concept, anxiety, despair, and alienation.

## A NOTE ABOUT RESEARCH METHOD

For this self-study, I initiated data analysis by reading each journal entry and coding each entry in which I explicitly made a (cognitive) reference to an emotion (e.g., I am angry or I feel good). My research questions emerged during the initial analysis, as I noticed the enormity and range of my emotional response to teaching, and then during my reading of the research literature on emotions and feminist theory. I was intrigued with how I managed to negotiate the emotional landscapes of my work; this led me to questions related to emotion rules, the functions and dysfunctions of emotions, and strategies for emotion management. These questions guided the analysis and categorization of the data. For example, following Armon-Jones's idea (1986) that emotions can effectively alert us to problems, I searched the data for incidents when an emotional expression was followed by an action plan to address the problem that precipitated the emotion. Following Hochschild's work (1983) on feeling rules, I searched the data for self-talk that suggested how I ought to emote, particularly if I wanted to be successful or effective. I also used emotional labor as a heuristic with which to search journal entries that reflected conscious behavior aimed at changing my emotional state (deep or surface) in accordance with the feeling rules in the school. The specific research questions follow:

1. What are the feeling rules that govern teachers' emotions?
2. What is the nature of teachers' emotional labor as they work to accommodate their emotions to the feeling rules of a school?
3. How are teachers' emotions functional, or useful, in their everyday work?
4. How are teachers' emotions dysfunctional in their everyday work?

The emotion categories presented in the next section are not comprehensive or exhaustive representations of my emotional experience. There are other categories of emotion that I do not display in this report, such as joy and satisfaction. I certainly experienced much joy in my teaching, but I tended to write more about the dark emotions in my journal. By focusing on the dark emotions, I employ a type of purposeful sampling that Patton (1980) calls intensity sampling, an approach that focuses on cases that are especially rich in information. Furthermore, the study is bounded as a self-study of the emotions of a middle-aged, Euro-American male who, although he had been in the field of teaching for twenty years, was once again a "novice teacher" who had not done everyday elementary classroom teaching since 1985. Finally, it is worth acknowledging that the representations of emotions, in my journal and here in this study, are undeniably partial because the written reflections in the journal only describe a small portion of my emotional life, and my selection of particular emotional experience to write about (in the journal) was done in a natural and unsystematic manner. It was not until I completed the sabbatical year and the journal that I decided to study this particular topic.

## RESULTS

My emotional life as a teacher can be characterized as functional and dysfunctional. It was functional when my emotions alerted me to teaching problems. I was also fairly skilled at using strategies to modify my emotional display or experience as feeling rules of the situation suggested. My emotions were dysfunctional when I appeared to psychologize my emotions, by experiencing them as individual phenomena and not as expressions of the sociopolitical context. The emotions described in this chapter often were expressions of self-flagellation, blaming of students and families, or resignation regarding the nature of teachers' work.

This section examines four dimensions of teacher emotions, and the display of data describes four central observations.

1. There are rules that guide teachers' emotional behavior in schools.
2. Teachers do emotion work, or emotional labor, in response to these emotion rules.
3. Teachers experience emotions that have functional outcomes; that is, the emotions alert teachers to problems in their work and then action to address those problems.
4. Teachers experience emotions that have dysfunctional outcomes; that is, the emotions lead to self-accusatory behavior by the teachers, or they lead to the blaming of others, such as students, parents, or administrators.

### Feeling Rules for Me as a Teacher

Five feeling rules are reflected in the analysis of the data. These rules are:

1. Teachers have affection and even love for their students.
2. Teachers show enthusiasm for subject matter as well as for students.
3. Teachers avoid overt displays of extreme emotions, especially anger and other dark emotions. They stay calm and tend to avoid displays of joy or sadness.
4. Teachers love their work.

5. Teachers have a sense of humor and laugh at their own mistakes as well as the peccadilloes of students.

*Rule one*: Teachers have affection and even love for their students.

In my journal, I point to at least two justifications for this rule. The first is instrumental: if the students like the teacher and vice versa, both teachers and students will work harder.

Certainly, teachers who like or even love their students will respond to student deviance with a greater caring for the long-term well being of the student. Perhaps this personal affection will give the teacher the psychic will to engage the student in the lengthy task of working through problems and the sources of the misbehavior. (February 5, 1999)

A second reason for the affection between teacher and students is that it satisfies what I believe is a natural need to be around people who like each other. I, like most teachers, chose teaching because I like being around young people, and in some way, warm relations with students nurture my sense of self.

One dimension of my work that sustains me is my relationship with the students. We genuinely like each other. I really enjoy talking to them and being with them. Some kids clap when I enter the room. I get many hugs. I just read a study that examined kids' perceptions of the "good teacher." The data pointed to the interpersonal dimension of the teacher–student relationship. Kids said that good teachers care for kids, have a sense of humor, treat kids fairly, don't lose their temper, etc. In spite of my struggle to implement an academic curriculum, and in spite of my struggle to help them control their social behavior, I recognize the imperative of a caring and easygoing persona for me as teacher. (December 16, 1998)

*Rule two*: Teachers have enthusiasm for subject matter and students.

Early in the year, I worried because I was not feeling enthusiasm about students in a way that I felt I was supposed to. I began developing a "theory of teacher dispositions," which recognized the importance of teacher enthusiasm for both subject matter and students.

As I wake up each morning and feel an emotional response to getting out of bed, and as I feel the butterflies at 12:15 as the kids are about to rush in, I wonder about how I *should* feel. I suppose I should, instead, be excited and happy to see the kids. I worry a bit now, since I don't have a whole lot of positive feelings at 12:15.

I think that a so-called good teacher has a particular disposition about the task of teaching and the work with youngsters. There might be a dispositional component with the following criteria:

- wholeheartedly enjoys working with young people,
- desires to effect the intellectual and social development of young people,
- and looks forward to most days in the classroom as an opportunity to help young people further their development and learning. (September 16, 1998)

Part of my theory of the "good teacher" has to do with teaching with passion. In order to do this, the teacher needs to feel some passion for the subject matter (along with care for students). It is crucial that we teach subjects and topics about which we feel great interest. (December 10, 1998)

*Rule three*: Teachers avoid overt displays of extreme emotions, especially anger and other dark emotions.

Teachers almost always stay calm, and their use of darker emotions (such as anger) is occasional and tactical. In the next excerpt, I give a student teacher directions on how to emote when disciplining students.

I said, "Just give them a choice: to comply or leave the group. Be very matter of fact about it. Don't get explicitly emotional. Calmly give them the choice. Say 'thank you' and walk away. This strategy tends to work for me. It is simple and effective." (December 7, 1999)

Repeatedly in my journal, I write about the importance of staying calm and maintaining emotional distance, particularly when faced with student insubordination. With certain students, the calm demeanor sometimes did not work, so when I resorted to more histrionic displays of emotion, particularly anger, I was uneasy.

I lost my cool for about five minutes, and for this I feel guilty. I don't want to treat students in this way. I have other strategies for dealing with chaos, but for some reason I let my anger take over. . . . I know that some teachers might applaud the occasional use of explicit anger to control students. I don't. I want my students to behave in a civil manner because they care about having a respectful community and because they care about themselves as self-respecting people. (March 3, 1999)

When I tell Nathan to leave the room with an aggressive voice, he goes. However, recently, if I am calm and affectless, he doesn't listen to me. I hate using the aggressive voice, but it works. (May 19, 1999)

It is not uncommon for teachers to use anger to resolve interpersonal conflicts with students or regain control of the class. While generally a violation of the rule, extreme emotion such as anger is tolerated if it is used only occasionally and in a way that makes sense to the participants. Especially if one is simply *acting* angry (i.e., not actually feeling this way) and the anger display is short and planned, the use of anger is only a mild deviation from the rule.

I was tired and wasn't responding decisively to the chatter, so Barbara called out in a no-nonsense manner, "All right, everybody. That's enough talking!" I then proceeded to threaten individual kids with a loss of recess if they talked when I was talking. I looked and talked as though I was really angry (I wasn't), and they really responded. It was so quiet you could hear a pin drop. Barbara said that's how many of the kids are treated at home, so this ad hoc tough-guy strategy is a management approach with which students are familiar and responsive. (November 4, 1998)

It is interesting how, as Barbara does in this excerpt, we find justifications or rationalizations for behavior that is at variance with our self-conceptions.

In the following situation, my use of anger was not particularly effective. However, I was able to make sense of and empathize with the student's resistance to my anger strategy.

I used anger to intimidate the boy, but this didn't work. He simply refused to talk. His response to my emotional outburst was a sane one, and one that I use in my everyday life. (If someone won't talk to me calmly, I often refuse to engage them in further discussion.) (November 6, 1998)

*Rule four*: Teachers love their work.

This rule is part of the corporate identity (Nias, 1989) of teachers. We commonly see references to this on bumper stickers and elsewhere in the

United States. Even if teachers do not truly love their work, there seems to be an expectation that they at least like their work. I worried throughout the year when I was not loving or even liking the work.

Part of the corporate identity of teaching is that "teaching is fun." I think this idea derives from the original motivation of many teachers to go into teaching because they "love working with kids." Implicit in loving what one does is the notion that "fun" will follow. I wonder if a more broad, more complex description of teaching is in order . . . such as teaching is fun and enjoyable at times, onerous and excruciating at other times, and just tolerable at other times. . . .

Certainly, to maintain a creative and effective role as teacher, it is important that the teacher experience a majority of the time as enjoyable and, yes, fun. So I suppose a more realistic expectation is that this work is (or can be) "fun" but, at the same time, there is space in our heads that acknowledges that much of our work life may be unambiguously dismal. And the times that we feel pessimistic or dark about our work will vary and will be highly unpredictable (we may have a difficult class one year, or several difficult children who drive us crazy; we may be experiencing serious stress in our personal lives; and the time of day, week, or year may signal different pressures on our evenness of mind). (September 3, 1998)

I'm not sure right now if I have the dispositional "knowledge" to be a teacher. When people see me in the school or around town, they often ask me something like, "are you just loving it?" or "don't you just love being with the kids?" Right now, I am not "loving it," nor do I want to go to work. It's just too hard right now. (September 16, 1998)

*Rule five*: Teachers have a sense of humor and can laugh at themselves and the peccadilloes of students.

I sense that humor is an essential part of the teaching repertoire, particularly in holding students' attention.

I'm not deluding myself into thinking that all the kids are cognitively attending to me. Often, they are just appearing to attend by the direction of their eye gaze. However, when the room is quiet as I talk and I have the impression of attentiveness, I feel more at ease and able to use humor. The use of humor and, in general, the expression of my personal self (warm, friendly, funny) allows for a bit of role distance, which then can effectively promote students' cognitive engagement. When I am more human, I find that students are more inclined to connect with my interests. The catch is that many students interpret my use of humor as an invitation to become silly and out of control. (February 3, 1999)

## Strategies for Following Emotion Rules

A persistent and perplexing challenge for me was managing the tension between my felt emotions (how I really felt inside) and the "rules" for how I was supposed to feel. In response to my understanding of the feeling rules, I used three strategies to *change* my actual felt emotional experience. Reflecting what Hochschild (1983) called *deep acting*, these three strategies included the following: physical manipulation of my body, self-exhortation, and cognitive heuristics, or reframing. These strategies tended to result in changing my actual felt emotion, so I was able to feel what I was supposed to feel, according to the emotion rules for teaching.

I also engaged in what Hochschild called "surface acting," which is when I only show, or display, a particular emotion without actually feeling that emotion. I present data that illustrate two surface-acting strategies: faking it and rationalizations.

The first strategy I employed to change my emotional state (i.e., deep acting) was physical manipulation. I did this in two ways: by increasing my actual physical movements (smiling, laughing, moving around, and animation) and by initiating affectionate physical encounters with the students (e.g., hugs).

I am continuously walking around the room, monitoring students, cajoling, encouraging, redirecting, threatening, raising my voice, lowering my voice, gesticulating with arms and legs and head, etc., etc. I need to be able to project my voice so everyone can hear me. And my voice needs to be animated and provocative so the kids will be more inclined to tune in to my messages. (November 4, 1998)

As difficult a time as I am having, it is crucial that I'm upbeat and happy with the students, at least on the surface. When I let them in the room after lunch break, and I feel a bit of a knot in my stomach, I greet each individual student with a handshake or hug. When things go awry, I almost force myself to laugh. When students really bug me, I will occasionally hug them. (September 24, 1998)

Another reason that I am beginning to look forward to school is the warm response of the children. Our students are important "reference groups" for teachers (Nias, 1989). By far, we see them more than our colleagues or principal; they do indeed create our reality as much as we create their reality. The warm affective response of the kids supports my self-concept as a warm, caring person. The hugs, joking, high-fiving, and laughter validates me; it affirms me as someone who is important and consequential in their school lives. (October 7, 1998)

A second strategy was self-exhortation; that is, through self-talk, I cajoled and admonished myself to feel in a way that was consistent with the feeling rules for teachers in my school.

As lousy as I feel, it is crucial that I be "up" with the students. I need to laugh, smile, and stay grounded when teaching. The work to maintain a positive outward persona is, itself, stressful, since my authentic feelings are anxiety, depression, and sometimes anger. (September 21, 1998)

However, I am less concerned about my future integrity as a teacher educator than I am about my present mental health. I feel myself falling into an anxious depression that is difficult to ignore. I am at the outset of a five-day weekend (without students), and I have spent too much time ruminating about my teaching problems. I realize that this is unproductive thinking, and I need to simply stop myself from thinking these kinds of thoughts. (November 24, 1998)

Cognitive heuristics are strategies that I construct to help me reframe my emotional state. By far, this was the most common strategy I employed. Here is a poem I wrote that summarized a group of these strategies. Typically, I would use these to reframe an angry, sad, depressed, or embarrassed state of mind.

1. Remind myself of
   that bird on the shoulder whispering
   tomorrow you die.
2. Don't sweat the small stuff . . .
   and it's all small stuff.

3. Take deep breaths
   and smile and
   remind myself that the gig
   is just for one year
   and half time at that!
4. Don't worry, be happy.
5. Que sera, sera,
   whatever will be will be.
6. Everything is perfect.
7. Remember my mother
   who at eighty is due for bypass surgery
   along with a nodule in her breast.
8. Nothing matters
   say the existentialists.
9. I can only do my best
   and that's all.
10. It's alright.
11. Let it be.
12. Let it go. (November 8, 1998)

Another cognitive strategy I used was to simply remind myself that the students were, indeed, just children, and that I should avoid the trap of imagining them to be something they were not.

Dorothy and I would cross paths as she prepared to leave the building around 11:30 a.m., and I entered the class to take over for the afternoon. Her last words to me, almost every day, were, "Love those kids!" After a few weeks of this, I theorized that her meaning of these words was that I should remember that the students are, ultimately, still children and that I should accept them as such. As children, they inevitably were going to be irascible, antsy, emotional, bored, talky, etc. I often used Dorothy's reminder to help me reframe my emotions so I would be calmer and more accepting of the children's peccadilloes. (September 16, 1998)

I often used my relationship with my own children to guide how I should feel when working with the students.

I got to school yesterday and saw one of my students, sitting in the office. He explained, "I have lice." His parents were unavailable, so he had to sit in the office all day. In the rush of the afternoon, I forgot about him. I didn't go back once to visit him and see how he was doing. I realized this oversight after I had gotten home. I tried to call the student at home, but all I got was his father's voice mail. I felt guilty that I'd forgotten him.

I sure would want my daughter's teacher to behave more compassionately to her if she had to sit in the office all day, with head lice. As a criterion for how I ought to interact with my students, I think about how I want my daughter's teachers to interact with her. The Golden Rule. . . . (September 26, 1998)

I would think of others less fortunate then me, and this would help me reframe, as I did when I thought of my mother in the poem.

I felt pretty much out of control for most of the afternoon. Whenever I felt myself become hot with stress, I focused my mind on a friend who was just diagnosed with cancer. My problems with classroom management pale in comparison with my friend's problems. (January 19, 1999)

Finally, I would do deep acting by engaging in sarcasm and humor. The comment in the next excerpt became almost a mantra in my interactions with Barbara, when we had to cope with student resistance.

When things go totally awry, I might look at Barbara, laugh, and say, "I love this class!" We smile at each other and I am be able to let the tension fall away. (September 24, 1998)

There are two strategies I employed that can be described as surface acting (Hochschild, 1983). I manipulated my outer appearance, so I appeared as if I was emoting in a certain way. The first (and most common) strategy here was faking it. I simply put on a face that hid how I was really feeling.

Nathan received an in-school suspension today. He threatened another child before school. This is part of the school district's new zero-tolerance policy on violence or the threat of violence. I visited him to leave some math work. He didn't express sadness at being left out of the class for the day. When I told him that I'd missed him, he said, "Well, I didn't miss you." He may have sensed that I was lying. (October 6, 1998)

Another example was when I pretended to be angry (see the November 4 excerpt earlier in this section), using this fakery to influence the behavior and emotions of the students.

Rationalizations are attempts to reframe a bad experience by finding some positive outcome in a particular experience. I often reframed a mistake, and the accompanying embarrassment, for example, by calling it a "learning experience."

When I make a major miscalculation, I've begun to ask myself, "What can I learn from this?" (September 24, 1998)

In another incident, a parent wanted his child out of my class, and this was public knowledge throughout the school. I was embarrassed. In my journal entry describing this, I engaged in rationalization in order to protect my self-concept from attack.

Donnie is lucky to have a parent who is aware of what's happening in his school life and has the ability and confidence to voice his concerns to the teacher. I find the father's concerns to be legitimate, and I will act on them. I worry about the rest of my students, whose parents don't have the wherewithal to advocate for their children. For these children, I need to be their advocate. I need to critique my curriculum and continually ask myself, "Am I challenging these kids? Am I meeting their needs? Would I be happy with their school experience if I were their parent?" (October 15, 1998)

## Functional Dimensions of Emotions

Throughout the journal, references are made to a panoply of emotions. On the dark side, I experienced emotions such as sadness, anger, embarrassment, and disgust. Particularly when I described a dark emotion, I often followed each journal excerpt with a plan to address or resolve the situation. In these cases, my emotions were functional in the sense that they alerted me to the problem and the need to take some action to ameliorate it. In the examples that follow, the journal excerpt representing the "action plan" is in italics.

The end-of-day procedure was chaotic. With ten minutes left in the day, I blanked out on what else to do. I brought the students to the rug for some sharing. I forgot to review my expectations for circle behavior. I struggled with many students to stay quiet when someone (including me!) was talking. My language was ineffective: "I am looking for quiet listeners. I need your eyes.

How are we supposed to behave when we are in circle?" With a minute before the bell, I tried to give my farewell meditation, "May we learn to find calm and peace in our lives, at school, and at home, etc." No one heard me, since there were too many other voices. I tried to have everyone sing a song. A lot of the kids used silly voices. Finally, the bell rang and I persisted with the end of day cheer. This led to group screaming. I was embarrassed when a parent stuck his head in the door, and he gave me a sympathetic look.

*Tomorrow, I need to establish expectations and enforce them. I read a great chapter on time out, one strategy for enforcing rules, in a humanistic approach to classroom management by Ruth Charney (1992). I will try it tomorrow.* (September 16, 1998)

I am less concerned about my future integrity as a teacher educator than I am about my present mental health. I feel myself falling into an anxious depression that is difficult to ignore. I am at the outset of a five-day weekend (without students), and I have spent too much time ruminating about my teaching problems. I realize that this is unproductive thinking and I need to simply stop myself from thinking these kinds of thoughts.

*I realized today that I need to do three things. First, develop a curriculum that I am excited about. Second, make sure the curriculum is well structured and hands on. Third, implement a system of outcomes (positive and negative) for student behavior.* (November 24, 1998)

I am getting anxious about the collection of student assessment data. Student-led conferences are in five weeks, and I don't have any samples of student work in science and social studies. We've done a lot of work, especially in science, but I have overlooked the collection of student work. *Luckily, in math, I've saved everything, so I can go back and pull out samples of problem-solving sheets the kids have done since September. For the next five weeks, I will be concentrating on having the kids generate paper copy of everything they do. If I show a movie, I will have them respond in writing or in picture. In math, I'm going to focus on problem solving, especially problems that are evaluated using the state guidelines.* (February 9, 1999)

## Dysfunctional Dimensions of Emotions

Throughout the journal, there are entries describing dark emotions that did *not* lead to action. Instead, these emotions led to self-recrimination or complaining about others. These emotions often led to continued dark emotions, such as when anger led to fear, or when anxiety led to depression and despair. Occasionally, I engaged in angry polemic aimed at the larger political system. These angry diatribes, however, are not accompanied by any kind of action to address the source of the emotional outburst.

I speculated that much of my emotional experience leading to inaction and self-flagellation tended to reflect two cultural norms of schools, at least my school: teacher isolationism (Lortie, 1975) and political passivity. By teacher isolationism, I mean the tendency for teachers to work primarily with children and in isolation from other adults, and the tendency for teachers to avoid explicit discussion and examination, collectively, of the emotional experience of teaching. By political passivity, I mean teachers' tendency to avoid explicit and organized expression of anger and subsequent action directed toward structures or individuals who are in positions of influence, such as administrators, legislators, or policy makers.

### Emotional Dead-Ends That Reflect the Isolation of Teachers

Much of my emotional response to working with students had dysfunctional outcomes, which reflected norms that encouraged privacy and isolation among teachers. For example, on many occasions, I felt embarrassment that I was not able to meet the needs of all students. Early in the year, a meeting was called to address a parent's concern that I was not meeting his child's needs, with the recommendation that one of my colleagues take this student.

> I feel badly, even embarrassed, that I was not able to meet the needs of the student and parent, and that I have to depend on the good will and expertise of a colleague in order to bail me out. (October 29, 1998)

In this situation, my "failure" as a teacher was very visible, very public, and this led me to feel great embarrassment. I remember talking to no one in the building about my shame, and I wonder if my colleagues avoided talking to me about the event because of their own embarrassment. The dysfunctional outcome of this emotion is that I just felt badly and there was no effective action that emerged from the feeling. There was no opportunity for me to reconcile my feelings of inadequacy. I did need the help of my colleagues, but neither they nor I felt at ease to get together. While my personality, gender, and status (as the teacher educator) may have been factors in my being left alone, I also attribute this outcome to a school culture that isolates teachers and, in effect, reduces opportunities to engage in meaningful professional conversations.

At other times, I felt a sense of despair that I was not able to meet the needs of all my students.

> I work with these kids every day, and I feel frustrated that I can't meet their needs. I am not comfortable in acknowledging this. Most teachers I know embrace the myth that their job is to meet the needs of all students. The problem with this expectation is that, for the most part, it is unreasonable.
>
> I am stricken by the increasing self-doubt about my ability to meet the needs of all my students. This goal is part of the corporate self-concept for teachers: meeting everyone's needs. Even in the best of circumstances (e.g., a class of conformist students), it is virtually impossible to truly meet individual students' needs. I am not sure how I am coping with this threat to my teaching self-concept. (November 12, 1998)

Again, I did nothing with these emotions. I despaired, but I did not engage colleagues in a discussion of my feelings or strategies to improve my situation.

I felt more embarrassment when a colleague wanted to observe me, since he actually thought he could learn from me! I never shared with him my real feelings: that I was not a competent teacher.

> [W]hen he asked if he could observe me, I felt my face flush, and I became embarrassed. My voice said, "Yeah, sure, any time." But I suppose my nonverbal signal was obvious to him, so he backed off, saying, "Great . . . uh . . . I can't observe today, but I'll come back soon." And he was out the door.
>
> I was embarrassed to have him observe me, because I don't feel good about my math program. I have a fuzzy image of what it should look like, but I am light years away from this image. I was also embarrassed at being embarrassed. I will talk to him and explain why my response to him was so unenthusiastic. (November 5, 1998)

One of the greatest fears of teachers is losing control of the class. I certainly had this fear, but I usually kept it to myself. The fear manifested itself in both my conscious and unconscious mind.

I had two nightmares last night. In my sleep. First, I was walking around town, looking for a teacher in my school. Suddenly, a tornado appeared out of nowhere and began chasing me. Eventually, I found shelter in an ice cream parlor. I looked out the window at the devastation and noticed some kids trying to stay afloat in a pond nearby. I ran out to rescue them.

Later, in the predawn, I dreamed that my kids were out of control. Joey assaulted Nathan, so I had to send him home. I lost my temper with Stevie, and I hit him. He thought I was just playing, so he started wrestling with me. In the entire dream, we were wrestling. Meanwhile, the remainder of the class was out of control, hanging from the rafters, having a good old time. (February 19, 1999)

Often, I felt anxiety about my ability or inabilities as a teacher, and I would simply keep it to myself. This unexpressed anxiety would then have a deleterious effect on my motivation to teach as well as my relationship with my own children.

I became really anxious over this problem. Even as I struggled with curriculum and management, I have always had the sense that the students and I liked each other. Now I struggle with interpersonal conflict with a student and parents who are giving their children negative signals about me. My immediate response to this is anxiety. Yesterday, after school, I couldn't enjoy my own children, because my two-hour power struggle with Donnie had rattled my peace of mind. This kind of problem really diminishes my motivation: to teach, to work hard. I counted the number of student contact days between now and winter break. There were thirty-two days. With the passing of each day, I put an "X" on that calendar date in my mind. I am counting days already. This isn't a good sign.

It seems like the emotional health of the teacher is so fragile. (October 27, 1998)

I did not feel safe to talk about my experience, at least not openly outside my intimate circle of wife and several friends. However, early in the year, I blew my cover by talking too openly about my teaching experience at a Thanksgiving dinner attended by a bunch of local teachers.

I was embarrassed at the apparent rumor around town that I was failing as a teacher. I failed at "impression management" (Goffman, 1959) when I let my guard down and spoke honestly about the experience. I was still holding on to some vestiges of feelings that I was a "good teacher," and much of this self-image was connected to my standing in the community as the teacher educator, the accomplished and expert practitioner who supposedly knew what he was doing. Widespread knowledge of my struggle among the general community would pose a real threat to my self-concept, and it is a threat that I want to minimize. (November 30, 1998)

Clearly I would become embarrassed when colleagues and parents observed me to be incompetent—for example, when parents observed my students being out of control, when my student teacher watched me struggle with resistant students, or when outsiders came to the class to see some "demonstration teaching." My modus operandi when faced with embarrassment was not to address it openly and explicitly with colleagues and others; rather, my game was cover up.

> Student-led conferencing reflects a more constructivist approach, in which the students are led to theorize on their learning and its products. Naturally, given my concern with order and classroom management, it is no great wonder that I haven't fully prepared the students for this gig. I was embarrassed at how poorly prepared my kids were for this. I am doing some impression management (Goffman, 1959) here by planning a huge number of topics, so there really isn't time for in-depth discussion of a single topic. My thinking: overwhelm the parents with a lot of "stuff" and maybe they won't think too much about the details. (March 8, 1999)

I covered my anticipated embarrassment of not being ready for the student-led conferences by inflating the conferences with too much information, thereby diverting parents from a more thoughtful discussion of their children's progress. In the next excerpt, I reduced my embarrassment by framing student misbehavior as my student teacher's problem, divorcing myself from the situation and responsibility.

> I was also embarrassed that my students had behaved as they did. I hid my guilt and embarrassment through some deft "impression management" (Goffman, 1959), by giving the student teacher suggestions to help her deal with this, "her" problem. In reality, she and I were in the same boat. (October 29, 1998)

*Emotional Dead-Ends That Reflect Political Passivity*

I often observed that my colleagues and I avoided open displays of anger when faced with difficult or irrational institutional structures or expectations. What I find interesting is the relative absence of any outward displays of anger, except the occasional angry expression of teachers toward children or children toward other children. Adapting an idea from Eisner (1985), the null emotion is the amazingly *absent* teacher emotion of anger. Certainly, there was much complaining or grumbling about the political state of affairs, but the norm here was that people inhibited angry display or, when there were occasional anger expressions, they did not take political action.

Periodically, in the journal, there are situations in which I allude to anger, or I suggest that I am entertaining the idea of anger, but never do I really show it. For example, the superintendent came to the school and talked about the state of affairs in the district. In my journal, I write about becoming "quietly angry" (November 6–7, 1998) when he explained why our high-poverty school shouldn't receive more support than the high-income schools. There was an incident early in the year when the special education personnel were being overrun with discipline problems, and at a staff meeting there was agreement that the school needed more resources to address this problem. One teacher (a male) argued that we needed to go to the newspaper and blow the whistle on the school district. However, the "other teachers worried that the strategy of confrontation would scare some of the remaining middle-class families away from Woodbridge" (October 7, 1998). People were concerned that any open display of anger would have negative political consequences for the school.

Later in the year, I (and other teachers) got the impression that the superintendent was avoiding a meeting with us teachers.

> The superintendent was scheduled to visit the staff at our regular meeting last week, but he couldn't come due to a conflicting appointment. The staff was disappointed. We are the only school he has yet to visit. He has rescheduled to visit us in January. I flew off the handle. I had been reading about the organizational and structural impediments to good teaching, such as large class sizes, large numbers of special needs students, planning time, and lack of resources. It has always perplexed me, since I came to Woodbridge, how uniform class size formulas are used when schools have different populations and

vastly different needs (e.g., the schools show great variations in student-family income, special needs, and second-language learners). (December 6, 1998)

In retrospect, I realized that my "flying off the handle" was merely a cognitive event. I did not visit with my union representative, organize teachers, write a letter to the editor, or take some kind of social action to address resource inequities. I shared my anger about the inequities in the system with my colleagues, and for most of the year I blamed dysfunctional families or insensitive administrators. By late March, I had stopped blaming families for the sorrowful state of their children and began pointing my finger at the system. Still, none of this anger moved me to take action.

> I now sense that *the* essential factor is not the families and the home life of the kids. By not pointing out the inequities built into the larger economic system, we implicitly endorse the system as fair and not responsible for poverty. Certainly, many of my families are dysfunctional, and this home experience results in huge challenges for its children. By defining the essential problem to be one of dysfunctional families, attention is diverted from our examination of an economic system that, itself, may be the problem. (March 29–30, 1999)

I did much ranting and raving in the journal, variously directed at the principal, superintendent, district administrators, the state department of education, the state legislature, and in general, the entirety of the patriarchal/capitalistic/market-driven economy. However, while my journal language had angry tones, never did this angry writing ever lead to any kind of political action by me.

## DISCUSSION

One obvious conclusion a reader could draw from this chapter is that teaching is profoundly emotional work. Of course, anyone who has taught or who lives with a teacher knows this. Professional and literary writing provide rich descriptions of the emotional lives of teachers, representations that show both the joyous and dark sides of teaching (Blanchard & Ursula, 1996; Hargreaves, 1998; Kelchtermans, 1996; Kidder, 1989; Kozol, 1968). I realize that this is a self-study, and in my account there is the subjectivity that goes on in any autobiography. At the risk of sounding delusional, I do believe that my emotional life was largely functional. For example, I used my emotions as a cue in my planning of subsequent teaching (Armon-Jones, 1986). My strategies for doing emotional labor, particularly my deep-acting strategies, appear sensible and normal. I have shared contents of this chapter with other teachers, including preservice teachers. The heuristics I used to manage my emotions made sense to these teachers, and they reflect similar strategies of workers in other service professions (Ashforth, 1993; Hochschild, 1983).

I found that I was somewhat effective in using my emotions when a situation revolved around questions of particular teaching practice. For the most part, my self-conception as a teacher does reflect the feeling rules delineated earlier in the chapter. I believe that the "good teacher" has affection for students, has enthusiasm for subject matter, and usually enjoys or even loves the work. The emotion work I did (to behave in ways that reflected the rules) was not alienating, which is a danger when there *is* a disconnect between the rules and the individual's real feelings (Hochschild, 1983). But the rules reflected a sense of how I believed teachers should behave and emote. I controlled much of my emotional labor, and this tended to lead to a sense of satisfaction with the work (Ashforth, 1993; Tolich, 1983). Even when I did surface acting, I was doing what Rafaeli and Sutton (1987) would call faking it in good faith: I had internalized the spirit of the rules, so it is more likely I would find my emotion work appropriate and even pleasurable.

Ashforth (1993) found that a healthy emotional situation existed when the worker's actual feelings are consistent with the feeling rules for those particular situations and settings, and extensive "deep acting" was not necessary to maintain the rules. I sense that this category of emotional experience was much more present in my experience than was reflected in my journal, because there was a tendency for me to write more about those experiences that were troubling or problematic. I know that there were many times when there was alignment between my felt emotions and the feeling rules of my classroom and school. However, this type of emotional experience was not a focus of this inquiry.

There were many instances when I experienced dark emotions, such as embarrassment and anger, that were simply left unresolved. I often questioned my competence when I had the inevitable problems with classroom management and teaching. I felt embarrassment, anger, fear, and anxiety in relation to my teaching performance and my perception of how my colleagues and parents viewed me as a teacher. However, I tended to keep these feelings to myself and, exacerbating my emotional disequilibrium even more, I engaged in self-accusatory and self-blaming behavior. My self-blaming behavior reflected the dominant discourse of teaching, which tends to focus on the "failings" of the individual, to suggest that failure or struggle is the teachers' fault alone and that their working conditions or the larger structural conditions are less influential than the individual's own performance (Rousmaniere, 1994). This self-accusatory stance is common with preservice teachers with whom I work.

There seemed to be a clear relationship between my emotions and working conditions. I did feel dark emotions when I lost control of the class, and some of my working conditions influencing these emotions had their antecedents in the material and structural context. This included a school ethos that might have been inappropriate for these students, the high number of special needs students in one class, the poverty of some of my students, and even physical constraints of the classroom and school. The expectation that teachers are paragons of virtue, self-sacrifice, and modesty (i.e., not ambitious) places extraordinary pressures on teachers to do emotion work to maintain the right mask at the right time with the right audience (Hochschild, 1983).When my emotion (e.g., anger or disgust) was directed toward the hierarchy, administrators, or the state legislature, my emotional expressions never developed into anything more than a grumble, which is the most benign form of political resistance (Scott, 1990). This inaction was a dysfunctional outcome of my emotions because what anger I was able to muster led nowhere in terms of improving my working conditions. Reflecting the culture and history of public schools, particularly as gendered organizations, the absence of any organized response to my anger or the anger of my colleagues makes sense and is a familiar pattern of behavior (Boler, 1999; Grumet, 1988). The culture of public schools and even teacher education, reflecting modern masculinist organizational culture, tends to privilege dispassionate, emotionally flat, and rational discourse (Boler, 1999; Putnam & Mumby, 1997). Our anger at the hierarchy has always been restrained and guarded, reflecting the women/teacher ideal as kind, gentle, and nurturing (Rousmaniere, 1994). Even if female teachers do engage in demonstrably angry behavior in reaction to some injustice, there is still an anxiety that those in superordinate positions will dismiss them as incompetent or as incapable of self-control (Campbell, 1994). It is safe to conclude that my colleagues and I were not predisposed to vent anger in explicit ways; we were not socialized to use anger to incite organized political action.

Outrage represents an early stage of political/emotional consciousness, when a person may use her anger and actually begin to take action to address some injustice (Barrows, 1996). My colleagues appeared to be feeling just a mild uneasiness and some inchoate anger over their working conditions. I did not observe much, if any, outrage from teachers. Still, it seems to me that my colleagues and teachers in general do know what they feel. According to Harrison (1985), therefore, the "moral question is not 'What do I feel?' but rather, 'What do I do with what I feel?'" (14)

The central implication of the present study is the recommendation that teachers ought to engage systematically in the examination of their feelings, or emotions, as they are reflected in working conditions. In these venues, teachers would provide description of their teaching/emotions and then work together to plan action to address those experiences. Sometimes, the simple validation of peers (that a particular emotion is normal or functional) is all that is required, and at other times discussion of emotions may lead to more extensive plans for political action at the building, district, or state level. In the absence of forums for teachers to study their emotions, share them, and use them for social change, it is easy for teacher emotions to become mired in accusatory and blaming self-talk (Lortie, 1975), which is itself a dysfunctional outcome in the emotional life of teachers. Schools could profitably give voice to teachers' emotions for the purpose of examining these emotions. There are some teachers and schools that take their anger and use it to organize politically to make schools and society more democratic and equitable (e.g., Bigelow, Christensen, Karp, Miner, & Peterson, 1994; Casey, 1993; Crocco, Munro, & Weiler, 1999). There are exceptions to the private world of teacher emotion, where teachers do openly share felt emotional experience, honestly and explicitly, and emotional (and spiritual) experience is recognized as a dimension of teaching worthy of formal examination and study (e.g., Lantieri, 2001; Palmer, 1998).

Preservice teachers would benefit from the explicit study of emotions, even before they go out into the field as licensed practitioners. For my preservice teachers, reading this chapter has tended to provoke expressions of relief that someone in a position of authority as a teacher (me) can feel the same way they feel. Preservice teachers have said that my story demystified some of the sacred cows of teacher emotions for them (e.g., teachers have to love all their students, they are a failure if they do not meet the needs of all students, good teachers are always happy and having fun). With some study of these nonpedagogical dimensions of teaching, beginning teachers might be in a better position to critique the interrelationship between their emotions, biographies, personalities, and immediate situations and the cultural and structural dimensions of their work as teachers. The profession would be well served if young teachers have opportunities to reflect on their own psychological readiness to help children who need a lot of emotional support. After his observation of how endemic anxiety is to the teaching experience, Jersild (1955) went so far as to argue that *"the concept of anxiety should be regarded as an essential topic in all teacher-training programs"* (italics in the original, 7). Teacher education programs in which students can explore their own selves (e.g., Tickle, 1999) seem warranted.

Teacher education has recognized, for some time, the power of story in the development of teachers (e.g., Clandinin & Connelly, 1995). The idea is for teachers to come together and share their stories for the purpose of helping each other deepen their understandings of the teaching experience. Particularly in helping teachers understand their own vulnerability in a hostile environment, the narrative experience gives teachers opportunities to share their stories and, in effect, affirm each others' worth and the validity of each others' experience (cf. Kelchtermans, 1996; Noddings, 1996). Of course, it is crucial that teachers do, indeed, feel free to tell the truth, and that their stories accurately depict dimensions of their work that are pleasurable as well as unpleasant. Newkirk (1992) said, "I confess that I have become increasingly estranged from much of what I now read. There is an emotional turbulence and a frequency of failure in my own teaching that I don't see reflected in many accounts, including ones that I have written or edited myself" (23). As teacher education increasingly makes authentic stories available, especially for beginning teachers, they will have models from which to tell their own. In teacher education classes, in teacher lounges, at staff meetings, in NCATE standards, and elsewhere, it is time to recognize the emotional experience of teaching and to let these stories be told, studied, and acted upon: stories good, bad, and ugly.

# THEORIZING FLEXIBILITY: TEACHER AS HIGH-WIRE DANCER

When I started the year, I had some vague ideas about what I wanted to do with the students and who I wanted to be as a teacher. But as my teaching began, and throughout the year, I never quite completed this vague plan for what I wanted to do and become as a teacher. In fact, I seemed to be in a perpetual state of change about my identity as a teacher. My ideas for what it meant to be a teacher, what I should teach, and how I should do it never quite found closure and completion. For example, I thought I was a student-centered teacher, but I sometimes uneasily entertained notions that I needed to do more top-down, teacher-dominated teaching with these students. This chapter examines my search for identity as a teacher.

My reading of the journal data suggests that teacher identity is a social construction, an outcome in large part of on-going negotiations by the person with multiple and often contradictory discourses, a project/product of situations and history. I will argue that the task for teacher education is to help preservice teachers become conscious of many identities for teaching, identities that reflect the interaction of the micropolitical (immediate situation, biography of individual, etc.) and macropolitical dimensions (school district structures, state standards, history) of their everyday work. By doing this, I believe that teacher education can enhance the ability of beginning teachers to reflect critically on practice and more effectively survive and even thrive during the often tumultuous beginning teaching period.

## CONCEPTUAL FRAMEWORK

I believe the teaching self is a process of social construction. It is an ongoing process that leads to a self that is provisional, contested, partial as well as situational and historic. This view is contrasted with several other conceptions of self, for example, as unchanging and unitary, unblemished by contradictions and change; as driven by biological and/or psychological impulses (Freud); and as determined primarily by circumstances external to the individual, such as larger economic forces (Marx) or cultural forces as they relate to one's ethnicity, gender, race, and so forth. Mead's central idea (1934) about self informs this study: self reflects and emerges from the individual's social interactions over a lifetime. We take our cues for what we say and how we think from others, including what they say to us and how we imagine they think of us (Blumer, 1969; Mead, 1934). These cues happen at the immediate level of personal interaction, including past interactions, as well as in patterns of behavior structured in the community and society.

> [T]he reality of the person is both individual and social, anchored in the numerous situations of everyday life and created anew in each situation, as well as in biographies people construct for themselves and in the ones built for them by others. (Hewitt, 1989, 85)

Our identity is historical, since our thinking derives from language and mental structures that precede us and provide us with our frames of reference. Bakhtin's idea (1981) of heteroglossia is useful here.

> [A]t any given moment of its historical existence, language (our thinking) is heterglot from top to bottom: it represents the co-existence of socio-ideological contradictions between the present and the past, between different socio-ideological groups in the present, between tendencies, schools, circles and so forth, all given a bodily form. (291)

The "socio-ideological contradictions" means that there are conflicts between the various discourses swirling around in the head of the individual, struggles between the individual's own voice or purposes and the voice and purposes of others. In our lives, we come to internalize the words of others, including language that is historic and ideological, and we usually are not even aware of this assimilation.

> [L]anguage . . . lies in the borderline between oneself and the other. The word in language is one half someone else's. It becomes "one's own" only when the speaker populates it with his own intention, his own accent, when he appropriates the word, adapting it to his own . . . intention. (Bakhtin, 1981, 293)

The task for the teacher, as it is for me in this study, is to understand one's motivations and intentions by analyzing the contradictions and competing discourses reflected in one's use of language.

I am intrigued by the idea from symbolic interactionism (e.g., Hewitt, 1976) and poststructural feminism (Britzman, 1986) that we have many identities. The symbolic interactionist maintains that our identity changes to adjust to changing situations (e.g., Becker, 1964). Weedon (1987) suggests that we have a "subjectivity which is precarious, contradictory and in process, constantly being reconstituted in discovery each time we think or speak" (33). Britzman (1986) suggests that we have many voices, "always contingent upon shifting relationships among the words we speak, the practices we construct, and the communities in which we interact" (12). Particularly when new situations are problematic, individuals will often construct a new role for themselves and, in effect, carve out a new identity. When identity is transformed, we become conscious of our identity, and this can

> serve as reminders to people that they have other identities than the currently operative one. Thus, integration is brought to the fore as an issue, for we are reminded that the role that makes us whole in this situation is not all there is to us. Continuity is momentarily challenged, for we are more conscious of ourselves shifting from one line of action to another. (Hewitt, 1989, 163)

I am interested in how and where self happens, how my teacher identity developed, and how I have come to know what I know. Jenkins (1996) maintains that "identities are to be found and negotiated at their boundaries where the internal and external meet" (24). (The tension here is between the person's self definition [internal] and the definitions of reality given by others [external].) The boundary that Jenkins refers to is what poststructural feminists might call battle sites, where different discourses are "constantly vying for status and power. The site for this battle is the subjectivity[1] of the individual and it is a battle in which the individual is an active but not sovereign protagonist" (Weedon, 1987, 41). This boundary area is a place where the emergent self presents itself as "a rich repository of cultural resources: organized biographically as memory, experientially as knowledge; some conscious, some not; some of them in contradiction, some in agreement; some of them imperative, some filed under 'take it or leave it'" (Jenkins, 1996, 46). As the individual grapples with the contradiction of competing discourses, or ways of behaving/thinking, she has some agency and control to affect her destiny. However, the individual is also a product of her biography, history, and a culture that is often out of consciousness, so her choices are limited and constrained.

It is in the gray area between the internal and external, between my sense of the ideal (my self-conception) and the reality of teaching, that I construct my sense of self. Phelan characterizes this gray area as a "rackety bridge between self and other" (Ellsworth, 1997, 158), a place where the individual never completely bridges the gap between one's intentions and those of others. Instead, perhaps the task when standing on the bridge is to appreciate the differences between self and other and to engage in dialogue so, using Bakhtin's idea, we are able to infuse our use of language with our own intentions. Similarly, Britzman (1986) found that, for teachers, "the capacity for contradictions . . . can serve as the departure for a dialogic understanding that theorizes how one understands the given realities of teaching as well as the realities that teaching makes possible" (15). It is the language we use to grapple with the contradictions of everyday life that "constitutes us as conscious thinking subjects and enables us to give meaning to the world and to act to transform it" (Weedon, 1987, 32).

My struggle as a teacher was to reconcile the tension in the boundary between my self-conception as a teacher and the material reality of the teaching situation. My subjectivity as a teacher was constructed in this messy and ill-defined boundary area. The present study is an examination of my teaching self as it wavered on the rickety bridge, doing boundary work. In this chapter, I examine two questions related to teacher identity:

1. What did I do to manage the tension between my self-conception as teacher and the reality of teaching?
2. In the boundary area between my self and the hard-core reality of everyday teaching, how did I reshape my self?

## RESEARCH CONTEXTS AND METHOD

There are four contexts that are germane to this study of self. First, there is the psychological context of my self-conception as teacher: the historic ideas I had about myself as teacher, particularly my ideas before the onset of the sabbatical. Second, there is the demographic context of my students, my colleagues, and the school culture. Third, there is the context of what happened in my class: the outcome of my intentions and my work as a teacher. Fourth, there is the context of the school district and the state education scene. I briefly describe these contexts here and in the introduction.

I had a self-conception[2] as a teacher that reflected some popular discourses for what it means to be a teacher. Before the sabbatical, my identity as teacher tended to reflect the following beliefs:

1. The teacher is able to maintain order.
2. The teacher is able to implement a curriculum that is academically viable, and he effectively influences student learning; the teacher also teaches social skills.
3. The teacher has warm personal relations with students.
4. The teacher engages in collaborative relations with students.
5. The teacher is (nearly all) knowing, expert, and confident.[3]

Certainly, there were working conditions that persistently challenged my beliefs, rendering them quite problematic, and I briefly list these conditions below:[4]

1. As many as eighteen of my twenty-five students had special needs, or they were "high profile" students who had trouble self-managing or

avoiding conflict with peers and authority figures. About the same percentage of the students were on free or reduced lunch. Many families lived in poverty or in near poverty conditions.

2. The school ethos privileged student-centered, constructivist pedagogies, and this included teachers' work in the academic subjects as well as student behavior.[5]

3. I had last been an everyday teacher thirteen years earlier, so I no longer had the practical fluency of an everyday teacher. I had never taught primary-aged students, and I had no experience teaching a grades 1–3 blend. I was in charge of the teaching of mathematics and science, but my areas of expertise were in reading and writing. I had a lot of theoretical knowledge about teaching, but my practical knowledge was undeveloped.

4. I had to give the ***** standardized test to my third graders in April. I was responsible for preparing the students on the mathematics portion of the test. The test tended to focus on lower-level mathematical knowledge.

5. The political and economic environment was hostile to teachers and public schools. School funding was on a continuous downward trend (since 1990). Legislators were regularly introducing legislation to more closely monitor and regulate the behavior of teachers. State requirements for the assessment of student learning entailed oftentimes quite onerous layers of bookkeeping and paperwork for teachers. The state standards and benchmarks for learning were imposed on our students, even if they were not ready developmentally. While our school promoted developmentally appropriate practice, the state standards and tests grouped and evaluated our students based on their grade level.

6. I had a somewhat collegial environment in which to interact with other adults. I had a full-time instructional aide, and for much of the year a student teacher and other clinical students from the university worked in our classroom.

These six conditions worked together to challenge my presabbatical identity. In my classroom, my teaching intentions (reflecting my self-conceptions) were often thwarted, leading to outcomes that were not what I envisioned for myself. The list below summarizes the central outcomes of my work:

1. There was often disorder and much deviant student behavior, especially in the first four months of the school year.
2. My teaching was often thwarted; I was unable to effectively teach and affect student learning.
3. I often had adversarial relations with students.
4. I was often confused, full of self-doubt, and had feelings of helplessness and hopelessness.

## Data Analysis

I used a grounded theory approach to data analysis and my representation of identity in this study (Charmaz, 2000). I read the journal and coded every instance when "things did not go well": that is, when I had a bad day, bad lesson, or dark emotion; when the students were out of order; when I had conflict with students; and so forth. Undeniably, I used my background knowledge, or what grounded theory practitioners would call sensitizing concepts, to cue my initial coding of the data. I coded each paragraph, examining each action taken or thought generated, by asking "What does this paragraph say about my identity? What beliefs or values does this action or thought reflect?" I began to reduce the initial codes into a smaller set of more conceptual categories, such as blaming, changing beliefs, finding reference groups.

After reading Britzman, Weedon, and Jenkins during the period of initial and conceptual coding, I conceptualized my identity getting constructed in the space between my self-conceptions and my material reality (which included interactions with other people, available resources, and the school culture). Referring to my research questions, I first asked, "What did I do to cope when there was a discrepancy between my self-conception as a teacher and the reality of my situation?" I then read the data again to determine what I did whenever I had a problem or whenever one of my intentions as a teacher was thwarted. (I chose the identification/analysis of problems as the unit of analysis, since problems lead us to a type of reflection that is more transparent and apparent than, perhaps, successes do.) I identified some new categories, such as problem solving and managing impressions. Reflecting Goffman (e.g., 1959), I defined each response as a "strategy" for self defense. Strategies served to help me protect myself from criticism, save face, or appear competent

(Goffman, 1959). I aimed to protect myself from criticism from others as well as from my own critical self. Then, referring to my second research question, in the description of each of the (five) strategies, or the boundary area between myself and my actual reality, I read the data to determine how my self-conception was reshaped by the experience. Finally, I synthesized the strategies to construct a theory of my own identities as a teacher.

## STRATEGIES: FINDING SPACE TO CONSTRUCT IDENTITY

I used five general strategies to reconcile or negotiate the tension between my self-conceptions and the reality of my teaching. I did not use these strategies in a planned or conscious manner. Rather, the strategies were spontaneous and unplanned moves aimed at coping with my teaching problems. It is inside these spaces (between my ideal and the real) that I constructed teacher identities that worked for me in particular teaching situations. The strategies are blaming, changing beliefs, problem solving, managing impressions, and finding reference groups. Below, I describe how I used these strategies to entertain new identities.

### Blaming

Blaming is a way of making sense of failure. It can explicitly serve to protect the self, by shifting responsibility for the problem away from the self. It is not unusual for teachers to engage in self-blame (Lortie, 1975), and I did much of this. More often, however, I blamed other factors, most of which were outside my control. These factors included my politically passive colleagues, dysfunctional families, mentally disordered students, large class size, too many special needs students, inadequate resources, school ethos, my own inexperience, my biography, the flaws of developmentally appropriate curriculum, table groups and the furniture, the assumptions underlying public education and schooling, the hierarchic/bureaucratic/capitalistic system, poverty, school district intransigence, state mandates and testing, and even the weather.

The focus of my blaming reflected three interrelated dimensions: the individual, the micropolitical, and the macropolitical. By blaming individuals, I mean blaming the performance of particular teachers, students, and parents, including my own performance. A second dimension of blaming was more ecological or micropolitical. Failure was due to some problem in the local structure, such as the school ethos, inadequate support for families, or the inappropriateness of some curriculum. A third dimension of blaming reflected a critique of the larger structural conditions of school. Here, the responsibility for my failure derived from some distant location, where amorphous others such as state legislators and policy makers took actions that adversely affected the working conditions for teachers and students. Critique of the larger cultural and social structure also entailed problems with the assumptions underlying schooling and teaching.

In the first month of school, I tended to criticize my own technical and personal skills as a teacher as well as the inappropriateness of my classroom structures for problems with particular students. Throughout the year, but especially in the beginning, I was harshest on myself, for my weaknesses as a teacher. Here is an illustrative journal excerpt:

> The end-of-day procedure was chaotic. With ten minutes left in the day, I blanked out on what else to do. I brought the students to the rug for some sharing. I forgot to review my expectations for circle behavior. I struggled with many students to stay quiet when someone (including me!) was talking. My language was ineffective. (September 16, 1998)

I also criticized my teaching for its "inappropriateness." When there was disorder in the classroom, I often questioned the match between the structures of my teaching and the needs of particular students. This idea of finding the right structure in a diverse class of students was a theme throughout the year.

> After break, at 2:00 p.m., it was time for creative drama. We are beginning with pantomime. Again, the kids were disruptive. . . . I presented a scenario, such as eating an ice cream cone on a hot hot day, and then invited students in small groups to the front to act out. I invited anyone who wanted to come to the front to pretend to hold a bird with a broken wing. Twenty students came to the front. I should have had them come to the front in small groups. I am not sure how to structure drama differently. But I am sure that it needs to change. By 2:25 . . . I was physically and emotionally exhausted. I felt like a policeman—one who did a very poor job.
>
> I think these kids need different structures. (September 21, 1998)

From around October to April, my critique increasingly focused on the structural conditions of my work, both at the local level and the societal level. At the local level this reflected, for example, my sense that the social constructivist school ethos was inappropriate for many of the school's students. I was critical of the political passivity of my colleagues and their unwillingness to express more anger and even take action to improve our working conditions. I blamed the school district for not giving more money to high-poverty schools in the district. I was critical of the lack of support for economically stressed-out families. In the following journal entry, I was critical of the appropriateness of the school ethos for many of our high-poverty students:

Woodbridge has emphasized a developmentally appropriate, hands-on, open-ended/problem-solving curriculum for years (DAP). Teachers and administration here have abandoned a direct-instruction, skills-based program in favor of developmentally appropriate practice. The problem with an extreme DAP approach here is that it may not match well with the needs of these kids. In middle-class schools, the kids tend to come to school with some grounding in basic literacy concepts, such as phonics knowledge or knowledge about numeration. I think that middle-class kids are academically and emotionally ready to learn from open-ended, discovery-type activity, and they tend to have more self-management skills. (December 18, 1998)

My analysis of student disorder after a particularly difficulty day in October reflected a more interactionist perspective. Here, I examined the folk wisdom that the weather or holidays can influence students to be unruly:

I wonder how teacher behavior is a factor in how kids do or do not get ansty before holidays or days off. I wonder if teachers consciously and unconsciously give kids signals that a vacation is looming, so rules and expectations will be more loosely enforced. There seems to be what Pollard (1985) calls temporal rule framing: time is a factor in how rules are framed, with either sharp boundaries (strictly enforced) or weak boundaries (loosely enforced).
It seems that teachers do frame expectations differently before vacations. Friday afternoons are often occasions for art activities or movies; the days and weeks before Christmas break are dominated by the weak curricular boundary represented by craft activities. (A sharply curricularly bounded activity would be to have students do some pages in the math textbook that are rou-

tinely evaluated by the teacher.) In many schools, it is a common practice for teachers to dress less formally on Fridays. This change in attire might cue students that rule frames are going to be looser. And teachers' moods (Pollard calls this "personal rule framing) tend to be more easy and tolerant of student antsiness just before holidays.

A holiday is imminent, teachers and students are both anxious for a break of the routine, and already the anticipation of the break influences both parties to let their guard down a bit (by weakening the rule frames). Teachers and students' past experiences with preholiday school days come into play, and teachers and students then cue each other to define the situation so the Friday afternoon of "talky kids" makes sense. Kids sense the acquiescence of teachers, so this gives them license to "be excited about the weekend." The important idea here is that this redefinition is a mutual and dialectic process between teachers and students, informed by their past experiences, in which teachers and students "take each other into account when they act and are thus at least partially affected by each other." (Charon, 1979, 133) (October 9, 1998)

This journal entry shows a more flexible and interactive perspective on making sense of classroom events, in which I avoid blaming any one group or factor.

At a more distant, societal level, structure had to do with decisions and policies generated far from the schoolhouse door. I was critical of the state legislature for not funding public education adequately; the vulnerability of public education in a capitalistic market economy; my students' poverty; and finally, the assumptions of mass compulsory education. In this journal excerpt, I blamed certain assumptions of schooling in a somewhat fatalistic polemic after a particularly difficult day.

I am coming to realize that the entire enterprise of mass public education is irrational and unnatural to children and to the adults who for noble, selfish, or expedient reasons have chosen to participate in this madness. Is school nothing more than forced confinement of an adult with a group of young people around an agenda that is somewhat irrelevant to the youngers and often the adult!? We have children caught in a physical, intellectual, and social trap that, to an adult, would be inconceivable and intolerable. Besides prisons and mental hospitals, where else are people subjected to forced confinement for long periods of time? At least in prisons there is the chance of parole for good behavior. (January 22, 1999)

Other assumptions I critiqued as problematic included the historic practice of filling twenty to thirty students in the cramped quarters of the typical classroom; technology as the savior of public education; and idea that teachers can reasonably affect the learning of a large groups of students.

Perhaps the largest quandary for teachers involves the assumption that our job is to influence the cognitive and social learning of students. The dilemma here is that no one can make someone else learn. It's a maxim among psychotherapists that the patient has to want to change before any change can occur. It's the same with any kind of learning, with any aged person. People have to want to learn, or change. So, as teachers, we initiate educational experiences that might facilitate learning, but it is problematic how students will interact with these experiences. (December 18, 1998)

Especially with large classes that include a lot of special needs students, the situation seemed rigged to work against creative and collaborative types of teacher–student relations.

In large classrooms, kids learn to comply to a more powerful other (teacher), how to defer gratification, how to be punctual, how to defer to the needs of others, and how to follow rules and experience consequences for violations of those rules. Because teachers have no choice but to generate academic tasks that are directed to the group (and not individuals), students in large classes learn to manage tasks, like they would in any bureaucracy, that they wouldn't do naturally, if they had a choice. The explicit academic curriculum is really secondary in purpose to the "hidden curriculum" of learning the "ropes" of an impersonal hierarchy of bureaucratic life. (February 18, 1999)

In April, a psychologist friend showed me a guide to mental disorders, and I became almost obsessed with diagnosing the mental "disorders" of my students. When I experienced failure or struggle, I now focused blame on my students and their individual, in-the-head characteristics (e.g., reactive attachment disorder, attention deficit hyperactivity disorder, attention deficit disorder). I psychologized my students' resistance and nonconformity (along with my own incompetence, at times) to make sense of failure or frustration.

We were talking about my students, and as I described them she began naming them as attention deficit disordered (ADD) and attention deficit hyperactivity disordered (ADHD). When **** came into our conversation, she named him as oppositional defiant disordered (ODD). She showed me the *Diagnostic and Statistical Manual of Mental Disorders* (DSM-IV), and I read the criteria for these disorders. It suddenly made sense to me. I went through my class list and figured that at least fifteen of my students showed behaviors typical of ADD, ADHD, or ODD.

... [U]ntil now, I have been trying to fit square pegs into round holes. I have tended to blame the students and have wanted to change them so they conform to my model or standard for behavior. (April 19, 1999)

Even when I complained about students' psychological failings, I also tended to criticize myself for not restructuring the classroom environment appropriately. I vacillated in my criticism of the students and myself for frustrating teaching experiences. Occasionally, I took a nonjudgmental stance, instead of my earlier self-flagellation or student bashing. In the next excerpt, I found a space in which I dispassionately reflected on the student–task interaction.

Last week, we gave Nathan's group a worksheet of double-digit addition problems with a dot-to-dot task, in which the kids were to draw lines from each of the answers to make, eventually, a face. Nathan couldn't handle the task. His face went into pained contortions, and he plaintively asked, "Why are you making me do this? Why did they have to put these (dots) in here? It doesn't make sense!" I'd explained it to him twice and even began the task with him. However, the extraneous visual information (the dots) was too much for him. A few days later, I read that this type of extraneous information creates an excessive perceptual load on some children. The page of exercises and dots appears to be a wild and often indecipherable page of mishmash for these children. (April 22, 1999)

I used three discourses during the year to make sense of frustration or failure: critique of the individual, the local structure, and the larger societal structure. Although I tended to use these discourses at particular times of the year, all three discourses were expressed throughout the year. Interestingly, many of my explanations for frustration were contradictory, and I often expressed contradictory perspectives in the same journal excerpt, sometimes in the same breath. The discourses also seemed to coexist quite easily, even when they were blatantly contradictory, such as when I explained school failure to be an effect of poverty and an inequitable economic system at the same time I psychologized a student as having an in-the-head disorder that resulted in much classroom dysfunction, all in the same paragraph. For example, in a long and rambling February 17 journal entry, I included multiple discourses to make sense of my teaching difficulties: I was angry about a student (a motivation problem!) who completed work only if I was sitting next to him; the inhumanity of having students constrained all day at little desks alongside others not of their choosing; a state legislature that was "strangling public education"; a school district that was mismanaging a poor budget situation; and my own miscues when negotiating with students. In my reading of the data, I noticed that when I shifted from one discourse to the next, I did not ever explicitly critique a previous discourse as inappropriate or wrong. The fact that I cycled continuously among the multiple discourses suggests that they all held out some usefulness to me in my theorizing of school failure or, more specifically, my struggle or frustration as a teacher.

## Changing Beliefs

My beliefs about what it meant to be a teacher changed and were reshaped by the realities of everyday teaching. These beliefs had to do with my metacognitions on teaching and curriculum and, particularly, what I believed to be the right way to teach as well as a curriculum that was worthy of public education in a democracy.

My metacognitions about teaching and curriculum also included ideas about the dispositions and attitudes of the teacher. Early on, I believed that teachers tended to be optimistic, and they experienced teaching as "fun." I believed that all students can learn. I had made little room in my identity for pessimism about myself and my students or the notion of teaching as "work." Gradually and throughout the year, I began making comments that framed teaching not only as "work" but as "impossible" work. I became more pessimistic about the notion that the "good teacher," alone, is able to influence learning and achievement. Certainly, I expressed optimism about teaching, and I did articulate beliefs that describe teaching as fun and hopeful. However, the pessimistic motif in my thinking dominated, especially in the beginning of the year.

> I am struck by the increasing self-doubt about my ability to meet the needs of all my students. This goal is part of the corporate self for teachers: meeting everyone's needs. Even in the best of circumstances (e.g., a class of conformist students), it is virtually impossible to truly meet individual students' needs. I am not sure how I am coping with this threat to my teaching self. (November 12, 1998)

In this excerpt, I expressed self-doubt about my efficacy as a teacher. Entries that expressed self-doubt and uncertainty permeated the journal.

I constructed a set of heuristics that reflected a view of "teaching as work." I used these heuristics to rationalize or make sense of bad days, or when presenting a face to the public. When people in the community would ask me how I "enjoyed being back in the classroom," my standard response was, "Oh, yeah. I'm learning that teaching is hard work." I found myself feeling an emotional lift on Fridays, the last day of the week, and I found myself feeling a little depressed on Sunday nights.

> It's Sunday night, and I am grieving. The weekend is coming to a close. Tomorrow, I enter the culture of at-risk children. I recall several times in the past few weeks when teachers at the school asked me if I am having fun yet. I'm not having fun at all. (I wonder if they are having fun, but I don't have the nerve to ask them. I would be crushed if they said, "Yes.") I respond, with a smile on my face, "Teaching's hard work." It's one of an emerging set of mantras I use to cope with or frame this experience. (September 13, 1998)

My beliefs about the curriculum were also reshaped during the year. Before the year started, I was unambiguously student centered in my orientation to curriculum and teaching. There was also an expectation among the other teachers in the school that my behavior reflected the school's ethos (developmentally appropriate/child centered). This expectation wore heavily on me, especially as people expected my teaching to be student centered when, in fact, I was shifting to a more text-centered and skills-based orientation. I believed that some students needed to be given fewer choices about academic tasks, more didactic skill instruction, and more direction regarding their behavior.

Even as I expressed a more skills-based and teacher-centered belief system, I worked to find spaces in the day to do more "meaningful" teaching. I did this in the storytelling units, by having the students write original math story problems, by teaching math problem-solving heuristics, and by conducting social studies units on racism, African American history, and gender bias. In these units, students posed their own questions, pursued independent projects, and generally had more control over the content of their activity. These units of study gave me much satisfaction. I noticed that doing more "meaningful" teaching was dependent, first, on my strong background knowledge in these subjects and, second, on the students' willingness or ability to engage in this work. However, my weak background knowledge in mathematics, resistant students, and the pressures of the state tests led me to teach more algorithmic and arithmetic-based mathematics than I was comfortable doing. This led me to some embarrassing experiences with friends and colleagues who assumed my old (student-centered/conceptually oriented) identity was still my operative point of view.

Tonight, before bed, I surreptitiously (in my head) went to Kinko's to do some copying. I didn't tell anyone what I was doing, not Melinda, Dorothy, or anyone else. I made copies of basic fact sheets—drill and practice. I do more of this than I am comfortable with, and I am slightly embarrassed that I've resorted to this. I am concerned that my students will not be facile with basic number operations by the end of the year. But I also rely on paper–pencil arithmetic as a management device. When I work with multiple math groups, I need the groups with whom I am not working at the moment to be engaged in work that can be accomplished without my help.

Today, a friend who is the director of the local Montessori school walked in and saw the copies of the drill and practice. I leaned over and tried to cover the copies. To my horror, I left one pile of papers uncovered, and he picked them up and immediately rolled his eyes as if to say, "You've got to be kidding." He offered to loan me a book on teaching math developmentally. I sheepishly accepted his offer, as I lamely tried to reassure him that skill/drill is not the emphasis of my math program.

Kinko's is open twenty-four hours a day. Next time, I will copy this stuff between midnight and 6:00 a.m. Under the cover of night. (March 10, 1999)

As I struggled with the tension between student centered and teacher centered, I was confused by contradictory messages in the professional literature. In some of the literature, there is a "consensus" that students in high-poverty schools will achieve and thrive in instructional environments that give students more control in the performance of authentic literacy activity. However, there are other respected educators who argue that high-poverty students may need more direction and less control. Teachers in my building whom I respected, such as my job-share partner Dorothy, believed that child-centered approaches would work with these students if the school were more consistent and adept at implementing this approach. Still, I observed very good teachers in my school struggling to do meaningful teaching to certain types of students.

I struggled with the school ethos, which favored student-centered structures, and my own emerging identity, which recognized the usefulness of other perspectives. I found myself constrained by the culture of the school as well as the availability of resources, such as furniture. In the spring, I wanted the students to sit in their own seats and in rows, a very traditional arrangement. However, I did have a teaching self-conception that valued a more social, collaborative classroom arrangement: students sitting at tables, group problem solving, and even peer conflict as a healthy antecedent to learning and development. However, some of my students were not ready for the intense interaction of table groups, nor was I proficient enough at teaching social skills at this time.

> Something is not right about how we do teaching, the curriculum, and the physical arrangement of classes. My sense is that we need to be much more structured, do more direct instruction, give the kids fewer choices, and rearrange the layout of classrooms to account for distractability. Not all kids need this hyperstructured environment.
>
> ... I would love to get desks and put my kids in rows. I would like to find some credible textbooks and get the kids focused on this work. I would like to implement a tight behavior modification program for the kids who need it. I would like to enforce a rule that all classrooms are quiet places where the student's job is to generate hard copy. I would like to have students working alone more than they are now. I would like to give students their own desks, so they can learn to take care of their own place. And then, when there is some calm and quiet and focus, only then must we begin teaching the kids how to cooperate, how to make decisions over an increasingly complex number of choices, how to find the answers to their own questions, how to work cooperatively, how to solve their own problems, and yes, how to think critically both of text as well as their social lives.

But I am scared about making these suggestions, in general and certainly at this school. In the 1990s, this school was renowned in the region for its implementation of developmentally appropriate practice and nongraded classrooms. (April 27, 1999)

I was constrained by fear, fear of my colleagues' disdain and rejection. I was also constrained by the fact that at this time there were no available chairs and desks in the school district furniture supply. Perhaps I was most constrained by my own technical skills at managing groups of students that, if I had continued my sabbatical for a second year, I would have learned to manage well enough that table groupings would have been more successful. I will never know.

Still, as my beliefs moved away from the child and toward external structure and order, I had doubts about the right balance, and I played with the idea that the tension between child and curriculum was both natural and inevitable. This reminded me of Dewey's (1938) warnings about "false dichotomies" and the dangers of tilting the balance in curricular orientation too rigidly in one direction or the other.

> The solution is not simply in the imposition of a teacher-centered, didactic, highly structured approach, and neither is the solution the implementation of a child-centered approach. We certainly want our students to find meaning in academic activity. . . . But, at the same time, we need the kids to attend to and focus on these tasks, and well-defined tasks, such as working out of textual resources and being able to sit and attend (cognitively) and learn "skills." We want our kids to learn to make good decisions, but if they have too many choices, they are simply not ready. So the quintessential task is to find the right balance between the "child and the curriculum." (May 13, 1999)

Changes in my beliefs were also psychological in the first three months of school, in the sense that changes in beliefs did not affect my practice, such as my metacognition that teaching *is* hard work. These changes were in my head and my head alone. Another example is my concept of the "good day."

> My notions of success, or a "good day," have really changed in the first five weeks of school. Earlier, I remember being thrilled if the students simply lined up quietly. Then, once this task was accomplished with a bit of consistency, I

found myself excited when the students were engaged quietly in anything. It didn't have to be a learning activity. I remember the students, a few weeks ago, were doing some mindless craft activity, like coloring a picture with crayons. A teacher from down the hallway stuck his head in the door, looked around, smiled at me, and gave a thumbs up. "Hey, you have 'em real focused. Nice!" he said. I was ambivalent about this compliment. Still, I took the compliment from him as a sincere expression.

Now, success means that the students are on task, and they are working on the tasks wholeheartedly and thoroughly. However, I do not yet have the time to closely observe students, talk to them about their activity, and more thoroughly come to understand how they are making sense of their activities. My head is still too busy with planning, gathering materials, and implementing lessons. (October 7, 1998)

By early February, after the students and I had constructed a working consensus and we had more order than before, compliments about my classroom control no longer figured in my conception of the "good day." By the end of the year, my "good day" depended on meaningful learning and quality interactions.

It is important to point out that these phases in my conceptions of the good day were not simply sequential and linear. I sometimes had bad days late in the spring when the students were out of control. In September, I experienced some bad days when no learning occurred, but at least the students were all sedate(d). Or I had some great days early in the year when some meaningful learning occurred. As I experienced days as either good, bad, or something in between, there were certain unpredictable factors at play, such as an unexpected comment from a peer or parent, a conflict with a student at the end of the day, or on a day that was otherwise a disaster, some sublime act of beauty performed by the students in the last twenty minutes. The quality of a day could be contingent on the teacher's and students' moods, the unwitting cues the teacher gives the students, or even the weather.

My move toward teacher-centered instruction was driven by at least three factors: I had less background knowledge in an area; the students were impatient with my indecisiveness as I haltingly or nervously engaged in teaching subjects in which I had less background knowledge; and the state tests. I wanted to have a more democratic classroom, for example, using class meetings as a place for dialogue between and among students and me. However, there was a group of nonconformist students who made my democratic/collaborative ideals difficult to implement, especially given my inexperience at managing a classroom. I wanted to implement a more meaning-oriented approach to the learning of mathematics. However, I was a novice at teaching this subject conceptually and, again, the students were unforgiving with a teacher who was indecisive pedagogically. I was also concerned about the state tests to be administered in April. The tests contained much algorithmic arithmetic and low-level mathematics, and I believed the most efficient way to prepare my students for the tests was to have them work their way through the mathematics textbook.

## Problem-Solving Behavior to Improve Practice

I engaged in problem-solving behavior when I found that my teaching was not working well. Problem-solving behavior here is defined as behavior that proactively aims to change my practice or my behavior as it relates to perceived problems or discrepancies. This category of behavior permeated the journal as it does the life of most practitioners. This problem solving entailed simply my work to change my teaching or my thinking, in order to address some problem in my work.

The focus of analysis here as it relates to my problem-solving work is the *planning* I did to address problems. Planning behavior is a metacognitive behavior that is representative of my identities, as it is for most teachers.[6] Two planning behaviors, however, were less obvious and surprised me in the frequency of their occurrence in the journal. These are the *self-exhortation behavior* and the *use of my private life* to inform and structure my thinking. While these behaviors may be commonsensical, I rarely make these planning behaviors explicit in my work with preservice teachers, and I do not recall much mention of these in the teacher education literature.

### Exhorting the Self

I did much self-exhortation as I responded to the tension between my self-conception and the reality of my teaching. These journal entries are prefaced with language such as, "I need to be more, . . ." "I should, . . ." or "I want to. . . ." Self-exhortations were responses to frustrating experiences. This self-exhortation entailed talk that was aimed at two dimensions of my work: improving my teaching practice and improving the quality of my relations with students, parents, and colleagues.

I consistently articulated support for a meaning-based and holistic curricular experience, and a discourse of "meaningfulness" permeated my thinking throughout the year. I was always exhorting myself to more effectively develop curriculum that would excite students or would draw on their curiosities.

> Kids *want* to be interested. They want to be engaged wholeheartedly in activity that matters. Of course. With the readings, discussion, and videos done in the black history unit, I noticed that the kids have been really interested. The topics are about real struggle, real lives, and people who are different than them. I am planning a month-long unit on ecology to end the year. I want to make this unit provocative. I am hopeful that these kids can wholeheartedly engage in academic work if the content is interesting. (April 7, 1999)

I was uncomfortable with my skills-based teaching in certain areas of the curriculum, so the self-exhortations to teach meaningfully served to defend myself from my own criticism.

Along with this, I repeatedly exhorted myself to care for all my students, and I even evoked the Golden Rule on several occasions to guide my relations with students and colleagues. In what I call the discourse of "caring," I envisioned how I ought to treat others. For example, after I forgot a student I had sent to the office because he had head lice, I was gripped with guilt, and I used my daughter to inform an ethical response.

> I sure would want my daughter's teacher to behave more compassionately to her if she had to sit in the office all day, with head lice. As a criterion for how I ought to interact with my students, I think about how I want my daughter's teachers to interact with her. The Golden Rule. . . . (September 26, 1998)

I expressed an interest in caring relations with students, both at the interpersonal and professional levels.

> I want to be a caring teacher. This means, among other things, that I insist that all my students do their work, and they do it well. A caring teacher cares about

the academic or intellectual well-being of the students. But this type of caring takes time and organization. It's very labor intensive. (February 22, 1999)

Countering the pressure to focus my attention on group needs, I continually exhorted myself to care for the individual student.

> I am concerned because I believe that my students . . . need a caring adult who is going to listen to them. Really listen. Often, I have to say, "Oh, I'm sorry. We just don't have the time today," or "Can we talk about this after math?" or "Can I look at your work later?" Stevie brings a book that he wants me to read to the class. It is inappropriate for the class, and I have other read-alouds planned that would have more positive impact on the group. But if I read his book, his heart would swell and he would feel like a million dollars. I could deflect his request by my reading his book privately and talking with him about the book. Still, he would feel a slight disappointment because he wanted me to read this favorite book to the whole class. (October 15, 1998)

Ironically, in contradiction to this idea of caring for all students, I exhorted myself to limit my caring for all students. I recognized the inherent frustration reflected in the ideal that teachers meet the needs of all students.

> Why do teachers complain so much? I think it's because the job is inherently doomed to failure. If we buy into a prevailing teacher discourse, our responsibility is to meet the needs of all children. I think it is virtually impossible to meet the needs of all students, especially when we have (typically) large classes (twenty to thirty students), which include many high-needs kids. (December 18, 1998)

The tension here is between one voice that aims to meet the needs of all students and another voice that recognizes the realities of everyday teaching and the limitations of one teacher working with a large group of needy students.

I also directed myself in how I thought about colleagues. Here, I cajole myself to be less judgmental.

> Perhaps I should not rush to judgment by attributing teachers' political inaction simply to some basic core conservatism. The material and institutional context of teaching has much to do with how they make sense of political action. (October 7, 1998)

The self-exhortations were responses to moments when I behaved in ways that conflicted with my self-conception. The self-exhortations suggest a tension between my identities and the demands of the situation, often represented in contradictory discourses that never quite were resolved. I sometimes felt that I was not behaving in a caring manner with the students. I would be brusque and more concerned with classroom order and the accomplishment of work. Hence, I would respond with a self-exhortation that reflected my core belief about the imperative to care for all students. Or I would be overwhelmed by the high number of students who needed my attention, and I simply could not get around to everyone. The material reality of my work made it virtually impossible to care for all the students in a way that made sense to me. In response, my exhortation would be a refrain about the importance of meeting all students' needs. I also found that meaning-based curriculum was too messy and, instead, the use of worksheets and seat work made it easier to keep the students quiet and busy. The historic school discourse that privileges order and busy-ness conflicted with another historic discourse, meaningfulness.

*Personal Life Merges with Professional Life*

As a way of dealing with problems, my personal life seemed to merge with my professional life in two ways. First, I used my children and my identity as a parent to reference and inform relations with students. Second, I found that I worked as a teacher on my own time: at home, on trips, in my dreams. This work entailed actual physical labor, such as organizing materials to develop curriculum plans, or it simply entailed nonstop thinking about school during my time away from work.

As I wrote earlier in this chapter, I used my own children to inform my thinking about how to treat my students. When I would lose my temper with a student or do something with a student that was questionable, I would often ask myself, Is this how I would want some teacher to treat my own children?

> When I think of my own children and their teachers, I would like their teachers to take the time to talk to and get to know my kids. I realize how little time there is for teachers to do this, but a teacher who works at it can squeeze a bit

of socializing into the cracks that creep into the daily schedule. I am constrained a bit by my half-time schedule. (October 12, 1998)

I also used my parent perspective to inform my thinking. When a parent criticized my teaching, I rationalized his criticism as the right of all parents.

I also recognize the parent's right to . . . demand an appropriate education for his child. I have the same concerns about my child, who is now in first grade. Initially, my feelings were a bit ruffled by the parent (and student) criticism. Once I'd gotten used to the idea, my thoughts were more driven by questions and solutions for how I can develop a more challenging math program for this student. Still, my professional ego is bruised from this criticism. (October 21, 1998)

School was on my mind virtually all the time, especially when things were not going well. The thinking I did about my teaching, on my own time, was a type of planning behavior that was a response to a felt discrepancy between my teaching self-conception and my actual teaching situation/performance. One obvious manifestation of this blurring of the personal and the public was insomnia.

This morning, before I knew I was staying home this morning, I woke up at 4:30 a.m. with high anxiety about the week looming ahead. I couldn't fall back to sleep. I worried about my observation by Judy, the principal, tomorrow, a day without Barbara since she is going to a reading methods workshop. I worried about my next unit after the food chain, a social studies unit I have yet to plan. And I worried about facing my kids for another week. (February 1, 1999)

Besides insomnia, I spent an inordinate amount of personal time engaged in lesson planning.

I got home from an ice cream social at the school. It's 8:15 p.m. I thought about tomorrow afternoon. There was so much to do and think about. I put a poem about clouds on butcher paper for a whole-group choral reading. I also made a cloud painting, a model for the kids today when I want them to do the same. I couldn't find white paint in my school (for the cloud paintings), so I drove to a store, only to find that they sold white paint in very small quantities at a high cost. I asked Melinda, my wife, if she had any in her classroom. She said yes, so tomorrow morning before I go in to work I will stop by her school to pick up some paint from her.

I practiced doing a math center as I prepared to introduce it to the students.

I perused several books on creative drama in the elementary classroom. I planned pantomiming activities for tomorrow.

I called Mary, one of the students who has been absent for three days. She has been sick and is coming back to school tomorrow. Her mom appreciates my call.

I watched a thirty-minute videotape on classroom management. I took notes. Before the tape ended, I got tired, turned off the TV, and went upstairs. All the lights were out. Melinda had gone to bed. I climbed into bed around 11:15 and was unable to fall asleep. I thought about the next day for about an hour. I woke up at 5:30 a.m. thinking about what I need to do. (September 15, 1998)

I realized early on that the (self-imposed) work regimen as a teacher was going to adversely effect my quality time with my own children. I sensed that, in order to maintain my self-conception professionally, I would have to immerse myself in work, and as a result I would have less emotional energy for home.

I got home and was impatient with my own children, and I felt guilty. I worried about the implications of a stressful teaching assignment on my life as a parent. I anxiously put my two-year-old to bed. I was scared because tonight I didn't have any psychic energy for my own children. (September 2, 1998)

There was a tension between my identity as a parent and my identity as a teacher. I found that my temper was shorter with my children, and I had less psychic energy to devote to them.

Later, at home, I was depressed at dinner and didn't talk. Later, I yelled at Claire for something that really didn't matter. . . . Sometime after dinner I really lost it. I went outside in the cool April evening and cried. I cried as I thought about how we had failed these kids, how the system had failed their parents, how their parents had failed them, as had the school system and teachers. I blamed my own novicedom and my own tendency to take the expedient strategy when faced with difficult teaching or social problems with the kids. (April 2, 1999)

There are other aspects of my teaching that affected my personal life, behaviors that are unexceptional for many teachers. I spent much money, out
of my own pocket, for classroom materials. I spent time with some of my colleagues outside school, and we inevitably talked about school. I attended
some of my students' birthday parties, visited students in the hospital, and
took students out to lunch occasionally. I sometimes ate lunch with the students during the school day, a practice that reduced down-time opportunities for me.

In the boundary area of my self-conception and the reality of teaching, I
used my personal life to make sense of the confusion and frustration of teaching. Throughout the year, I struggled with the competing tasks of caring for
myself as a teacher, caring for my students, caring for myself as a person, and
caring for my own family. My identities as a parent certainly gave me a useful
reference point in my caring for students. However, I was so immersed with
work that it disrupted my identities as a parent. I simply did not have the
same amount of time and emotional and physical energy for my own children. I suppose that this blurring between the public and private spheres is
not unusual for other kinds of work, especially for the beginning practitioner
in any type of complex work.

## Managing Impressions

A frequent response to problematic teaching outcomes was to pretend that
things were going well, or to create the public impression that I was at ease
with my struggles when, indeed, things were not going well or I was not at
ease.[7] Following the "feeling rules" for teachers at my school, I perceived an
expectation that I had to be (or appear to be) caring, competent, and confident. The audience for this performance was the usual suspects: the students, their parents, the other teachers, the principal, people in the community, and even myself. The psychological reality of my teaching identities,
especially in the beginning of the year but certainly throughout the year, was
that I was full of self-doubt and often frazzled before, during, and after working with the students. On the surface, however, I constructed a teacher voice
of confidence and control, since I wanted people to think that I was competent. However, very early in the year, I feared that people would see through
my mask.

I don't know the kids, they don't know me, and I don't know yet what kind of curriculum is appropriate for them. In my stomach, I sense that this is going to be a difficult year. A feeling that I've had under my skin is now surfacing: I am almost like a beginning teacher, and I think the kids have already picked up on this fact. Uh, oh! The jig is up. (September 3, 1998)

Saul, another primary teacher, asked if he could come into my room and watch some "demonstration teaching from the master." His language was a bit tongue in cheek, but he expected to see me do some good teaching.

I felt my face flush, and I became embarrassed. My voice said, "Yeah, sure, any time." But I suppose my nonverbal signal was obvious to him, so he backed off, saying, "Great . . . uh . . . I can't observe today, but I'll come back soon." And he was out the door.

I was embarrassed to have him observe me, because I don't feel good about my math program. I have a fuzzy image of what it should look like, but I am light years away from this image. I was also embarrassed at being embarrassed. I will talk to him and explain why my response to him was so unenthusiastic. (November 5, 1998)

I did let my mask down purposefully, but only in very safe settings, such as with my wife, with some trusted friends, or with my therapist. Occasionally, I inadvertently let the mask fall in public settings, such as at a huge Thanksgiving Day party at a friend's house. There were ten or so local teachers at the party. I spoke frankly about my struggles and doubts about teaching. The next Monday, my principal asked me, "So I hear around town that you are really struggling. You want to talk about it?" I was mortified that people around town were talking about me, and my status as a competent teacher was at risk.

Later in the year, the school counselor at my wife's school said to me in passing, "So, I hear you're getting pretty scarred this year. Tough class?" This comment put a chink in the armor of my front. I had a sense of myself as a competent, in control, and confident teacher. I did not *think* I was getting scarred. My response to him was to go into denial. "No, no, not at all. I'm doing quite well. Teaching *is* hard work, isn't it?" As I thought about his comment later on, I feared that he was right and I was actually getting scarred. The incident, described earlier, when I was discovered by the director of the local

Montessori school running off copies of drill and practice late at night at Kinkos, is another example of the mask inadvertently falling away. I wanted to be known as a teacher who taught from a conceptual, or meaningful, orientation, not as a skills-based, skill-and-drill aficionado. In the space between my self-conception, which reflected the idea that teachers ought to be confident, controlled, competent, and conceptual, and the reality of my teaching, I constructed a regime of impression-management stances that reduced the threat to my identities. Sometimes these "face" strategies worked; I imagine that sometimes people saw through my mask; and sometimes I accidentally let my backstage reality slip out. The tension between my felt emotions and the emotional requirements of the role seemed to be unrelenting, ineluctable, and wearing. Impression management was part of my teacher identity, as it is part of other aspects of my everyday life.

## Aligning with Reference Groups

When my goals for teaching were, at best, partially realized, I found myself aligning myself with others who validated me and my emerging beliefs. These reference groups served to reassure me that I was a competent teacher and a good person, self-images that were at risk in the disorderly world of my classroom. These reference groups included a special education specialist from an area education service office who affirmed my new belief that "all students have special needs" and that teachers are hugely underprepared to work with special needs students. Using my friend's idea, I deflected criticism of my failure with these students by blaming teacher education programs, by rationalizing that teacher education had not done a good job of preparing teachers to work with special populations.

I also found several colleagues in the school who shared my belief that the students in the school were, indeed, exceptionally difficult and that some of the existing academic and management structures were inappropriate for this population. These colleagues affirmed my sanity and my emerging sense of the situation. These individuals shared my cynical self, so we were able to complain about things without self-consciousness. Our complaining usually focused on forces outside ourselves and the school, such as the district administration, an inequitable economic system, and the lack of support for our families.

Dorothy, Barbara, and Fran also served as a reference group simply by their nonjudgmental stance toward me. I sensed that they knew that I was struggling and was prone to mistakes, but they never criticized me once to my face all year. I felt safe with them as a "beginning teacher." This sense of safety made it easier for me to fail, since these individuals were usually in the room and observing me as I taught.

> Fortunately, my colleagues at Woodbridge were caring and supportive of me. I felt safe. The principal was an old friend with whom I was able to talk frankly. And Dorothy, Barbara, and Fran, people who watched me everyday, were nonjudgmental and caring people. My colleagues never showed any negative evaluation of my work, and they appeared to accept me for who I was: basically, a mixed bag. . . . Over the first several months of school, my teaching self changed to fit this experience, and the emotional pain that I felt early on about my "failure" as a teacher gradually gave way to acceptance. I became more comfortable with my new self, as novice teacher. I doubt that I could have transitioned to this new self as easily if it hadn't been for my significant others (Dorothy, Barbara, and Fran), who accepted me for who I was. (September 16, 1998)

The students were a key reference group for me. In spite of my frustration with my ability to maintain order and to teach, the students all liked me, and so did most of their parents. Each day, I was greeted with hugs and smiles. Students invited me to their homes for birthday parties, and one rather needy boy wanted us to spend the weekends together. In the journal, I often emphasize the primacy of relations with students and the idea that it is the interpersonal stance of the teacher that is the most enduring lesson for students.

> Another reason that I am beginning to look forward to school is the warm response of the children. Our students are important "reference groups" for teachers (Nias, 1989). . . . [Students] indeed create our reality as much as we create their reality (Riseborough, 1985). The warm affective response of the kids supports my self-concept as a warm, caring person. The hugs, joking, high-fiving, and laughter validate me and affirm me as someone who is important and consequential in their school lives. (October 7, 1998)

For the most part, I had positive personal relations with students. I drew on this aspect of teaching to deflect or blunt my uneasiness with the frustration

I felt with my teaching of the academics as well as the classroom disorder. In spite of the problems I was having maintaining order and constructing a functional learning environment, I found solace in the fact that the students (and even most of the parents) liked me.

> One dimension of my work that sustains me is my relationship with the students. We genuinely like each other. I really enjoy talking to them and being with them. Some kids clap when I enter the room. I get many hugs. . . . Perhaps one essential benefit of my work with the kids this year will be their association with an adult (me) who is caring, thoughtful, and easygoing. Perhaps the model of who I am as a person is the most significant lesson for my students. (December 16, 1998)

I had other, more distant reference groups that served to validate my self-concept. I focused quite a bit on problem solving in mathematics, and I regularly had the students write their own story problems. I also taught storytelling to my students, along with units on gender studies, African American history, and racism. I found support for this curriculum in the educational literature, such as the National Council of Teachers of Mathematics (NCTM) Standards (1989), the *Rethinking Schools* journal, and Donald Graves (1983). In addition to significant professional allies nearby, I used these more distant reference groups to reassure me to continue with this kind of curriculum.

When faced with problematic situations, I drew upon my reference groups to reconcile or make sense of the tension. For example, when my class was out of control, I had colleagues who listened to my frustrated voice and responded by saying, in effect, "Yes, our students do the same thing. It's not you." I felt validated when my special educator friend agreed that most regular classroom teachers were inadequately prepared to teach special needs students, so I blamed myself less for my struggles with these students. My teacher education program was at fault, not me! When I felt insecure about my teaching, I found solace in my interpersonal relations with the students. When I found myself moving away from conceptual teaching, because of my need for control, I used my memory of the NCTM Standards to remind myself to keep one foot in teaching for meaning.

## IDENTIT(IES) AS CONTINGENT, CONTESTED, AND DEFENSIVE

The persistent challenge for me as a beginning teacher was the construction of identities that *worked* in my current teaching situation. My emergent identity was constructed in the space between what I imagined to be my stable, or core, beliefs as a teacher and the everyday conditions or realities of this work. There was an unrelenting dance between often changing teaching conditions and my identities. As the reality of the job changed, as my circumstances changed, my identity then responded, shifted, and changed. Identities were contingent and temporary, dependent on changing situations, including my own evolving knowledge of teaching.

My reading of the data is suggestive of a teacher identity that is not stable and uniform but, instead, teacher *identities* that are multiple, competing, contradictory, historic, and contingent on immediate circumstances. Like the chameleon's color, which changes as the environment changes, so too does teacher identity change as the teacher's environment changes, through changes in students, developing teacher skills, colleagues, parents, policy (local, state, and federal), as well as the minutia of everyday life (such as the weather, mood, and time of day/week/year). There are certainly more stable, perhaps core, dimensions of identity, and these relate to one's personality, one's history as a student, family background, and the larger culture and history of schools. But the contingent in our lives does significantly influence identity, and it is the continual interaction between the contingent and permanent that shapes and reshapes identities. The following is a synthesis representation of my teacher identities as reflected in my reading of the data.

1. In the United States, popular images often represent the teacher as happy, self-assured, confident, and satisfied in her relations with students. Implicit in many texts for preservice teachers is a representation of teachers as rational, dispassionate, decisive, and enthusiastic about their work. Of course, anyone who has spent any time in classrooms knows that the dispositional and psychological experience of teaching is not so unambiguous and unproblematic. While I did find joy and satisfaction in my work, I also disliked this work as well. I experienced work at times to be deeply meaningful and at other times to be odious and repugnant. I thought of myself as having

passion for my work, and I tried to evoke passionate responses in my students. However, my identity had to make room for unhappiness, self-doubt, uncertainty, and dissatisfaction with my relations with students. I was both pessimistic and optimistic about teaching and public education, at various times and as the circumstances varied.

2. The ethos of my school, reflecting a particular tradition in elementary education in the United States, was student centered and social constructivist. This reflects my personal theory of teaching and learning as well as my work as a teacher educator. However, my identities had to make room for alternative discourses, such as more didactic, teacher- and text-centered, skill-oriented, and custodial classroom arrangements. I found that to get any work—any learning—done, I had to impose more control on the students; some students were given fewer choices; small groups were "inappropriate" at many times with many of the students; and sometimes, I taught less conceptually. The circumstances driving this more teacher-centered identity were a group of students who were difficult to control, my inexperience with the teaching of math and science from an inquiry perspective, and my inexperience managing behaviorally challenging students. Woods (1990a) and Dudley-Marling (1997) also found there to be more pressure on teachers to be text centered when they had fewer resources: that is, they had less experience, they had less training and education, and their personal abilities, beliefs, attitudes, and commitment were insufficient to sustain student-centered teaching. Certainly, a huge factor in my reliance on skills-based approaches in mathematics was the April state tests, which emphasized lower-level knowledge.

3. My parent and teacher identities each competed with and enhanced the other (cf., Bullough & Baughman, 1997; Pajak & Blase, 1989). My teaching identities were reshaped, diverted, and subordinated to my parent identity. Concomitantly, my parent identity was reshaped, diverted, and subordinated to my teacher identity. My knowledge as a parent informed my relations with students, but my responsibilities as a parent reduced the amount of time I thought about teaching and engaged in planning. Similarly, the mental space that teaching took up in my head made me more distant to my own children during the year.

Teaching, especially beginning teaching, was a totalizing experience. It dominated my consciousness and unconscious. It seeped into my dreams, my personal conversations, and my thinking just about every day. There seemed to be a merger of my personal and professional identities that, perhaps, is an inevitable and unsettling dimension of beginning teaching (Danielewicz, 2001; Huberman, 1993). Goffman (1961) studied how certain institutions, such as the military and mental hospitals, dominate and shape the identities of individuals living in those institutions. While "beginning teaching" is not an institution per se, the effect of beginning teaching is similar to what is seen in Goffman's rendition of the totalizing effect of institutions such as asylums and the army. For beginning teachers, there is a danger that the weight of everyday teaching might powerfully impress teaching identities that reflect the need to survive, to protect self-conceptions, and to maintain a public persona as a competent professional when, in fact, the reality may be very different.

4. I cared much about what other people thought of me, and these people were first and foremost other teachers, in my school and around town. Waller (1965) claimed that a key moment of assimilation into the teaching world is when the teacher understands that it is peers' opinions that matter most. "This means that the teacher enters negotiations with the pupils with a predetermined intention of living up to the expectations of his colleagues" (Hargreaves, 1972, 147). I did much impression management (Goffman, 1959). My concern with my public self and my sense of how others perceived me did drive much of my behavior. I wanted to be viewed by my community as competent. Fundamentally, this motivated me to problem solve and become a better teacher. However, it also led me at times to *feign* competence. I became acutely aware of impression management, as part of my identity. I do not view the need to "look good" as particularly indigenous to the teacher role, since our "presentation of self in everyday life" is, basically, part of the roles we play in life. Since my concerns with how others perceived me motivated me to be more effective as a teacher, this aspect of my identity may be, in part, a functional dimension of my identity. However, I think one's focus on impression management can also be a dysfunctional dimension of identity when there is a large and persistent gap between reality and the impressions one is projecting to others. For example, a teacher who continually pretends to be happy when, in fact, he is depressed, can experience deep feelings of alienation from work, or what Hochschild (1983) refers to as "going robotic."

5. I also sense that my personal ethics interacted in some way with what I believed were the ethics reflected in the teacher's role, and these ethical considerations framed or informed my teacher identity, including what impressions exactly I wanted to construct. So much of my thinking, when faced with frustration, was to cajole myself to behave more ethically: for example, to be more caring with students or to help students find more meaning in curricular experience. I thought a lot about being a good person with my students. The role itself (as teacher) motivated me to be more patient, more curious, and less judgmental, since these traits reflected my conception of the role. Similarly, other teachers have noted that, as they work to construct a role as teacher, they strive to achieve a higher ethical standard. These teachers find that "teaching broadens and deepens their human sympathies, their imaginations, and their desire to learn" (Hanson, 2001, 852). It is not unusual for teachers to use their moral or spiritual goals in life to inform their work with students (Buchman, 1986; Pajak & Blase, 1989).

My sense of teacher identities now is more complex, multifaceted, flexible, and contradictory than it was before the sabbatical. I suspect that what for me are "ideal" teacher identities, if there is such a thing as ideal, comprise many perspectives and many positions, at different times and under varying circumstances. This requires that the teacher is able to entertain contradictory discourses at the same time, discourses that both hold appeal and then allow a teacher to assertively make decisions while somewhat conscious of the dilemmas and contradictions inherent in those decisions. As Bakhtin suggests, the challenge is to bring our own intentions and voices to the language we use. While psychological wholeness can result from taking the perspectives of multiple others, Hewitt (1989) argues that it is important for the person to keep one community dominant in one's mind, on a day-to-day basis. This is a "community of reference and the source of the generalized other . . . (a mainstay community). . . . [H]aving a major purpose and a main community . . . makes it possible to work towards other purposes and to identify with others" (227). When challenged, the individual has "at least temporarily established the priority of one social context and its associated identity over another context and its identity" (Hewitt, 1989, 225).

As much as I am arguing for a more fluid and hybrid[8] type of teacher identity, some recurrent beliefs did provide me with an overarching framework as a point of departure for other purposes and other identifications, such as my commitment to conceptual teaching and caring relations with students; my opposition to the bureaucratic nature of school life and interest in humanizing teacher–student relations; and a holistic curriculum that strives toward meaningfulness and authenticity. It is *from* these core self-conceptions that I found myself constantly moving back and forth among various discourses for teaching, in a way similar to Hewitt's (1989) characterization of the pragmatic identifiers who "live on a wire" (225). Perhaps a useful metaphor for teaching identity is the tightrope walker, who uses the rope as a base structure to keep from falling into the abyss, while there is continuous movement back and forth, among different positions and perspectives, with the body always tilting back toward the middle.

I also am more sensitive to a notion of teaching as inherently incomplete and partial work (Britzman, 1986; Burbules, 1995). Burbules goes as far as to characterize teaching as a tragic endeavor in which the protagonist acts in good faith but without realizing the folly of her actions (the audience knows of the protagonist's imminent demise). All teaching is inherently frustrating, since our intention as teachers is almost always going to be only partially achieved, given the free will, diversity, and resistance of our students and the constraints of our teaching situations. The teacher who is welded to an idea or belief, in spite of circumstances that conflict with the idea, may be doomed to failure or frustration. The task for the beginning teacher is to understand that all teaching requires trade-offs, that there is a silver lining in any cloud of failure, and that there are problems associated with any success (Lampert, 1985). Hargreaves (1972) argues that flexibility is perhaps the quintessential characteristic of the successful teacher.

It is important that beginning teachers have access to a wide set of beliefs and perspectives with which to make sense of the many discourses and pressures that await them as first-year practitioners. Obviously, after twenty years as a teacher, I had the benefit of years of teaching and study of the professional literature, so my reflections on "beginning teaching" were more mature and multifaceted than those of the typical beginning teacher. When I struggled, I was able to shift from one discourse to the next: full of angst, complaining, but always interrogating and deconstructing. Preservice teachers are well served to study the relationship between the macro- and microdimensions of teaching: how larger structural forces such as the economy and culture influence our behavior and identity as teachers, as well as how teachers engage in resistance in spite of external pressures to conform to a dominant discourse. Similarly, it may be useful for beginning teachers to have some understanding of the historical, biographical, cultural, situational, and psychological factors that interact to constitute identities. It can only help beginning teachers to begin thinking about the contradictions inherent in teaching, between child and curriculum, academics and social learning, whole language and part language, teaching as work and teaching as love, and so forth (cf., Berlak and Berlak, 1981; Dudley-Marling, 1997), so they have the anticipatory schemata with which to make sense of these tensions when they inevitably occur. It is this work of making new identities, including the preservice teacher's work to clarify her more stable core self-conceptions, that may enable beginning teachers to weather the storm and stress of the first year and to grow from this experience.

## NOTES

1. *Subjectivity* "refers to the conscious and unconscious thought and emotions of the individual, her sense of herself and her ways of understanding her relation to the world" (Weedon, 1987, 32). Subjectivity recognizes that identity is a social construction instead of an endeavor accomplished by the individual, self made and working alone.

2. Turner (1968) defines *self-conception* as the permanent, stable core self, the "vague but vitally felt idea of what I am like in my best moments, of what I am striving for and have some encouragement to believe I may achieve" (98). Self-image, by contrast, consists of our ideas about ourselves that are more susceptible to change, based on changing situations. The self-conception changes more slowly than self-image, and it is often viewed as permanent and inescapable by the individual. Self-conception can be viewed as an averaging of one's self-images.

3. My teaching self-conception, or identity, was somewhat typical of teachers, especially elementary teachers. For example, Lortie (1975) found that teachers strove to maintain order and student compliance with rules; effect student learning as well as love of learning; and evoke respect and affection from the students. For the teachers Lortie studied, earning the respect of students was crucial. Ironically, studies that examine students' conceptions of the "ideal" teacher match up closely with teachers' conceptions. Woods (1990b) found that students like teachers who know how to talk to young people, are able to distance themselves from the teaching role and be a

bit human (can have laughs), get students to get the work done, and maintain class-room control.

4. For a more detailed description of the school, my teaching situation, and my research method, see the introduction.

5. For a more detailed description of constructivist teaching, see the introduction.

6. The following list comprises my planning behaviors as I engaged in the problem-solving process:

1. I engaged in self-exhortation behavior.
2. To improve practice, I used external resources, such as books, journals, and videotapes.
3. I engaged in informal collaborative relations with faculty.
4. I engaged in introspection, including journaling.
5. I involved parents and solicited their ideas and support.
6. I attended workshops on curriculum, classroom management, and special needs.
7. I used other staff and personnel to assist me, including the school counselor, colleagues, and outside speakers.
8. I used my private life to inform and structure my thinking.

7. See chapter 3 in the current volume for a fuller examination of impression management and emotional labor.

8. Bhabha (1994) writes about the emergence of hybrid cultural identities, given the movement of immigrant people around the world. He uses the image of the stairway as a place of continuous movement of identities that never permanently become attached to one pole or the other. "The stairway as liminal space, in-between the designations of identity, becomes the process of symbolic interaction, the connective tissue that constructs the difference between upper and lower, black and white. The hither and thither of the stairwell, the temporal movement and passage that it allows, prevents identities at either end of it from settling into primordial polarities. This in-terstitial passage between fixed identifications opens up the possibility of a cultural hybridity that entertains difference without an assumed or imposed hierarchy" (4).

# 5

# CONCLUDING ON AN
# OPTIMISTIC NOTE

Teaching *is* hard work. Of course. It is complex, unnerving, relational, draining, joyous, confusing, satisfying, conflictual, consensual, collaborative, full of contradictions, and hugely demanding on time and mind. Like most first-year teachers (Roehrig, Pressley, & Talotta, 2002), I had a challenging year. Some of it was dismal, some of it was encouraging, and some of it was pure joy.

Looking at the glass as half full, however, I can say that there were good reasons to have been plunked down in such a difficult teaching situation. My struggle amplified and made salient many issues of beginning teaching that may have been hidden if I had taught reading to a single-graded class of "ready for school" affluent students. My research goal prior to the start of the year was to study and write about the uses of writing in learning math, science, and social studies. I wanted to write a book about teaching writing across the curriculum to primary-aged students. Early in the experience, however, my research focus morphed into the questions, "How does order get constructed in classrooms and how does a beginning teacher construct a professional identity?"

I learned much about teaching, students, the learning process, and myself. Especially through the early struggle and pain, I came to understand myself as a teacher. Sometime in late January or February, I had *constructed* an identity as a teacher that was somewhat confident and optimistic. My good days became more routine beginning in late January, and I started to look forward to coming to school. I managed to construct the kinds of teaching routines that made it possible for me to feel like a teacher. For me, this meant that there was some order in the class, some learning was happening, and the students and I felt some satisfaction in the worlds we had created together.[1] I would say now—five years after the sabbatical—that my work now has been enhanced by the sabbatical and the years I have spent reflecting and writing about the experience. With my preservice teachers, my teaching now is more nuanced, more relevant, more tentative about "what works," and more sensitive to the students' felt emotional experience of beginning teaching.

In the first few weeks and months of the first year in the classroom, it is normal for the beginning teacher to experience self-doubt and anxiety about his or her ability to control the class. Even experienced teachers I know describe "students-out-of-control" dreams just before the first day of school each year. I think this anxiety reflects the absence of a negotiated order, a set of understandings that get constructed between the teacher and students during the first minutes, hours, and days of the school year. Veteran teachers have the schemata with which to engage more fluidly in the negotiation process with students, in order to establish the working consensus. At this point, most beginning teachers do not have available the well-rehearsed pedagogic routines—including the multiplicity of routines that structure and order all classroom life—and they have to figure out who they are, with the students. While I did not construct a consistent confidence until the winter, there are some beginning teachers who are able to construct this confidence after the first week of school. I think most beginners tend to figure out this identity by midyear, and still others may take the entire year.

Teachers have always struggled with their working conditions (e.g., see Rousmaniere, 1997). Difficult conditions include large class sizes, inadequate resources and funding, and the pressure of negotiating order with diverse groups of students. Still, every generation of teachers has its unique problems and expectations. Currently, teachers have to cope with the increasing poverty of families, a federal law (No Child Left Behind) that seeks to control and punish teachers and schools, and attacks on the whole system of public education. In spite of these difficult working conditions, young people still line up to get into teacher education programs, and teachers endure and even thrive year after year, coming back to work each September, in spite of working conditions that are often harsh and unforgiving.

Sonia Nieto (2003) interviewed a group of accomplished teachers, asking them the question, "What keeps teachers going?" Nieto found that the metacognitive trait common in these teachers' responses was a sense of hope. These teachers had hope that their work mattered, that their efforts would result in increased student learning, better schools, and a more just world. For these teachers, there was much truth to the proverbial bumper sticker "Teachers Make a Difference" as a summation of teachers' collective aspiration. Sometimes the difference teachers make in students' lives are easily observable. The difference we make for our students may not be apparent until years later, when an unexpected note from a student arrives thanking us for our work. And regretfully, there will always be some students for whom teachers and schools simply do not matter and for whom our work is ineffective.

Nieto suggests that hope is tied to teachers' actions. Hope is not some amorphous and psychological state unrelated to our work in the world. Some teachers she studied found hope in their love of students and a deep commitment to their learning and welfare. There was a powerful undercurrent of hope for teachers that they could effect how their students learned and saw/felt the world. Other teachers found hope in teaching for social justice and taking political action to improve their schools and communities. Other teachers were motivated by teaching as intellectual work, by doing collaborative work with other teachers interested in systematic, deliberate, thoughtful inquiry. Some teachers found that their hope derived from their anger and desperation about working conditions, which they used as a catalyst for making some change or taking some action.

In my teaching at Woodbridge, I found hope in my passion for subjects that reflected my core identities as a teacher, such as my units on racism, African American history, mathematics problem writing, gender equity, and storytelling. I found hope in my anger at central administrators, inadequate school funding, and some of the more irrational assumptions underlying mass compulsory public education. I believe that my anger could have been the first step in my taking action to solve the myriad social and economic problems facing schools (Scott, 1990). I also found hope in my relations with students, including my caring ethic—about how I cared for their social/emotional needs as well as their academic needs. Finally, I found hope in my own emerging professional competence. As my teaching skills developed and I noticed this development, my belief that I could make a difference in my students' lives was enhanced.

In the end, the identity that I may have found most meaningful and enduring revolved around the personal relationships I developed with my students and some of my colleagues. The centrality of the relational may be typical in the work of elementary teachers (Nias, 1996). Like my elementary colleagues, I spent time every day with the same twenty-five children for almost ten months. The outcome of this involuntary marriage is that I grew to know my students deeply and I constructed an affection for most of them that endures even now, five years later. My personality and my self-conception as a caring, empathetic, and sensitive person influenced a teacher identity that put a high value on empathetic and friendly relations with students. Clearly, my personal identity affected the professional identity, and my identity as a *caring* teacher influenced my beliefs about teaching. For example, I believe that the quality of teachers' interpersonal relations with students is crucial to the learning experience of students and the teacher's working conditions in the classroom. I believe that one can teach others only when the others believe the teacher likes them. It was important to my motivational state that (I perceived that) my students liked me and that I liked them. I often rationalized my pedagogic flaws by noting that it was my interpersonal relational work with the students that would be the most significant lesson for them. Thinking back to my year in the classroom, it is the everyday relationships that dominate my memory. I remember Crystal's jokes, Kathleen challenging my every move, racing Cesar at recess, spilling my soda and laughing with the kids when they thought I was drinking iced coffee, and all their innocence, optimism, resistance, exuberance, sadness, and joy. It was in the contexts of the personal that I developed a deeper motivation to persist in my work to teach them the academics. It was in the context of the personal that I constructed a commitment to the learning of all of my students, regardless of special needs, gender, race, whatever.

Based on what I've learned, certain aspects of teacher education programs and in-service programs for beginning teachers seem self-evident to me. In the chapters on emotions, negotiations, and identity development, I concluded each chapter with a set of recommendations regarding teacher education and early teaching. Instead of repeating myself, I offer here several overarching recommendations not included in earlier chapters (and then I repeat myself at the very end).

Teacher education programs matter! My advocacy for teacher education programs is not trivial, since there are powerful interest groups that aim to deregulate university teacher education (Cochran-Smith, 2004). Voucher systems, which have proliferated in the United States in the past ten years, are a real threat to university teacher education, since teachers in private schools do not need to have a formal teaching license and do not need to have graduated from a certified teacher education program. States have begun to adopt alternative pathways to teacher licensure. University teacher education programs in the United States tend to take the blame for much of what ails public education in the United States. In the rhetoric of the perennial cycles of blame and crisis in education, teachers are the focus of blame for what is wrong, and the university teacher education system that prepared them for teaching is often subjected to similar virulent criticism. Simply holding teachers accountable for school success or failure ignores larger structural factors, such as school funding, the control of curriculum, and poverty. It is far easier for conservatives to focus their criticism on teachers and teacher education by calling for more testing and deregulation of licensure systems than it is to significantly increase school funding, give teachers greater control over the curriculum, reduce the testing frenzy, and end poverty!

In spite of the criticism of university-based teacher education, there is a considerable body of research that shows that teachers who graduate from university teacher education programs are more effective than teachers who earn their teaching licenses through alternative means (Darling-Hammond, 2000). Furthermore, the research indicates that teachers who earn their licenses through quick pathway approaches suffer a much greater attrition in the first few years of teaching than do university-trained teachers (Darling-Hammond, 2000). Quality university teacher education programs provide beginning teachers with the conceptual tools with which to analyze teaching experience. There is so much for teachers to think about. The press of everyday teaching and the inevitable crush of problems can be overwhelming for the beginning teacher. Unlike a simple reactive stance of using "what works," study of the psychological, sociological, and philosophical dimensions of teaching and their interaction with curriculum can provide the beginning teacher with some theories to make sense of and to learn from experience. Darling-Hammond (2000) argues that university teacher education, when it works well, prepares teachers to convey subject matter to others, particularly others who do not share the cultural perspective of the teacher.

[P]eople who have never studied teaching or learning often have a very difficult time understanding how to convey material that they themselves learned effortlessly and almost subconsciously. When others do not learn merely by being told, the intuitive teacher often becomes frustrated and powerless to proceed. This frequently leads to resentment of students for not validating the untrained teacher's efforts. Furthermore, individuals who have had no powerful teacher education intervention often maintain a single cognitive and cultural perspective that makes it difficult for them to understand the experiences, perceptions, and knowledge bases that deeply influence the approaches to learning of students who are different from themselves. The capacity to understand another is not innate; it is developed through study, reflection, guided experience and inquiry. (171)

Because of my understanding of various cognitive, motivational, and cultural perspectives, I had the wherewithal to consider many factors in understanding my teaching experience. University teacher education can help young teachers develop these multiple perspectives.

I realize that some teacher education programs are more effective at doing this than others. I realize that teacher education has long been criticized by preservice teachers as being irrelevant to the concerns of everyday teaching. I do think there is some value when teacher educators have some recent experience as everyday classroom teachers so they can speak more honestly to the dilemmas and contradictions of teaching. Our preservice teachers want honesty from teacher education faculty, an honesty that is rooted in their own experiences as committed and enthusiastic as well as imperfect and ambivalent practitioners. I also think there should be clearer integration of methods/experience with the conceptual frames from sociology, politics, psychology, and other fields (e.g., Bullough & Gitlin, 2001; Pollard & Tann, 1993). I am not recommending more foundations coursework per se.

Rather, I am recommending the study of foundations that is embedded in everyday practice. In this way, for example, young teachers can bring more powerful analytical frameworks and skills to consider student behavior as reflecting some interaction of psychology (of the student/teacher) with culture and power relations (between the student/teacher and the immediate setting as well as the structure of the school and society).

Once beginning teachers are hired and begin teaching, they should not be left alone. Good induction/mentor programs for beginning teachers also matter (e.g., Costigan, 2004; Howey, 1988). Beginning teachers have a profound need to talk about their experiences in the classroom with other teachers, primarily other beginning teachers. Without the opportunity to share and examine their experiences with knowledgeable and empathetic others, beginning teachers may develop a perspective that is narrow, dysfunctional, and prone to the expedient modus operandi of "what works." Talk and reflection with knowledgeable others support the development of multiple perspectives and teaching identities. Induction programs can facilitate more collaboration, peer coaching, sharing of resources, and conversation to reduce the typical isolation in which teachers find themselves. I think I would have struggled less if I had had active and direct support of others, such as a more veteran teacher in the same grade level who could have done regular observations of my teaching and helped me plan more effectively. I would have benefited from on-going support group meetings of other beginning teachers coming together to share their feelings and ideas. While these groups may include more experienced teachers, beginning teachers need this reference group to validate each others' realities, to reassure them that it is a normal condition of beginning teaching to be struggling, failing, confused, and fearful. In most cases, beginning teachers share common challenges and struggles (Roehrig et al., 2002), so regular and open-structured meetings during which beginning teachers freely talk and support each other can serve a validating and affirming function.

The second overarching recommendation is that schools need to become social/collaborative places of learning for adults. Lortie (1975) long ago decried the isolationist culture of schools, and recommendations regarding the importance of collaborative school cultures are not new (e.g., Fullan, 1993; Lieberman, 1988). Isolationist schools leave beginning teachers alone to fend for themselves, often in the swirl of chaos, contradictions, and conflict typical of, at best, just the first few weeks and months and, at worse, the entire year. In a collaborative school, teachers engage in the joint planning of curriculum, routinely share resources and seek out external support, collectively establish goals and objectives, team teach, and most important, engage in professional conversations on a regular basis. The challenge of beginning teaching can be softened considerably in the context of a supportive, interactive, and caring community of adult learners. Collaborative school cultures enhance the development of professional communities that help teachers mitigate the inherent pressures of teaching and, hopefully, advocate for more equitable school systems and a more just society.

The common sense of collaborative school cultures, however, does not lead to common practice. There is a nontrivial set of conditions that needs to be in place in order for collaborative school cultures to develop (Little, 1990), and these conditions ought to be examined by beginning teachers. As a teacher educator, I need to consider how I am preparing my preservice teachers for this dimension of their work. I need to support my own department and its development as a collaborative culture. Our program, how we relate to our teacher education students, and our syllabi should reflect genuine participation and feedback from our students. It is useful to make the notion of collaborative culture explicit to preservice teachers. When they begin looking for jobs, preservice teachers should be able to assess the cultures of the potential job sites. We need to help them also develop strategies to be change agents once they get jobs, so they have the skills and motivations to begin influencing the development of more collaborative, democratic workplaces. Given the challenges and pressures of teaching and a political environment that is unfriendly to public education, it makes sense to engage young teachers in the study and practice of collaborative cultures.

My final point is a response to the focus of traditional teacher education programs on pedagogy and teaching technique. The focus on technique leaves teachers unprepared to understand fully, critique, and then act to improve their working conditions and the learning conditions of their students. Linking the teachers' classroom experience with the cultural, the economic, and the political can only increase teachers' abilities to generate a broader set of explanations for what is happening and options for managing these problems. The recommendation that teacher education programs engage preservice teachers in the study of the relationship between the micro- and macrodimensions of teaching is contained in the three studies in this book. The study of the nonpedagogic dimensions of teaching and their relationship to pedagogy and the emergence of teacher identity, therefore, is a central implication of my work here.

## NOTE

1. Nias (1989) examined the notion of "feeling like a teacher" among experienced primary teachers. She found that this feeling depended on four conditions: feeling relaxed with the students, feeling able to integrate one's personal life with teaching, being in control, and establishing a caring relationship with students focused on both academic and personal needs.

# REFERENCES

Adler, P. A., & Adler, P. (1994). Observational techniques. In N. K. Denzin & Y. S. Lincoln (Eds.), *Handbook of qualitative research* (pp. 377–92). Thousand Oaks, CA: Sage Publications.

Apple, M. (1989). *Teachers and texts: A political economy of class and gender relations in education*. New York: Routledge & Kegan Paul.

Armon-Jones, C. (1986). The social functions of emotion. In R. Harre (Ed.), *The social construction of emotions* (pp. 57–82). Oxford: Blackwell.

Ashforth, B. E. (1993). Emotional labor in service roles: The influence of identity. *Academy of Management Review, 18* (1), 88–115.

Atwell, N. (1987). *In the middle*. Portsmouth, NH: Boynton/Cook.

Bakhtin, M. M. (1981). *The dialogic imagination: Four essays*. M. Holquist (Ed.). Austin, TX: University of Texas Press.

Ball, S. J. (1984). Initial encounters in the classroom and the process of establishment. In M. Hammersley & P. Woods (Eds.), *Life in schools: The sociology of pupil culture* (pp. 108–120). Milton Keynes, England: Open University Press.

Barrows, A. (1996). *The light of outrage: Women, anger, and Buddhist women on the edge*. Berkeley, CA: North Atlantic.

Becker, H. S. (1964). Personal change in adult life. *Sociometry, 27* (1), 40–53.

Berlak, A., & Berlak, H. (1981). *The dilemmas of school: Teaching and social change*. London: Methuen.

Bhabha, H. K. (1994). *The location of culture*. London: Routledge.

Bigelow, B., Christensen, L., Karp, S., Miner, B., & Peterson, B. (Eds.). (1994). *Rethinking our classrooms: Teaching for equity and justice*. Milwaukee: Rethinking Schools.

Blanchard, J. S., & Ursula, C. (1996). *Modern fiction about school teaching*. Boston: Allyn and Bacon.

Blumer, H. (1969). *Symbolic interactionism: Perspective and method*. Englewood Cliffs, NJ: Prentice-Hall.

Boler, M. (1999). *Feeling power: Emotions and education*. New York : Routledge.

Britzman, D. (1986) *Practice makes practice: A critical study of learning to teach*. Albany: State University of New York Press.

Buchman, M. (1986). Role over person: Morality and authenticity in teaching. *Teachers College Record, 87* (4), 527–43.

Bullough, R. V. (1989). *First year teacher: A case study*. New York: Teachers College Press.

Bullough, R. V., & Baughman, K. (1997). *First-year teacher eight years later: An inquiry into teacher development*. New York: Teachers College Press.

Bullough, R. V., & Gitlin, A. D. (2001). *Becoming a student of teaching*. New York: RoutledgeFarmer.

Burbules, N. C. (1995). Authority and the tragic dimension of teaching. In J. W. Garrison & A. G. Rud Jr. (Eds.), *The educational conversation: Closing the gap* (pp. 29–40). Albany: State University of New York Press.

Burns, M. (1992). *About teaching mathematics: A K-8 resource*. Sausalito, CA: Marilyn Burns Education Associates.

Calkins, L. M. (1986). *The art of teaching writing*. Portsmouth, NH: Heinemann.

Campbell, S. (1994). Being dismissed: The politics of emotional experience. *Hypatia, 9*, 46–66.

Casey, K. (1993). *I answer with my life: Life histories of women teachers working for social change*. New York: Routledge.

Charmaz, K. (2000). Grounded theory: Objectivist and constructivist methods. In N. K. Denzin & Y. S. Lincoln (Eds.), *Handbook of qualitative research* (pp. 509–536). Thousand Oaks, CA: Sage Publications.

Charney, R. (1992). *Teaching children to care: Management in the responsive classroom*. Greenfield, MA: Northeast Foundation for Children.

Charon, J. (1979). *Symbolic interactionism: An introduction, an interpretation, an integration*. Englewood Cliffs, NJ: Prentice-Hall.

Clandinin, D. J., & Connelly, F. M. (1995). *Teachers' professional knowledge landscapes*. New York: Teachers College Press.

Clandinin, D. J., & Connelly, F. M. (2000). *Narrative inquiry: Experience and story in qualitative research.* San Francisco: Jossey-Bass.

Coates, T. J., & Thoresen, C. E. (1976). Teacher anxiety: A review with recommendations. *Review of Educational Research, 46* (2), 159–84.

Cochran-Smith, M. (2004). Taking stock in 2004. *Journal of Teacher Education, 55* (1), 3–7.

Codell, E. R. (1999). *Educating Esme: Diary of a teacher's first year.* Chapel Hill, NC: Algonquin Books of Chapel Hill.

Collins, R. (1975). *Conflict sociology: Toward an explanatory science.* New York: Academic.

Conley, D. T., & Goldman, P. (1995). Reactions from the field to state restructuring legislation. *Educational Administration Quarterly, 31* (4), 512–38.

Connell, R. W. (1985). *Teacher's work.* Boston: Allen & Unwin.

Conway, J. (1987). Politics, pedagogy and gender. *Daedalus, 116*, 137–52.

Costigan, A. (2004). Finding a name for what they want: A study of New York's Teaching Fellows. *Teaching and Teacher Education, 20* (2), 129–43.

Crocco, M. S., Munro, P. & Weiler, K. (1999). *Pedagogies of resistance: Women educator activists, 1880–1960.* New York: Teachers College Press.

Danielewicz, J. (2001). *Teaching selves: Identity, pedagogy, and teacher education.* Albany, NY: State University of New York Press.

Darling-Hammond, L. (2000). How teacher education matters. *Journal of Teacher Education, 51* (3), 166–73.

Dewey, J. (1938). *Experience and education.* New York: Collier Books.

Dollase, R. H. (1992). *Voices of beginning teachers: Visions and realities.* New York: Teachers College Press.

Dudley-Marling, C. (1997). *Living with uncertainty: The messy reality of classroom practice.* Portsmouth, NH: Heinemann.

Dyson, A. H. (1993). *Social worlds of children learning to write in an urban primary school.* New York: Teachers College Press.

Eisner, E. (1985). *The educational imagination: On the design and evaluation of school programs.* New York: Macmillan.

Ellis, C., & Bochner, A. P. (2000). Autoethnography, personal narrative, reflexivity: Researcher as subject. In N. K. Denzin & Y. S. Lincoln (Eds.), *Handbook of qualitative research* (pp. 733–68). Thousand Oaks, CA: Sage Publications.

Ellsworth, E. (1997). *Teaching positions: Difference, pedagogy, and the power of address.* New York: Teachers College Press.

Everhart, R. (1983). *Reading, writing and resistance: Adolescence and labor in a junior high school.* Boston, MA: Routledge & Kegan Paul.

Feldman, A. (2003). Validity and quality in self-study. *Educational Researcher, 32* (3), 26–28.

Ferguson, K. E. (1984). *The feminist case against bureaucracy.* Philadelphia: Temple University Press.

Foucault, M. (1978). *The history of sexuality, vol. 1: An introduction.* New York: Pantheon.

Fullan, M. (1993). *Change forces: Probing the depths of educational reform.* London: Falmer.

Geer, B. (1971). Teaching. In B. R. Cosin, I. R. Dale, G. M. Esland, & D. F. Swift (Eds.), *School and society: A sociological reader* (pp. 3–8). Cambridge, MA: MIT Press.

Gerth, H. H., & Mills, C. W. (1953). *Character and social structure: The psychology of social institutions.* New York: Harcourt, Brace.

Glass, G. V., Cahen, L. S., Smith, M. L., & Filby, N. N. (1982). *School class size.* Beverly Hills, CA: Sage Publications.

Goffman, E. (1959). *The presentation of self in everyday life.* New York: Doubleday.

Goffman, E. (1961). *Asylums: Essays on the social situation of mental patients and other inmates.* Garden City, NY: Anchor.

Gore, J. (1998). Disciplining bodies: On the continuity of power relations in pedagogy. In T. Popkewitz & M. Brennan (Eds.). *Foucault's challenge: Discourse, knowledge and power in education* (pp. 231–51). New York: Teachers College Press.

Grace, G. R. (1978). *Teachers, ideology, and control: A study in urban education.* London: Routledge & Kegan Paul.

Graves, D. H. (1983). *Writing: Teachers and children at work.* Exeter, NH: Heinemann Educational.

Grimmett, P. P., & MacKinnon, A. M. (1992). Craft knowledge and the education of teachers. In G. Grant (Ed.), *Review of Research in Education* (pp. 385–456). Washington, DC: American Education Research Association.

Grumet, M. R. (1988). *Bitter milk: Women and teaching.* Amherst: University of Massachusetts Press.

Hammersley, M., & Woods, P. (Eds.). (1984). *Life in school: The sociology of pupil culture.* Milton Keynes, England: Open University Press.

Hanson, D. T. (2001). Teaching as moral activity. In V. Richardson (Ed.), *Handbook of research on teaching (4th edition)* (pp. 826–57). Washington, DC: American Educational Research.

Hargreaves A. (1994a). *Changing teachers, changing times: Teachers' work and culture in the postmodern age.* New York: Teachers College Press.

Hargreaves, A. (1994b). Restructuring restructuring: Postmodernity and the prospects for educational change. In P. Grimmet & J. Neufeld (Eds.), *Teacher de-*

*velopment and the struggle for authenticity: Professional growth and restructuring in the context of change* (pp. 52–82). New York: Teachers College Press.

Hargreaves, A. (1998). The emotional practice of teaching. *Teaching and Teacher Education, 14* (8), 835–54.

Hargreaves, D. (1972). *Interpersonal relations and education.* London: Routledge & Kegan Paul.

Harrison, B. W. (1985). *Making the connections: Essays in feminist social ethics.* Boston: Beacon.

Herndon, J. (1968). *The way it spozed to be.* New York: Simon and Schuster.

Hewitt, J. P. (1976). *Self and society: A symbolic interactionist social psychology.* Boston: Allyn and Bacon.

Hewitt, J. P. (1989). *Dilemmas of the American self.* Philadelphia: Temple University Press.

Hochschild, A. (1983). *The managed heart: Commercialization of human feeling.* Berkeley: University of California Press.

Hoffman, M. (1991). *Amazing grace.* New York: Dial.

Hogan, D. (1989). The market revolution and disciplinary power: Joseph Lancaster and the psychology of the early classroom system. *History of Education Quarterly, 29* (3), 381–417.

Holt, J. (1964/1982). *How children fail.* New York: Delta/Seymour Lawrence.

Howey, K. (1988). Mentor-Teachers as inquiring professionals. *Theory into Practice, 27* (3), 209–13.

Huberman, M. (1993). *The lives of teachers.* New York: Teachers College Press.

Hudson-Ross, S., & McWhorter, P. (1995). Going back/looking in: A teacher educator and a high school teacher explore beginning teaching together. *English Journal, 84* (2), 46–54.

Jackson, P. (1968). *Life in classrooms.* New York: Holt, Rinehart and Winston.

Jaggar, A. (1989). Love and knowledge: Emotion and feminist epistemology. In A. Jaggar & S. Bordo (Eds.), *Gender/body/knowledge: Feminist reconstructions of being and knowing* (pp. 145–71). New Brunswick, NJ: Rutgers University Press.

Jenkins, R. (1996). *Social identity.* London: Routledge.

Jersild, A. (1955). *When teachers face themselves.* New York: Teachers College, Columbia University.

Katz, L, & Chard, S. (2000). *Engaging children's minds: The project approach.* Stamford, CT: Ablex.

Kelchtermans, G. (1996). Teacher vulnerability: Understanding its moral and political roots. *Cambridge Journal of Education, 26* (3), 307–23.

Kemper, T. D. (1978). *A social interactional theory of emotions.* New York: John Wiley & Sons.

Kidder, T. (1989). *Among schoolchildren*. Boston: Houghton Mifflin.

Kozol, J. (1968). *Death at an early age: The destruction of the hearts and minds of Negro children in the Boston public schools*. New York: Bantam.

Lampert, M. (1985). How do teachers manage to teach? Perspectives on problems in practice. *Harvard Educational Review, 55* (2), 178–94.

Lantieri, L. (2001). *School with spirit: Nurturing the inner lives of children and teachers*. Boston: Beacon.

Lazarus, R. S. (1991). *Emotion and adaptation*. New York: Oxford University Press.

Lazarus, R. S. (2001). Relational meaning and discrete emotions. In K. Scherer, A. Schorr, & T. Johnstone (Eds.), *Appraisal processes in emotions: Theory, methods, research* (pp. 37–67). New York: Oxford University Press.

Lensmire, T. J. (1994). *When children write*. New York: Teachers College Press.

Lieberman, A. (1988). *Building a professional culture in schools*. New York: Teachers College Press.

Little, J. W. (1990). Teachers as colleagues. In A. Lieberman (Ed.), *Schools as collaborative cultures* (pp. 165–94). New York: Falmer.

Lortie, D. C. (1975). *Schoolteacher: A sociological study*. Chicago: University of Chicago Press.

Martin, W. B. W. (1976). *The negotiated order of the school*. Toronto: Macmillan of Canada.

Maslow, A. (1973). What is a Taoistic teacher? In L. Rubin (Ed.), *Fact and feeling in the classroom* (pp. 147–70). New York: Walker.

Mead, G. H. (1934). *Mind, self and society from the stand-point of a social behaviorist*. Chicago: University of Chicago Press.

Measor, L., & Woods, P. (1984). *Changing schools: Pupil perspectives on transfer to a comprehensive*. Milton Keynes, England: Open University Press.

*Merriam-Webster's new collegiate dictionary (7th edition)* (1965). Springfield, MA: Merriam-Webster.

Montandon, C., & Osiek, F. (1998). Children's perspectives on their education. *Childhood: A Global Journal of Child Research, 5* (3), 247–63.

National Council of Teachers of Mathematics (1989). *Curriculum and evaluation standards for school mathematics*. Reston, VA: National Council of Teachers of Mathematics.

Naylor, P. R. (1991). *Shiloh*. New York: Atheneum.

Newkirk, T. (1992). Silence in our teaching stories: What do we leave out and why? In T. Newkirk (Ed.), *Workshop 4, by and for teachers* (pp. 21–30). Portsmouth, NH: Heinemann.

Nias, J. (1989). *Primary teachers talking: A study of teaching as work*. London: Routledge.

Nias, J. (1996). Thinking about feeling: The emotions in teaching. *Cambridge Journal of Education, 26* (3), 293–306.

Nieto, S. (2003). *What keeps teachers going?* New York: Teachers College Press.

Noddings, N. (1996). Stories and affect in teacher education. *Cambridge Journal of Education, 26* (3), 435–47.

Ohanian, S. (1999). *One size fits few: The folly of educational standards.* Portsmouth, NH: Heinemann.

Pajak, E., & Blase, J. (1989). The impact of teachers' personal lives on professional role enactment: A qualitative analysis. *American Educational Research Journal, 26* (2), 283–310.

Paley, V. G. (1992). *You can't say you can't play.* Cambridge, MA: Harvard University Press.

Palmer, P. J. (1998). *The courage to teach: Exploring the inner landscape of a teacher's life.* San Francisco: Jossey-Bass.

Patton, M. Q. (1980). *Qualitative evaluation methods.* Beverly Hills, CA: Sage Publications.

Phillips, S. (1972). Participation structure and communicative competence: Warm Springs children in community and classroom. In C. Cazden, V. John, & D. Hymes (Eds.), *Functions of language in the classroom* (pp. 370–94). New York: Teachers College Press.

Pollard, A. (1985). *The social world of the primary school.* London: Holt, Rinehart & Winston.

Pollard, A., & Tann, S. (1993). *Reflective teaching in the primary school.* New York: Cassell.

Putnam, L., & Mumby, D. (1997). Organizations, emotion and the myth of rationality. In S. Fineman (Ed.), *Emotions in Organizations* (pp. 36–57). London: Sage.

Rafaeli, A., & Sutton, R. I. (1987). Expression of emotion as part of the work role. *Academy of Management Review, 12*, 23–37.

Riseborough, G. (1985). Pupils, teachers' careers and schooling: An empirical study. In S. Ball & I. Goodson (Eds.), *Teachers Lives and Careers* (pp. 202–265). London: Taylor & Francis.

Roehrig, A. D., Pressley, M., & Talotta, D. A. (2002). *Stories of beginning teachers: First-year challenges and beyond.* Notre Dame, IN: University of Notre Dame Press.

Rosser, E., & Harre, R. (1984). The meaning of trouble. In M. Hammersely & P. Woods (Eds.), *Life in school: The sociology of pupil culture* (pp. 204–10). Milton Keynes, England: Open University Press.

Rouse, J. (1994). Power/Knowledge. In G. Gutting (Ed.), *The Cambridge companion to Foucault* (pp. 92–114). Cambridge: Cambridge University Press.

Rousmaniere, K. (1994). Losing patience and staying professional: Women teachers and the problem of classroom discipline in New York City schools in the 1920s. *History of Education Quarterly, 34* (1), 49–68.

Rousmaniere, K. (1997). *City teachers: Teaching and school reform in historical perspective.* New York: Teachers College Press.

Ryan, K. (1970). *Don't smile until Christmas: Accounts of first year teachers*: Chicago: University of Chicago Press.

Ryan, K., Newman, K. K., Mager, G., Applegate, J., Lasley, T., Flora, R., et al. (1980). *Biting the apple: Accounts of first year teachers.* New York: Longman.

Sarason, S. (1971). *The culture of the school and the problem of change.* Boston: Allyn & Bacon.

Sarbin, T. R. (1986). Emotion and act: Roles and rhetoric. In R. Harre (Ed.), *The social construction of emotions* (pp. 83–97). Oxford: Basil Blackwell.

Schoonmaker, F. (2002). Growing up teaching: From personal knowledge to professional practice. New York: Teachers College Press.

Scott, J. C. (1990). *Domination and the arts of resistance: Hidden transcripts.* New Haven, CT: Yale University Press.

Shange, N. (1997). *Whitewash.* New York: Walker.

Sharp, R., & Green, A. (1975). *Education and social control: A study in progressive primary education.* London: Routledge and Kegan Paul.

Strauss, A. L. (1978). *Negotiations: Varieties, contexts, processes and social order.* San Francisco: Jossey-Bass.

Tickle, L. (1999). Teacher self-appraisal and appraisal of self. In R. P. Lipka & T. M. Brinthaupt (Eds.), *The role of self in teacher development* (pp. 121–41). Albany: State University of New York Press.

Tolich, M. B. (1993). Alienating and liberating emotions at work: Supermarket clerk's performance of customer service. *Journal of Contemporary Ethnography, 22* (3), 361–81.

Turner, R. (1968). The self-conception in social interaction. In C. Gordon & K. Gergen (Eds.), *The self in social interaction* (pp. 93–106). New York: John Wiley & Sons.

Vygotsky, L. (1978). *Mind in society: The development of higher psychological processes.* Cambridge, MA: Harvard University Press.

Waller, W. (1965). *The sociology of teaching.* New York: John Wiley and Sons. (Originally published in 1932).

Wartenberg, T. E. (1990). *The forms of power: From domination to transformation.* Philadelphia: Temple University Press.

Weedon, C. (1987). *Feminist practice and poststructuralist theory.* Oxford: Blackwell.

Weiler, K. (1988). *Women teaching for change: Gender, class & power.* South Hadley, MA: Bergin & Garvey.

Williams, C. L. (1993). *Doing "women's work": Men in nontraditional occupations.* Newbury Park, CA: Sage Publications.

Winograd, K., & Higgins, K. (1994). Writing, reading, and talking mathematics: One interdisciplinary possibility. *Reading Teacher, 48* (4), 310–18.

Wong, H. K., & Wong, R. T. (1998). *The first days of school: How to be an effective teacher.* Mountain View, CA: Harry Wong.

Woods, P. (1984). Negotiating the demands of schoolwork. In M. Hammersley & P. Woods (Eds.), *Life in School: The sociology of pupil culture* (pp. 225–37). Milton Keynes, England: Open University Press.

Woods, P. (1990a). *Teacher skills and strategies.* London: Falmer.

Woods, P. (1990b). *The happiest days? How pupils cope with school.* London: Falmer.

Yanay, N., & Shahar, G. (1998). Professional feelings as emotional labor. *Journal of Contemporary Ethnography, 27* (3), 346–74.

Zahorik, J. A. (1999). Reducing class size leads to individualized instruction. *Educational Leadership, 57* (1), 50–53.

Zolotow, C. (1972). *William's doll.* New York: Harper & Row.

# INDEX

Palmer, P. J., 228
Patton, M. Q., 208
Peterson, B., 228
Phillips, S., 19
Pollard, J., x, 12, 39, 41, 79, 173, 175,
  176, 178, 192, 240, 241, 274
poststructural feminism on identity,
  xiii, 233–34
power, xiii, xiv, xxii–xxiii, 41, 64, 66,
  84, 85, 93, 96–97, 98, 99, 104, 132,
  142, 144, 169–98, 202, 204,
  227–28, 234, 275
power struggle, xxii, 24, 47, 57, 62, 63,
  66, 76, 84, 98, 99, 105, 107, 128,
  132, 177, 178, 184–89, 197, 222
Pressley, M., 269
Putnam, L., 203, 227

Rafaeli, A., 207, 226
research method, xiv–xviii, 178,
  207–8, 235–38; Woodbridge
  Elementary School, xv–xvii;
  students, xvii
resistance, 171–72; disguised, by
  students, 196; student, 195–97
Rethinking Schools, 19, 260
Riseborough, G., 38, 85, 86, 259
Roehrig, A. D., 269, 275
Rosser, E., 53, 63, 64, 178, 185
Rouse, J., 171
Rousmaniere, K., 203–4, 227, 270
Ryan, K., xi

Sarason, S., 17
Sarbin, T. R., 201
schedule, of afternoon. See teaching
  schedule
Schoonmaker, F., xi

Scott, J. C., 172, 185, 187, 196, 227,
  272
self. See teacher identity
self-conceptions, 237, 265, 266n2
self-interest, 173
Shahar, G., 206
Shange, N., 97
Sharp, R., 51
Strauss, A. L., 195
student engagement, 195
subjectivity, xv, 51, 225, 233, 234,
  266n1
subordinated groups, 59, 172
Sutton, R. I., 207, 226
symbolic interactionism, xiii, 233

Talotta, D. A., 269
Tann, S., 274
teacher education, recommendations,
  197–98, 228–29, 272–77
teacher identity: hybrid identity,
  267n8; integration of personal
  ethics, 264; merger with parent,
  262–63
teacher identity, blaming, 238–44;
  changing beliefs, 244–50; managing
  impressions, 256–58
teacher identity, problem solving,
  250–56; synthesis of own,
  261–66
teacher identity, strategies to construct,
  238–60; alignment with reference
  groups, 258–60
teaching as hope, 271–72
teaching schedule, xvii; validity, xv
thesis of book, xii–xiii
Thorenson, C. E., 14
Tickle, L., 229

# ABOUT THE AUTHOR

**Ken Winograd** is an associate professor in the School of Education at Oregon State University. He teaches courses to preservice students and graduate students in literacy and research methods. Before coming to Oregon, he taught elementary school in Grand Junction, Colorado, and earned a doctorate at the University of Northern Colorado. Dr. Winograd is currently working on an action research project with local elementary teachers in the area of reading comprehension.

Dr. Winograd lives in Corvallis with his wife, two children, dog, rat, and hamster. He enjoys reading biographies, riding his bike, talking with the neighbors, and watching his children play soccer.